Praise for Roger Welsch's
Embracing Fry Bread: Confessions of a Wannabe

"If it can be said of anyone who is not an Indian (Native American, American Indian) that he or she has the 'soul of an Indian,' it has to be said of Roger Welsch. He offers the one thing that diverse groups of people, indeed the world, need to get along: understanding."
—Joseph Marshall III, author of *The Lakota Way: Stories and Lessons for Learning*

"Welsch's natural warmth and skill as a storyteller, and his obvious respect for the individuals he encounters, come through clearly in his writing, and it's easy to see why so many people, from so many backgrounds, might be honored to call him 'friend.'"
—*Publishers Weekly*

"Welsch's gratitude toward the Omahas and Pawnees is real, his outrage at their painful history is justified, and his story is proof that Native American culture is still alive and complex."
—*Kirkus*

"Though an anthropology scholar, Welsch is never pedantic or preachy. Instead, this is a heartfelt and very personal story, rich in wry and self-deprecating humor."
—Deborah Donovan, *Booklist*

"Welsch manifests himself as a listener who has spent fifty-five years involved in Native culture where he has made uncountable friends. His ability to write honest prose, both informative and erudite, captivates from the beginning."
—Wynne Summers, *Great Plains Quarterly*

"This is a watchful, thoughtful man's memoirs of how he has been drawn into three Indigenous families and communities through no particular volition of his own. This is the story for anyone who wakes up one morning and realizes he or she has somehow become something beyond what nature and nurture had originally provided . . . and is the better human for it. Welsch writes a compelling personal account that can resonate with us all."

—MARK AWAKUNI-SWETLAND, author of
Dance Lodges of the Omaha People

"A self-described wannabe, Roger Welsch has over many years absorbed a deep knowledge and appreciation of the Indian tribes of the Northern Plains. His writing, sincere and often humorous, reveals a personality that many Indian people and even one tribal council have come to trust, love, and adopt into their circles."

—CHARLES TRIMBLE, Oglala Lakota
journalist and author

"Once again my Heyoke friend, Roger Welsch, has captured the true essence of being a 'wannabe,' not afraid to take risks, staying close to the fire but not too close. Like our people, he understands what it means to live in two worlds. He does so with humor, gusto, and fearless dignity."

—JUDI M. GAIASHKIBOS (Ponca), executive director of
the Nebraska Commission on Indian Affairs

"We can all enjoy the wit and humor of my long-time friend and Native rights colleague Roger Welsch. He presents an important message, as we strive to live together as one great people joined together on the same land by a common heritage."

—WALTER R. ECHO-HAWK, author of *In the Courts
of the Conqueror: The Ten Worst Indian
Law Cases Ever Decided*

BISON
BOOKS

THE RELUCTANT PILGRIM

A Skeptic's Journey into Native Mysteries

ROGER WELSCH

University of Nebraska Press | Lincoln & London

Library of Congress Control Number: 2015931459

Set in Minion Pro by Rachel Gould.

For those who know or who will come
to know soon enough . . .

Der Wunder hoechstes ist,
Dass uns die wahren, echten Wunder so
Alltaeglich werden kennen, werden sollen.

[The greatest miracle is
that genuine, true miracles become
so utterly mundane to us.]
—Gotthold Ephraim Lessing (1729–87),
Nathan der Weise

"Religion is belief in someone else's experience;
Spirituality is having your own experience."
—Mystic Magic

"If you talk to God, you are praying; if God
talks to you, you have schizophrenia."
—Thomas Szasz

"The white man's equivalent of the Old Pawnee
Tawadahat or Omaha Wakonda would be 'Wow!'"
—Chris Welsch

"Trust those who seek the truth;
Doubt those who have found it."
—Anonymous bumper sticker in Denver

"If all of this should have a reason,
We would be the last to know."
—John Kay

"I am not a member of a congregation of believers.
Nor do I belong to a community of seekers. I
remain a singularity of amazement."
—George R. Schwelle

"Then said Jesus unto him, Except ye see signs
and wonders, ye will not believe."
—John: 4:48

"I guess somebody up there likes me."
—Malachi Constant in *The Sirens of Titan*

Contents

Preface

This book hasn't been easy to write. I figured if it ever found its way into publication, however, it would be my forty-some-odd book, so simply the usual problems of writing and publishing a book haven't troubled me. Instead, yes, I am about to reveal personal stories that I am a bit uncomfortable about making public; yet these events have had such a profound effect on me that I am eager to tell others about them even though they may seem preposterous to anyone who has not experienced them with me or who has not even experienced anything like them. I suppose there is something in this matter about wanting to save the world by shouting out the truth, but more than that, I would like to have other people, especially sympathetic friends, know what's going on with me—that is, simply put, Something *Is* Going On. I will repeat this phrase throughout the book because it is in brief what the book is about.

I'll admit I am reluctant to face the inevitable ignominy that comes with admissions such as those I am about to make here. Okay, I'm a coward. We no longer burn or drown witches, stone wizards, or commit to asylums those who think Something Is Going On around us other than officially sanctioned supernatural experiences, but we still make it damned uncomfortable for people who talk about things magical, mystic, unexplained, spooky, or even "crazy." And curiously, it is precisely those who insist there *are* supernatural experiences, the hypersanctimonious, who insist that only approved, official people can have them and can have them only through official channels sanctioned by them and their authorized social mechanisms. (More about that later . . . in fact, a *lot* more about that later!)

I am going to tell you as little about myself as possible, not simply because I am not ready to face the ridicule that would certainly follow my revealing the stories that follow. For one thing, if you are reading this book, you probably already know a bit about me. Over my long life I have acquired a small public reputation. I worked hard to acquire it, and as important as I believe the story of my spiritual journey is, I do not want to expose myself or my family to embarrassment even while I want to share what I know with them and others. I suppose we all know, at least to some degree, that we are mortal. But there are also varying degrees of possible avoidance of that reality. I am now of an age (seventy-eight at this writing) and condition (all at once this body, which has been such a reliable conveyance for me, is showing signs of substantial deterioration) that any reluctance I might have had to reveal unconventional personal experiences when I was younger is fading fast too. As I age, I have ever less to risk by way of reputation, status, and certainly wealth. (By way of validating that but certainly not bragging, I would like to note that my wife, Linda, and I have already divested ourselves of most of our property—at least our home and real estate holdings—by returning them to the Pawnee Nation from which they were stolen a century and a half ago. The return to us from that decision has been generous . . . with enough further mystic experiences directly coming from that return to fill a few more chapters in this book!) The bottom line is increasingly I have nothing to lose in baring these craziest occurrences of my life. So while I first wrote this book as an anonymous confession, I have now decided to face the music and make it clear that these are the personal experiences, impressions, doubts, hopes, and wonderments of me, Roger Lee-Flack Welsch. Not an easy decision.

Moreover, even though the following story is mine, it is also more than mine. By training I am an anthropologist and folklorist. *Folklore* is the study of the typical, the usual, the ordinary. Folklore itself is material that is transmitted from person to person by informal means—conversation, example, personal communication—rather than education, fine arts, formal performance, official publication, print, or broadcast. That is to say, folklore is *un*official culture, outside the sanctioned format, known and used among those who are not the authorized arbiters of taste, knowledge, or experience. Since that is the heart and soul of what I am going to tell you in these pages, who I am may be of no importance whatsoever. The spiritual experiences I have had may be available to anyone and therefore experienced by many. Anyone who makes himself open and available to such things not only *may* experience them but will almost certainly find them hard to avoid, as you will see, even if he insists such things make no sense at all in a modern, educated, logical, scientific world.

I have the impression I have had more than my share of "visions," or whatever they are, but I'll be damned if I know for sure what my "share" should be. Or why I have been so blessed with them. Since I am inside this body and mind, I have no way of knowing what goes on in other bodies and minds, especially since the opprobrium that goes along with "seeing things" makes the modern, educated, logical, scientific world unreceptive to reporting or sharing such experiences. More likely, my associations with Native American communities have given me the permission, means, and access to things not available to those who have not had such associations. I have been very cautious up to now to mention these experiences only to people I think might understand or at least be tolerant of them, but I have already been impressed that almost every person I have talked with about such things reports similar experiences. It suggests that sensing Something That Is Going On around us may indeed be a universal experience that is however almost completely unreported, at least in Western culture, in the twenty-first century.

My intention here is not to dazzle you that I, of all people, have had these experiences but to suggest that you might have had them too. And to suggest that if you open the door just a bit, you might have them. Or perhaps to wonder what the world would be like if we did not have them. And maybe to suggest that we should all talk more openly about them.

The following narratives describe what has happened to me. The same things could have happened to anyone, and perhaps they have. I sure hope so because they are wonderful experiences, and they have opened for me a world of wonder and awe . . . and even a few laughs. Of all the surprises involved in the process, none is more wonderful or obvious than laughter. I believe you can judge a religion by, among other things, the degree to which its gods laugh. Because the fact of the matter is, a lot of what is going on around us must be described as an enormous and grand joke.

Acknowledgments

I am deeply indebted to Dennis Maun for carefully reading and editing my manuscript for this book. I am notoriously bad at copyediting my own work, so while I am embarrassed at all the errors he found in the first readings of this book, I am also grateful for his patience and diligence.

I am as always grateful too to my beloved wife, Linda, who has heard all these stories before and who has always been kind in accepting my awe and confusion as I wrestled with the mysteries. She took time from her own artistic pursuits to comb through a muddled draft of these pages and, as she has done so often before, did what she could to save me from myself.

I have been more cautious in sharing my experiences with my children and friends. Being a first-person witness to such remarkable things who still stumbles in confusion myself, how could I, after all, expect *them* to find these baffling events plausible? But they nonetheless have listened with care and accepted my confused narratives with love.

Finally I want to thank all those who have heard me and then shared their own experiences with such mysteries, trusting *me* to understand. You'd be surprised how many they are. For those to whom I owe these unlikely understandings, I express my gratitude to Edgar Red Cloud, Earl Dyer, Naomi Gilpin, Frank Sheridan, Clyde Sheridan, Lillian Sheridan, and the Sheridan children and their families, Oliver Saunsoci Sr., Oliver Saunsoci Jr., Benny Butler, Calvin Ironshell,

Ronnie Good Eagle, Jess Flores, Colleen Flores, Michael Flores, Bill Canby, Alberta Canby, Joseph Marshall Jr., Marshall Gover, Elmer Blackbird, Frank LaMere, John Turner, Nicky Solomon, Shirley Cayou, Francine Philips, Francillia Philips, Carrol Stabler, Karma Stabler, Charles Stabler, Elizabeth Stabler, Russell Parker, Ago Sheridan, Dorrin Morris, Felix White, Rufus White, Clydia Nawooks, Reeves Nawooks, Louie LaRose, Nancy Gillis, Judi gaiashkibos, Dawn Adams, Jimmy Horn, Bill Howell, Clem Howell, Alice Alexander, John Mangan, Mark Awakuni-Swetland, Mick Maun, Pat Leading Fox, Vance Spotted Horse Chief, Adrian Spotted Horse Chief, Walter Echo-Hawk, St. Elmo Wilde, Ron Rice, Rob Bozell, Deborah Echo-Hawk, Ronnie O'Brien, Margot Liberty, Dorothy Howard, Jim Gibson, John Carter, Art May, Mert Moore, Paul Olson, Alan Dundes, Phyllis Stone, Francis LaFlesche, Reuben Delgado, Barre Toelken, Jean Lukesh, Liz Deer, Steven Bird, Gale Pemberton, and Peggy Lang. I also express my thanks to Alfred "Buddy" Gilpin Jr., Francis Morris, and Charles Trimble—three men of dignity, accomplishment, and strength who have blessed my life by calling me friend and brother.

THE
RELUCTANT
PILGRIM

1

A Lesson from Stones

S unday mornings have always been a lazy time around my home, a time to read, to drink some coffee, to watch news interview shows. That was as true forty years ago as it is today. And the first story I'm about to tell you happened that long ago. I was a lot younger then, but nonetheless I felt pretty weary one Sunday because I had spent the good part of the previous day helping my friend John pack up his household for a move out of state. I was happy to help him even though I was not happy to see him go. He was . . . probably still is . . . a really good guy. I haven't seen him since that weekend. No particular reason why. The opportunity to get together with him again simply hasn't come up.

Even though we had finished loading his household goods into a moving van and had said our good-byes already, it turned out that I hadn't seen the last of him that weekend. Still in my pajamas, I was lounging around my home the next morning, thumbing through a book that I had received in the mail as a gift from another friend the day before . . . T. C. McLuhan's *Touch the Earth: A Self-Portrait of Indian Existence*. My friend sent it to me with a note saying that for some reason, after she had read the book, she had the strange feeling that I should see it too. I had been deeply interested in Native American issues for twenty years up to that point, had been adopted by a nearby Native American tribe as a family member and friend, and had even published some essays about Native American culture. The arrival of the book, though, was a curiosity because this friend had no real reason to send me any book, let alone *this* book—a collection of statements from Indian speakers. But there it was. It seemed interesting enough, and that morning seemed a good time to begin reading it, if for no other reason than so that I could acknowledge the gift.

I had read only a dozen pages before I was brought to a dead stop, chilled by what I was reading. In her introduction to a short text from the Sioux Tatonka-ohitka (Brave Buffalo), McLuhan described Frances Densmore's discussion of the Sioux term for "God," or Wakan Tonka. It's not a particularly dramatic passage in either McLuhan's text or Brave Buffalo's speech, but for some reason it hit me and hit me hard. Simply put, the Lakota phrase is composed of two adjectives—*wakan* meaning "mysterious" and *tonka* meaning "great." Great Mysterious. No nouns. Just adjectives.

Of course. That was it. This simple, declarative definition hit me as an epiphany. God is not a noun; God is adjectives. We white folks in the mainstream have it wrong, and we've had it wrong for centuries, perhaps millennia. How much clearer it all is when you understand that simple and small truth: God is adjectives, not nouns!

Still sitting in my chair with the book in my hands, reeling from that utterly unexpected revelation . . . not at all what I had been looking for on that quiet, warm Sunday morning, after all! . . . but with a lingering confusion from this explosion in my head, I read on through McLuhan's few lines of introduction and into Brave Buffalo's text itself as taken from Densmore's *Teton Sioux Music* (Bulletin 61, Bureau of American Ethnology, 1918). Maybe I was flailing around for a twig to grab in this emotional, intellectual, spiritual maelstrom in which I suddenly found myself struggling for breath. (Adjectives! . . . Not nouns!) But this was not going to be a day of emotional tranquility for me.

For the moment, however, there was some peace in my confusion. What Brave Buffalo said, after all, seemed to have nothing to do with me. It was, if anything, utterly inconsequential. I read,

> It is significant that certain stones are not found buried in the earth, but are on the top of high buttes. They are round, like the sun and moon, and we know that all things which are round are related to each other, and these stones have lain there a long time, looking at the sun. . . . The Thunderbird is said to be related to these stones. . . . In all my life I have been faithful to the sacred stones. I have lived according to their requirements, and they have helped me in all my troubles. I have tried to qualify myself as well as possible to handle these sacred stones, yet I know I am not worthy to speak to Wakan Tonka. I make my request of the stones and they are my intercessors. (17)

I paused in my reading. It's a striking passage. What does Brave Buffalo mean by his words "I have lived according to their requirements"? What requirements would round rocks demand? And how would round rocks help someone like Brave Buffalo? "I have tried to qualify myself . . . to handle these sacred stones"? How does one "qualify" oneself? And how do you decide which round stone is sacred and which is just another round stone?

Well, you know those crazy Indians! They have strange ways. Strange ideas. Strange beliefs. I knew something of that. I had spent many, many days among the Native people in the city where I lived at that time and on the Omaha reservation a couple hours north of the city. I had participated in Native American religious ceremonies. I had been adopted as a brother by a dear tribal friend who served as the tribe's chairman, Alfred "Buddy" Gilpin Jr., a few years earlier and already had hints of things I didn't understand but that my Native friends did. Big things. Lots of things. This meaningful association with the round stones seemed to be one of those things. Perhaps I would ask my Lakota and Omaha friends. Maybe they could tell me something about this thing with round stones. Maybe I would do more reading about it. Maybe I would come to understand more about it later on. Maybe. As an academic and scholar, my natural bent was to investigate. As I would soon learn, however, there are other ways of learning and teaching than the ones I had come to know and expect.

I was sitting that day with the McCluhan book on my lap, open to that page, thinking about Brave Buffalo's words, when the doorbell rang. I closed the book, got up, and walked to the door. To my surprise . . . even a bit of confusion . . . there was my friend John. I thought he had left a couple hours earlier for his new home in Illinois, I think it was. It's been a long time, and I don't recall that detail now. That, after all, was the least important part of the avalanche that was about to sweep over me and had already started rushing by me even before I could realize what was happening. I sputtered my surprise to John: "I thought you were long gone! Is there a problem, John? What's up?"

"Well, Rog," he said, "I'm not sure what's up. To tell you the truth, I'm not even sure why I'm here." I could see by his expression that he was as confused at that moment as I was. It wasn't some kind of rhetorical device; he really did *not* know why he was there. "You're going to think this is really stupid, but I have something for you. We were just pulling out of the garage with the car all loaded up a couple minutes ago when I spotted something."

He held out to me a perfectly round white stone, about ten inches across. "My aunt found this on top of a mesa in Colorado thirty or forty years ago and gave it to me. She says it was a grindstone the Indians used for milling grain and seeds. I put it out in the garage and have used it to hold open the door the last couple years. For some reason, as we were pulling out of the garage, I noticed the stone, and the instant I saw it I had this overwhelming feeling that I should bring it right over to you before we left town. As silly as it sounds, I got the feeling I didn't really have any choice in the matter. So . . . well . . . here's a round rock."

He handed me the round stone . . . one that had lain for years on top of a mesa looking at the sun. I wish I could see now what my face must have looked like. I was so stunned, I was disoriented. John excused himself and rushed out to the moving van, where his wife was impatiently waiting to get on the road for their long drive. That was okay. I wouldn't have known what to say to him, because to this day I don't know what to say. John couldn't possibly have known about the McCluhan book or that I was reading it at that very moment or what Brave Buffalo had said so long ago about round stones.

John is a researcher and teacher in the sciences. How could I ever explain to him something so utterly unscientific as the coincidence that had just sucker punched me? I went back to my chair, McLuhan's book, and my confusion. I have no idea what I did the rest of that day. Nothing, I suspect. I know I read Brave Buffalo's text several more times and looked at that round stone, expecting some sort of answer. What had just happened to me was not simply unlikely or stunning . . . it was impossible. What are the odds of such a coincidence? There are no odds. The coincidence of a friend reading this book, thinking of me, and sending it to me just in time to be read on that morning and of my friend John having his own peculiar intuition while I was reading Brave Buffalo's passage at the very moment he brought me, of all things, a round stone from a mesa top . . . the string of coincidences around the McCluhan book, the Brave Buffalo text, and this rock is not just impossible . . .

it's absurdly impossible. No logical explanation could possibly account for it.

As I came later to understand, that was precisely the meaning and message of this gift of a round stone. No explanation *is* possible. There *is* no explanation. That is the lesson: there is no explanation. Not even the stone could give me an answer because the questions of its sudden appearance *were* the answer. Its insertion into my life in the most impossible of all circumstances is precisely the point, insofar as there is a point that I (or anyone else) can understand. The lesson is the mystery. My confusion is the clarity. The possibility of the impossible was the conclusion. The only thing that can be said of this is . . . Something's Going On. Something beyond our understanding. Something beyond our control. Something, well, mystic.

At least that's what I thought. I suppose the first and most human reaction to such a stunning experience is to share it with others, to share the wonder, to ask if they think it's as insanely unlikely as I found it to be. Meanwhile, there is also the enormous danger of being judged utterly loony when telling such stories. This is the kind of evidence involuntary sanity hearings and commitments to an asylum are made of! I don't recall if I told even my children or wife what had just happened, at least not that same day. It didn't take mere potential embarrassment to silence me; I was having enough trouble sorting out this whole thing in my mind without trying to report this curious set of events to someone else.

As I have since learned, however, while experiences like this one are ambiguous in the telling and maybe even in the initial experiencing, they do not long remain ambiguous for the person who receives the gift. Okay, yes . . . as preposterous as it might seem, perhaps it *was* just an enormously unlikely coincidence—if that is what you prefer to believe. Unthinkably unlikely . . . but, okay, just a coincidence. I mean, what else *could* it be but coincidence? You can't imagine, and yet deep in your psyche you know that as impossible as the reality is, the notion that it is mere coincidence borders on sheer lunacy. The concept of "coincidence," after all, stretches only so far. If there was an element of madness in the issue, however, it was not in the utter impossibility of the events or in seeing them as some sort of pattern but rather in denying the obvious rationality of them. As it turns out, Wakan Tonka was not done with me and this whole matter of round stones.

About the same time in my life as when my friend John brought me the gift of the round stone, I had purchased a piece of land on a quiet river about a hundred miles away from my former city home in Lincoln, Nebraska. I had stumbled on the beautiful piece of ground and have since come to love it with all my heart. I hadn't owned it a whole year yet when I walked to the top of a bluff overlooking my river bottom ground, the future site of my home, where I would write this chapter. As I stood there, I noticed something on the ground at my feet. Just as when I had found John standing at my front door with the round, white stone in his hands, I again felt my knees buckle. There at my feet was . . . a round stone . . . this time a reddish stone, perfectly round, about four inches across and two inches thick, lying on the ground, looking at the sun, just as Brave Buffalo had said. I later learned from an archaeologist friend that the fist-sized stone is a dimpled mano, or a hand grindstone. It was a gift to me from people whose names I could never know and used by people of a tribe many centuries removed from this entire region, probably pre-Pawnee, from a time eight hundred years ago, . . . and of a tribe whose descendants I would come to know personally, even intimately at a later time.

Okay, one round stone could be a coincidence . . . perhaps. But *two*? Weeks later I was in an antique store I frequented when the proprietor approached me and said, "I know this is silly, Roger, but I picked this up in a box of miscellaneous junk I bid on at an auction last week, and for some reason I thought I should pass it along to you. No charge. It's not worth anything. A dumb idea, I guess." Of course. A black, round rock . . . obviously (to me, at least) another grindstone. Please know this and believe me, I wasn't advertising that I was in the market for round stones! Not only had I not mentioned this curious attraction I seemed to have for round rocks to the people who were handing them to me, but also I hadn't told this nutty sequence of coincidences to anyone. If even close friends who know me and my ferocious skepticism about such things had been told all this, they would have laughed me out of town. Tell this story to total strangers then? No way was I about to pass along my confusion and growing suspicions to *anyone* about what seemed to be going on around me. Suspicions? About what? Increasingly I felt I knew "what." Increasingly the only conclusion possible was also becoming completely unavoidable: Something Was Going On.

Again not long after these events, I was in Wyoming on a research project, interviewing a taxidermist near Casper. It had nothing to do with Indians or rocks or anything of the sort, when out of the blue the man I was talking with reached under his workbench and said, "Here . . . I think this is something you should have." A perfectly round, pure white, Native grindstone, about two inches thick and ten inches across. By this time I was not so much amazed as I was amused. Another round stone. Not exactly a subtle message, huh?

It didn't stop. It seemed as if all at once everyone had a round stone for me. In the mail I received a small box from someone I'd never heard of before and haven't met since. It was a small, perfectly round black stone. She'd found it in a riverbed in the eastern part of our state and knew my name from somewhere or another and thought she'd send it to me. No reason. She just thought she'd send it to me, and so she did. I had never seen a rock quite like it, and I am an inveterate rock picker-upper. It is about an inch and a half in diameter, black, smooth, and as round as a marble.

When was the last time you sent someone a round rock? Someone you had never met. With no particular motivation. Why would anyone do that? I am seventy-eight years old now, and I don't believe I have ever given anyone a round stone for no particular reason. A remarkable coincidence, wouldn't you say? But that's not the way such things work in the world of the Great Mysterious, as the Lakotas call God. Points are not made subtly. They are hammer fisted home as if to make the message clear beyond mistake . . . even if the message itself is indecipherable.

My Lakota brother Charles Trimble decided about forty years after I had received this gift of the round black "marble" to entrust me with his vision bundle, the package that had been assembled for him in preparation and interpretation of his own vision quest many years before. He encouraged me to open it, refresh it, and contemplate it. He noted it was missing an eagle talon he had long ago passed to someone else, but there was a pipestone pipe and stem, a sage bundle, a few other objects meaningful only to him, and . . . a small, perfectly round, smooth, black rock, a bit smaller than the first black one I had been given but still uncannily the same. Gulp. I had not told Charles about the earlier gift of the round black rock; he had no reason to know of its existence. Even if he had, he wouldn't have had a way to obtain and pass along a rock like it since, as I said, I had never seen another like it. (For those of you who might be venturing guesses, it is not an Apache tear, Moqui marble—not even close!—or any other geological specimen I have ever heard of or seen.)

How does one explain something like this? What I had assumed was a single astonishing and unique item, a perfectly round, small black rock, suddenly had a double. Now I was really at sea. But not done, apparently. Only three years later a man approached me at a social gathering and said he had something he thought I would be interested in, something he felt he wanted to pass along to me before he was too old to get it done. You guessed it: a third, even smaller, perfectly round, black, smooth rock like a marble. Of course I was amazed, but now I was no longer taken totally aback. I took it as a message. But from whom or from what? And what is the message? And what is its meaning? And are the signals now at an end? (I very much doubt it but am obviously in no position to know.)

Now you might doubt my veracity or my sanity, but believe it or not, there was still more to this lunatic paradigm that was being built around me in stone. The events I have just described to you involving the first two gifts of round stones took place over a span of three or four years; the second two rocks, forty years later. Just about the time my astonishment over the last unexpected appearance of yet another round rock faded, suddenly there would be another to fire up my confusion anew.

And when round rocks weren't dropping into my life, there was McLuhan's book *Touch the Earth*. Again and again over the next few years I would open my mail to find that someone had sent me another copy. It's one thing for friends to send someone a book they think would be of interest or use, but I received copies of the book from strangers who had no obvious reason to send me books. Yes, I had some small public recognition by then and later as a teacher, writer, and researcher, but attached messages, if there were any, didn't suggest any logic to the gifts. "Here's a book I ran across and for some reason I thought of you. So I am sending it to you.

No need to respond. I know this is silly, but I got this feeling I should send it to you. Have you seen it before?" It got to the point where I kept a small stack of the gift books—all the same book, remember: *Touch the Earth*—and I passed them along to others.

Yes, occasionally someone sent me different titles, often books about Indians. It still happens. But I have received many more copies of McLuhan's book. It is not exactly a best seller, after all. The publisher and the author are both relatively obscure. There are lots of other books about Indians, even anthologies of Indian texts. But this book is the only one I have seen with Brave Buffalo's description of his relationship with round stones. And it is the only book people have sent me in astonishing numbers. The whole thing got to be funny to me. Another round rock . . . another copy of McLuhan! Okay, okay, okay . . . I get the point. You have made yourself perfectly clear . . . in an obscure sort of way. Something *Is* Going On . . .

And then, as if to make it perfectly clear that it was indeed a pattern, not a coincidence, not something that just happens all the time but that I had somehow not noticed up until now, it all stopped. No more round rocks. No more copies of *Touch the Earth*. Apparently that part of the lesson was finished. My attention had been focused. I had been confronted with something I was ferociously determined not to admit but now had no choice but to recognize—that is, Something Is Going On. It was not insanity to admit that now, in fact; it would have been insanity *not* to accept it. Something *Is* Going On. What it is doesn't really matter because this was such an enormous recognition and admission on my part that it was in and of itself beyond anything and everything I had been prepared to accept up to now. In defiance of everything I knew, believed, wanted to believe, and in the face of all logic, I was being forced into believing the unbelievable. Something I had adamantly resisted, even vigorously opposed, for most of my life. "No, there *is* nothing!" I had always insisted. "Be serious! Be logical. Forget superstitious answers. *There . . . is . . . nothing!*" And yet now I found myself forced—forced!—into a new admission: Something . . . Is . . . Going . . . On.

As if to remind me that not only is Something Going On but that a lot more is going on than I know, something curious came to my attention after the initial manuscript for this book had been accepted for publication. While reading the final draft, my wife, Linda, came to me and said that something strange had occurred to her. About the same time I was sent my first copy of *Touch the Earth* and long before Linda and I met, a woman with whom she was sharing an apartment in Lincoln, where I was also living, came home one evening with a copy of that same book. She gave it to her, saying she thought Linda should have it. Linda told me that she had never read the book; in fact, she had never opened it. After all, she had no reason. She had no interest in or connections with Indians. And she had no way of knowing that her life would be profoundly affected by someone who, in turn, was profoundly affected by this very book at about that same time. Or that she would live on Indian land. Or that she would herself be adopted as an honorary Pawnee.

Not knowing why, she had nonetheless kept the book through three moves of her household and for another thirty-five years. "In fact," she said, "it is somewhere here on these shelves." She looked on some shelves beside our bed, and there it was. Quite a coincidence, isn't it?

2

Lessons from People Who Know

I t's not as if I was just beginning my journey into . . . into whatever the hell this all was. But it was one of the first times I realized what was going on and that I had set out on a grand journey without the slightest notion that I was, let alone where I was going. My religious history was fairly conventional, I suppose, for a white boy in middle America through the 1940s and 1950s. I grew up in a German Lutheran household. My parents were laborers, lower middle class. During the Second World War when time, fuel, vehicles, tires, and all such resources were severely restricted, I no longer attended our family's Lutheran church across town but walked instead to a tiny Methodist church closer to our home. My parents considered themselves to be religious but found their spirituality in living decently and modestly and in working in their garden.

I was the first member of my family, ever, to enjoy a higher education, and I suppose that played a role in my growing skepticism and then contempt for organized religion, a disdain I still have. I did have an interest in theology, religious history, belief systems—all of which made me skeptical, even cynical, about religiosity and political structures around belief systems, a rejection I continue to harbor this very day. In fact, I believe even more strongly today than I have before in my life that organized religion—which is to say, "the Church"—is a curse.

While in college, I took classes in Latin and Hebrew with

an eye toward gaining insights into religion. I was a language major as both an undergraduate and a graduate student before moving into anthropology and folklore studies. I attended religious services in various churches, mostly out of curiosity. I never felt any particular spiritual emptiness in my life, having reason, education, sense, logic, and collective wisdom to fill whatever gap there might have been in that part of my life. I considered myself variously an agnostic, pantheist, deist, then quite firmly an atheist. I toyed with Unitarianism in my twenties and early thirties since it made allowances for knowledge, and that approach made sense to me. However, I never felt comfortable with the social aspects of the organization, the trappings of church services, sermons, "temple," hymns. (Is there anything worse than a Unitarian hymn, by the way?) But still I liked the Unitarian idea that its members are a community of seekers rather than a congregation of believers. I appreciated the notion that we can come to understand the nature of God through our own intelligence and by examining the thinking and conclusions of others before us and of our contemporaries in considering the same questions. Very tidy. Very logical. No embarrassment in that kind of common sense.

As was the case with round rocks, and with many other things along the way, my conventional line of thinking was quickly, easily, and quite unexpectedly destroyed. Beginning in 1956 I made contacts in the Indian community, primarily with tribal elders, of Lincoln. I established my Native contacts during a project for a linguistics class in the anthropology department of the university I was attending as an undergraduate. I worked on the vocabulary and structure of the Omahas' tribal language with a man I came to know and love as Uncle Clyde Sheridan. But at that time we met little more than an hour or two every week or so in the sterile context of an anthropology department office.

Eight years later, in 1964, I developed a new interest in traditional music in Lincoln, the city where I had been born, grown up, and taken my education. A friend who had many contacts in the Indian community told me that the members of the nearby Omaha Tribe still knew and used traditional music in many aspects of their culture, including the hand game, a friendly social competition with a rich musical matrix that at the time was a very active part of tribal community life not only on the tribe's reservation but also in Indian communities in nearby towns and cities. I began attending hand games in the city and on the reservation and made many friends in the tribe. My appreciation for the Omaha people . . . their generosity, kindness, good humor, and culture, especially their music and dance . . . grew quickly. My new Native friends became a central element in my life.

My first wife and I adopted an Omaha infant, and my connections with the tribe became ever stronger. In 1967 I had only been closely involved with the tribe for three years, but in that short time my affection for the people and apparently theirs for me had become very strong indeed. I camped on the tribal powwow grounds for the traditional weeklong gathering and harvest celebration during the August full moon, the customary time for tribal celebration even today. My old linguistic resource person and now dear friend, Clyde Sheridan, came to my campsite one day and said that the tribal council chairman wanted to have a word with me.

A tribal council chairman is like the grand chief of a tribe, a person of considerable importance, well beyond the status of meeting casually with a visiting white man like me. I had met Chairman Alfred "Buddy" Gilpin Jr., before and certainly knew who he was. Not only was he an important political figure in the tribe, but he was also personally imposing and culturally very important. I didn't know it at the time, but he was a central figure in tribal and community religious life, being a "road man" with a "fireplace." The non-Indian can perhaps best understand his position as being "ordained" in the tribe's predominant faith system, the Native American Church. Some use the term "peyote cult," but I find it inaccurate and even offensive.

I should perhaps also note here that I am struggling to avoid confusion and offense by skirting or blurring other dangerous terminology in these pages. For example, I am using "non-Indian" rather than "white man" because there are other races and cultures outside Native tradition besides that of the white man. I use the word "Native" much as the mainstream might use "Indian," but I avoid using "Native American" since we are all in some sense native Americans. I like the word "Indian," even though many tribal peoples— another evasion!—do not; and I like it for precisely the reason they do not: it reflects the really stupid misperception of early explorers, such as Christopher Columbus, who thought they were in India! To my mind, the word "Indian" stands as a remarkable and worthy symbol for a world of misunderstandings and misperceptions of Native peoples, culture, and world history. Therefore, I often find myself—almost by accident, I'll admit—using the word "Indian" for native peoples in their tribal settings, especially historically, and the word "Native" for people of "Indian" heritage in today's world.

I found my way to Chairman Gilpin's humble home, just across the main entry to the powwow grounds, where his widow and my beloved sister-in-law, Naomi, later lived until her death in 2007. Our meeting that day was more like an audience than a conversation. It was obvious that this leader of the tribe had something important in mind, something serious. I was intimidated just to be talking with this man of such importance, much less to be in his home. And when I realized that he wanted to talk with me about an issue of enormous import, I was truly humbled. When he told me what he had in mind, moreover, I was so flabbergasted, I couldn't find words. To my utter astonishment, he told me that it was his intention to adopt me as his brother. I told him I was honored and that I accepted his instructions. I left, walking onto the powwow grounds and to my campsite in a daze, completely bewildered by this incredible honor. I had never before heard of anyone being adopted as a brother in the tribe, nor had I seen what might be involved.

I wonder how many readers understand what it means to be adopted in the tribal sense. I certainly did not. Even today I have a hard time grasping the enormity of it. The whole idea of adoption, of being taken as a brother by an Indian, has been so muddied and muddled by romantic claptrap and by politicians wearing war bonnets and using names like His Voice Is Like Thunder that the true process and meaning of actual tribal adoption are easily dismissed as a courtesy or, at the most, a nice honor. That is not what it means at all, certainly not among other tribes with which I am familiar. When Alfred Gilpin said he wanted to take me as his brother, he meant I would become, literally, *his brother*. And as is the case in the tribal kinship system, his children would become my children, which they are to this day.

Up to then my interest in the tribe had been just that, a casual interest. I was not studying or researching anything . . . I was just sitting at the drum, enjoying the music, joining in the hand games, sharing food, and being among people I had come to love and appreciate. I had always been ignorant of the right way to do things in Omaha culture, and I knew I had made a lot of mistakes. But the Omahas, like many other Native peoples, are a forgiving people, and we had laughed off most of my social, cultural, religious, and political gaffes. This time, however, things were more serious. I needed help in getting this ceremony right . . . a lot of help. I turned to Clyde and my other friends in the urban tribal community—

Clyde Sheridan's brother, Frank, now family to me; Oliver Saunsoci; Bill Canby; Russell Parker; Charles and Elizabeth Stabler; Carroll; Francillia; Shirley—in fact, the entire tribal community that had taken me in as a friend, almost as an orphan. Not only did I need their guidance about how to prepare for the occasion of my adoption ceremony, a mere month in the future, but also, by way of demonstrating my respect, I would be expected to provide a celebratory feast for several hundred people. As a non-Indian I had never fed so many as a dozen people, much less hundreds.

The Omaha Tribe has a culture of open hospitality and universal generosity. The custom is that they feed everyone. They understand gift giving. And they instantly sprang to my side and guided me through the feast's process, dealing with such details as butchering and cooking hundreds of chickens, making mountains of fry bread, buying institutional-size tins of beans and peaches, piles of pies and cakes, coffee. It took dozens of people and days to prepare and transport all the food and gifts from my home city to the reservation a hundred miles away.

During the September day of the ceremony itself, I sensed some uneasiness among my tribal friends, and I deduced there were some problems with the name I would be given that evening in the ceremony. Elders conferred. One suggestion was that I be given a choice of four or seven or twelve names from which I could choose one. My new brother, Buddy, it seemed, was insisting on something that troubled the others. Much of the discussion was in their Native language, so I couldn't follow it. I think it was Frank Sheridan, a Native who moved with particular ease between his Native traditional culture and the non-Indian's mainstream society, who told me the problem: Buddy Gilpin had made it known that he was going to give me his own tribal name, Tenugagahi (Bull Buffalo Chief). In doing so he was opening himself to severe jeopardy. It is considered very bad luck in the culture, with the very real possibility of physical consequences, to share your name with another. (As it turned out, Buddy did indeed fall ill that next winter and was hospitalized a good part of the following year, events that many, including Buddy himself, interpreted as a result of his decision to share his name with me.)

All of which is to say Buddy's taking me as a brother was a good deal more than a minor honor. In fact, it is understood in this tribe (but not all tribes) that such an adoption equals becoming a full blood. After my adoption ceremony, the next time I stood up to do the Half-Breed Dance, my Native aunt Lillian Sheridan gently told me I could no longer do that dance because now I was considered a full blood and needed to follow the ways of the full blood. Only full-blooded tribal members can claim clan membership; as a full blood I became a member of a totemic KonCe (Wind) Clan and am obligated to follow all the prohibitions that go with that clan membership. I have done so faithfully now for nearly fifty years.

This discussion is to explain why I was sitting on a curb outside the tribal activities building in the tribal agency town on the Nebraska reservation at 2 a.m. one Sunday in September 1967. When the adoption ceremonies were all over and everyone had been fed and all the songs had been sung and everyone else had gone home, Buddy and I drifted out the front door and down to my old battered pickup truck . . . to find that I had a flat tire. We were exhausted from a long, long day and not eager to tear into the task of finding a jack and seeing if the spare on that wreck of a vehicle had air, so we sat down on the curb to suck in the cool night air . . . and talk.

As is so often the case with bad luck like that flat tire on the reservation in the middle of the night, this one too turned out to be actually a stroke of good fortune. Buddy and

I talked most of the night, and I had some real revelations in the process. For example, Buddy asked me if there was anything I wanted to know now that I was his brother and a full-blood Omaha. I said that yes, for several years I had wondered about the Native American Church prayer meetings and if they were still being held. I had mentioned to several of my tribal friends in Lincoln that I surely would like to attend one but could never pin down when or where one was planned, and more often than not, by the time I figured out when the next one was going to be, it was over already.

Buddy chuckled. "Listen," he said. I listened, and out somewhere in the dark reservation night I could hear singing and drumming not too far away to the southwest. "Huh!" my new brother said. "That's a meeting." And then another song came from farther away but to the north. And another to the east, far in the distance. It turned out that prayer meetings are as regular as clockwork . . . but not open to the general public for reasons of self-protection, for one thing, and because the Native American Church is not an aggressive proselytizer and most certainly not outside the Indian community. Within a few weeks, Buddy invited me to attend a prayer meeting at which he was officiating.

The sound of the drums and singing that night of the ceremony started us talking about religion. For his part, Buddy was curious about why white folks were making such a fuss about prayers in schools. (That was more than forty years ago; I can't imagine what he would think about the public chest pounding of pietistic religionists today!) I explained that some people were trying to inject official religion into all manner of public activities, including a minute of prayer at the beginning of each school day. He shook his head, as if commenting on the peculiar behavior of my race. "Among our people, you know," he said, "among our people, we feel every moment of life should be a prayer of gratitude." So much for the super-righteousness of those who think a minute a day constitutes a deep commitment!

"What is your religion?" he asked, using my new name—*his* tribal name—Tenugagahi; it was the first time I heard it in conversation. Now I was on firm ground. I was clear about this one thing here in this strange country among strange people with strange ways. "I am a Unitarian," I said.

"Unitarian . . . What's that?"

And I gave him the short-version brochure text of what I held to be about as wise an approach to understanding religion as I could imagine. "We Unitarians are a community of seekers rather than believers. We use our minds, the best of the gifts we are given, to do what we can to understand the nature of what is called God," I explained. "We use our brains to study, to learn, to investigate, to *think* . . . . In this way, we hope to understand the mystery of what we call God."

I thought I handled that pretty well. I was all set to be admired by Buddy for my rational, sensible approach to his question.

"So, Brother, you actually think that with your one mind, in one short life, you can figure out Wakonda . . ." Later I would come to know that the Omahas use the Omaha-Ponca variant "Wakonda" in the same way the Lakotas use Wakan Tonka.

"Well, my mind, and what everyone else has learned over the centuries and around the world."

"That surprises me. I would think that as enormous as Wakonda is, and as small as we humans are, even through all time and around the world we wouldn't be able to come very close to understanding that."

Gulp. Now that he mentioned it, for all my thinking and study, I hadn't made much progress in coming to an understanding of what God is. In fact, for all man's thinking and study, we really hadn't made a lot of progress. I decided to play it safe with Buddy and stay silent. I'm glad I did. Buddy continued in his slow, eloquent, wise way to explain to me how things really are. He spoke of the timeless, endless grandeur of the Great Mysterious and more about our own small insignificance. He said that all we can really hope for, at the very most, at the very best, is some small hint of the grand immensity. There's no way we can grasp the entirety, he said quite rightly. In fact, there is no way we can understand even the small glimpses we might get or from those fragments understand the entirety of the Great Mysterious. And yet, he said humbly, we must be grateful for what we are given even if we cannot understand it. The smallest gift tells us more than we probably deserve. For one thing . . . it tells us . . . Something Is Going On. Actually, he laughed, we probably can't even understand that . . . so why should we ever be so arrogant to think we can understand more? Or to feel a need to understand more?

Suddenly my Unitarian smugness and confidence in my own intellect and mankind's genius dissolved like a snowflake in the spring sun. I never again called myself a Unitarian. I never again presumed to think I was on my way to understanding Wakonda by strength and virtue of my powers of reason. And I began to do what the non-Indian should have been doing all along in his relationship with much wiser people, from Native Americans to the Nepalese and every native spiritualistic society in between: I decided to sit quietly and listen. That night on the tribal reservation in 1967 was an epiphany for me, but it was nothing compared to what lay in store for me over the following decades.

There have been other influences in the forces wrenching me from rational, European American, mainstream religious thought. I wrote but deleted from the previous sentence the word "Christian"; true Christianity is an Eastern, not a Western, tradition. Therefore, Europeans and Americans never have understood Christianity and never will. Its precepts are utterly alien to European, Anglo-American culture in which they often find themselves. Many Native Americans, for example, had no trouble at all accepting early nineteenth-century missionaries' biblical instruction. Offering open hospitality, giving to the poor, completely sharing of resources, even accepting the mystical contemporary miracle offered no problem for the Native mind. That's the way their culture worked on an everyday basis already. Where they had a problem was coming to understand . . . and actually they haven't done so to this day . . . that while we *profess* to uphold the teachings of the Bible, the average European American non-Indian has no intention whatsoever of *practicing* it. Christian principles are ideals, theories, thoughts. But they are most assuredly not common practices!

When preparing for my adoption ceremony, for example, I had approached Clyde and explained that I knew it would be my responsibility and privilege to "feed the people," as the tribal members phrase it. So, I had inquired, if I were to invite the Lincoln Indian Club, the Little Warriors (the young people's organization for local tribal members), and maybe from the reservation the tribal societies of, oh, say, the Big Crazies and the War Mothers, how much food should I plan on providing? How many chickens? How many pounds of pork? Or how many hogs? I had no idea. How much food should I buy?

When I finished my questions, Clyde looked at me as if I had just asked how many stars are in the sky. He was dumbfounded. I had asked an utterly incomprehensible question for the traditional Native community member. He had no idea of how to answer me. He tried, however. "Uh, well, Roger . . . you buy . . . well . . . all you can." Over the years I was to come to understand that that is the Native way. You buy all you can. You spend everything you have to share with the people.

Have you ever spent every cent you have to feed your people? No, of course not. Can you even imagine spending not just all you want to spend or all you think is necessary to cover the situation but everything you have? When was the last time you spent every cent you have to feed others? Maybe even borrowing more so no one will be hungry? It is simply not a non-Indian's way of thinking. To this day, even though I have moved within tribal society for most of my life now, I still cannot act in this way even though I understand how the system works. I am too much the non-Indian to spend everything I have. But my Indian relatives do that regularly.

Now which course of belief and action, to your mind, comes closest to what Jesus would indeed do? Spend whatever extra he had, beyond what he had saved for his retirement fund and maybe a new car, as a non-Indian would do? Or spend every cent he had to feed his people, as is the custom with many tribal cultures? No, if we speak of Christianity in the context of Indian ways, we have to differentiate between the philosophy and culture of the Middle East from where it came and the considerably altered and acculturated form practiced today in Europe and America. If anything, what I have learned of Native ways is closer to true Christianity than anything being taught in churches, cathedrals, and tabernacles.

Author's note: Another, in some ways more detailed, narrative of these events and others mentioned in passing in this book can be found in my book *Embracing Fry Bread: Confessions of a Wannabe*.

3

A Lesson from Elders

A major influence in my being wrenched from skepticism to—what, Native deism?—was a Sincanju holy man by the name of Richard Fool Bull. He was well into his nineties when I came to know him in the early 1970s. He's long gone now, and while I often lament not having known him longer and put more effort into learning from him while he was here, I am also grateful I knew him as long as I did and that he was kind enough to share with me so much of what he knew.

My first encounter with Mr. Fool Bull was another of the jarring experiences that have contributed to my conversion from skepticism. The "fool" in Fool Bull, by the way, is like the "crazy" in Crazy Horse. It is the closest translation from Lakota to English that our language would permit for words that might better be understood to mean fey, enchanted, magical, mystic, sacred, and holy, all wrapped up in one, and not what mainstream English speakers think of when they say fool or crazy. Again in my enthusiasm for telling you about all this, I am getting ahead of myself. I'll tell you more about the nature and contrariness of Coyote when I speak of Coyote in chapters 11 and 12.

I had heard about Mr. Fool Bull from several people, but mostly from Kay Young, an old friend who was a close friend of Mr. Fool Bull's and was learning from his vast knowledge about plants and their uses as medicine. Both Kay and I tried repeatedly to arrange a meeting, but you know how those things go. When he was in town, I was not. Or I was busy and he was just passing through. Or . . . well, it just never worked out . . . until one evening when Kay called. First she apologized for calling so late in the day. It was late for me because I had had one long, hard day and was utterly exhausted even though I was much younger and in much better physical condition then . . . about 1972 or 1973.

Kay also apologized for the purpose of her call, what she thought was an utterly ridiculous request for help. She explained, chagrined, that Mr. Fool Bull was in town and was staying with her. They got to talking about his skill at making Lakota love flutes and how hard it was for him to find the materials he needed . . . primarily red cedar (juniper) heartwood. He had tried substitutes such as true cedar from the Northwest Coast and even redwood, but they just didn't work the same as the traditional juniper heartwood. At some point during the conversation, Kay mentioned my name in regard to something else . . . maybe about getting together while Mr. Fool Bull was in town on this visit.

He instantly perked up and said, "Him! That's the man. He can get me the cedar heartwood. The man you just mentioned . . . he has the wood I need."

Now, remember, I had never met Mr. Fool Bull. And what he couldn't have known is that I lived at that time in a ultimately typical, suburban walk-out ranch-style home, the kind they build on streets named Sycamore, Chestnut, or Shady Lane right after they bulldoze out every tree on the thousand-acre tract. Kay knew that on my small city lot I had maybe two trees, both silver maples, and that neither of them had a trunk bigger around than her wrist. The idea that I would have cedar heartwood was the ultimate absurdity. She tried to explain that to Mr. Fool Bull, but he wouldn't hear of it. He insisted that she call me, and so here she was, calling me.

I didn't even know how to start my explanation. Kay finally

had to call me out of my daze . . . "Hello? Hello? Are you there? Hello?"

Maybe the problem was not just my surprise at her call and question but also because I was exhausted since . . . well, let me tell you the story. About that same time, I had struck up a friendship with a curator from a museum a couple hours from Lincoln, where I was teaching. The museum where he was working wanted to consult with me about a historical sod house replica they were thinking of constructing. I had done some research and had just written a book about sod construction, and it remains to this day the definitive book, so I certainly could offer the kind of information he could use to build one accurately. One of the things we needed for the project was cedar beams for the roof. So when I found out that the college where I was teaching was about to raze one of its oldest buildings . . . a building surrounded with ancient cedar trees . . . I hotfooted it over to the provost's office and asked if I could bring in some volunteers and a truck that Saturday and salvage all the cedar trees; otherwise, they would be piled up with the building's rubble and hauled off to the landfill. He agreed that I could help myself to the trees, and I gleefully notified my museum friend that I would soon be hauling out to him all the cedar trunks we would need. After all, we only needed five, maybe seven, trunks, but I was going to wind up with a good thirty trees.

So at that very moment, as Kay and I talked, I had piled up in my suburban side yard a monstrous inventory of huge red cedar trunks. No one else in the entire state had as many cedar logs as I did. I had little else in this world at that time, and was about to have a lot less as things would turn out, but I had red cedar trees. And more wood than Mr. Fool Bull could ever imagine . . . although it seemed that somehow he *had* imagined exactly that, without knowing me and without seeing my suburban side yard full of red cedar logs.

The next morning Kay and Mr. Fool Bull came early, not long after dawn. After all, he was excited about finally finding the wood he needed. When Kay saw the huge stack of logs, she was stunned. It made no sense at all. How could Mr. Fool Bull have known about them? It was, well, crazy. And what was Mr. Fool Bull's reaction to his astonishing prescience? Nothing. That's what. Nothing. He began at once looking over the wood, telling me how much he needed of this log and how much of that one. He showed not the slightest sign of surprise. He was clearly pleased but not surprised.

I commented on this, saying that, well, uh, wasn't he astonished to find that I had all this cedar heartwood piled up in my suburban yard? No, the only thing that surprised him was that Kay and I were surprised. The reason he had wanted to come here was the cedar wood. So why would he be surprised to find cedar wood? White people! They sure do think in funny ways!

I don't recall if it was then or later that Mr. Fool Bull expanded on how curious we non-Indians are. Years later he gave me one of the beautiful flutes he had made from the wood he got from me that day; I have since passed it along to my Lakota brother Charles. On one occasion, Mr. Fool Bull talked more about how different the world seemed to him than it apparently seemed to me and my white kin. He said that it was his impression that the white man's real religion is something called coincidence. He said he was constantly surprised at what faith the white man seems to place in the idea of coincidence. So much is made of it, he said, and yet what a leap of faith it is to believe that some things are simple happenstance, even some things that are obvious, common, glaring. And yet the white man prefers to stretch credulity by crediting so much of it to coincidence. He couldn't imagine why we work so hard to deny the obvious and at the same time embrace the ridiculous.

His conclusion to his own hypothetical question was that the white man is educated out of what should be natural—that is, recognizing the obvious, or that Something Is Going On. He said that he didn't think that the Indian . . . or any other peoples of the world . . . were born with special powers or even somehow acquired them within the workings of their traditional cultures. Nor, he said by way of encouragement, I guess, is the white man incapable of grasping the obvious. He concluded that it is the process and purpose of the white man's educational system to dull our senses to What Is Actually Going On around us. After all, he said, these remarkable processes and events truly are so obvious and so common. How can we miss them, unless we have somehow been purposely cleansed of the ability to recognize wonders? Sort of as if we put on a blindfold or maybe earplugs that allow us to ignore what otherwise would be apparent.

Mr. Fool Bull wasn't being at all insulting as he spoke of the non-Indian's loss of such wonderful abilities. In fact, he seemed just a bit sorry for us. He felt we were being deprived of something wonderful, and it wasn't really our own fault. Nor was it his intention to change me or anyone else. (Even though he did!) He was merely observing an obvious fact. Nor did he take any particular pride that he saw what we do not—that is to say, the magic of life around him—or, in the case of the cedar trees, that he was a part of magical events. (In that case, after all, all of us shared equally in the inexplicable. He was perhaps the most passive partner in the process and certainly the least astonished by what happened.)

Far from feeling that he possessed special knowledge, information, or skills, Mr. Fool Bull insisted on the opposite, as have other Native mystics I've encountered. I have, in fact, learned to be cautious about ascribing special knowledge to Indians because they almost inevitably find that notion silly. And that too is part of the power of it all. These visits from

Wakan Tonka are not out of the ordinary in their opinion. We all have them, so the only thing special about them is that some of us choose not to recognize them, accept them, or acknowledge them. They are for all the world so mundane that they are no more special than if a waitress were to offer us a cold salami sandwich.

And still we refuse the offer. That is what is extraordinary.

In fact, if there is a problem in my sharing all of this with you, it's making too much of something that is, in reality, quite ordinary. I am perhaps compounding the problem by telling you about the most spectacular coincidences I have experienced. The fact of the matter is that scarcely a day goes by now when I don't think to myself or even say to the few people with whom I have already shared the magic, "Just a coincidence, I'm sure." Those who are in the know with me—my children, my wife, a few friends—smile, maybe laugh, and echo, "I'm sure . . . just a coincidence." But we *do* know. The real leap of faith so peculiar to the white man would be the nutty notion that the preposterously persistent is only coincidence, that obvious patterns are only unconnected, irrational accidents.

I suspect there are coincidences, plain and simple accidents, things happening and coinciding purely by random chance. What becomes unsettling are the *patterns* of such coincidences. And the extreme unlikeliness of the ones that are truly impossible, so impossible in fact that they would be better characterized as ridiculous. And the intense, unavoidable feeling on the part of the person having the experience that Something Is Indeed Going On beyond pure coincidence. There are stunning, ordinary, but memorable human experiences . . . seeing the birth of a child; hearing for the first time Jimi Hendrix play "Purple Haze"; witnessing the raw ferocity of a plains blizzard, a tornado, or a volcanic eruption; realizing mutual and absolute love . . . and all those kinds of experiences are wonderful and profound. Maybe even mystical. But the kind of visions I am considering here are beyond that. They can be dismissed as peculiar coincidences only because the human mind has real difficulty accepting them, but once their nature begins to creep into the witness's consciousness and the utterly impossible becomes acceptable reality—that is, acknowledging that Something *Is* Going On!—there can be no more dismissing and no consideration of what is happening without knee-buckling awe.

4

Early Lessons

Because I have so little time to catch your attention and tell you about what has been essentially a lifetime of wonder, it may seem to you as if all these revelations began for me quite suddenly, happening in jerks and starts and with gigantic emotional peaks in my life. Actually each of the stories I am telling you were part of the normal fabric of my story, not so much beginning all at once as happening continually and consistently and with the realization of them coming to me slowly but surely, creeping into my consciousness so I could no longer ignore or deny that certainly Something Was and *Is* Going On. I have no idea when the first of these mystical events happened to me; they have always happened and not just to me but to all of us. I have no idea when I eventually came to recognize that in fact Something Was Going On and that a pattern existed—facts that suggested it was all not simple coincidence. I simply don't know. Perhaps it is a matter of my own maturation, but for all I know . . . or, more precisely, *think* may be the case . . . perhaps children have these awakenings all the time too but, Indian-like, accept them as part of the normal course of things. After all, how would children know the difference between mystic occurrences and ordinary wonders, which seem to be coming their way regularly anyway, since they are only early in the processes of learning what is usual and expected in life and do not yet see anything as extraordinary?

I do recall being absolutely stunned on repeated occasions

during the summer of 1959 when my former wife and I spent several months bicycling through Europe. As I look back on that time, the wonder of it becomes especially evident in retrospect, but even then I was puzzled by what seemed to be uncanny coincidences, one after another. The entire three months, the whole trip seems now to have been an adventure in innocent surrender to the mercy of the gods. We had no idea what we were doing, and yet we not only came out of the wacky adventure unharmed but also were graced again and again and again by remarkable good fortune.

In 1958 I was a graduate student in languages at the University of Nebraska, and my former wife worked at the city library. We lived in a basement apartment and lived on what today wouldn't even constitute poverty-level income. We had nothing. My mother thought I was crazy, in fact, when I squandered $14 on a guitar, which later in my life became the very basis of my career and fortune—that is, folksongs and folklore. We had a friend who was also interested in folklore, especially in musical instruments and building and repairing them. He later became a legendary guitar builder on the West Coast, but at that time he was a novice instrument designer, repairman, and builder who was even poorer than we were. He and his wife visited us one evening and told us they were headed to Europe to bum around the Continent, look for musical instruments, and take in the usual tourist sights.

That plan seemed to us the ultimate dream and even a necessity since both my undergraduate and graduate degrees were going to be in languages. After these friends left us and headed for a stop in Chicago on their way to Europe, my wife and I began to think and talk, ever a dangerous direction for the brainless young. And we decided we should go to Europe too. I even knew a couple of other graduate students in my department who were planning on going over that coming summer . . . so why shouldn't we?

Well, if we had had any brains at all we would have considered, for one thing, that we had no money and, for another, that we didn't have any idea what we were going to do if we ever got there. But again, being young, we saved up about $1,000 from our total income of $2,500 during the next six months, living on Kool-Aid and popcorn, and made plans to go to Europe. We would travel by foot and bicycle. We would sleep at hostels (and, as we did later, in haystacks and under bridges!). If the then popular guidebook said we could live on $5 a day in Europe, why shouldn't we *both* be able to live on the same $5 a day? And we did, even though we returned to our Nebraska home the next autumn without two dimes to rub together.

For almost a hundred days we stumbled through Europe, utterly innocent, totally ignorant, and apparently immune to consequences. All that good fortune could be attributed, I suppose, to our youthful vitality and flexibility and the realization that it was a different time. After the catharsis of total war, total horror, and total depravity across Europe, maybe then everyone realized it was time for nothing but goodwill, even toward former enemies, hopeless innocents, hapless tourists, mere children . . . At the time we didn't particularly notice. We were young enough that we presumed it was the way things should and would be, that the horrors of the preceding five decades had been the anomalies. So we children of rural America wandered through Hamburg, Amsterdam, Munich, Cologne, Paris, and London without any notion at all of having put ourselves in any kind of jeopardy. Even when we were utterly broke, totally lost, or completely flummoxed about what to do next. We moved around the Continent blithely ignorant and at the mercy of the Fates.

It was only later that I wondered about the fact that despite our ignorance, we managed to see what we really should have seen in our grand tour. I have a vague recollection, for example, that I had seen photographs of and had read about the wonderful Schloss Neuschwanstein, the castle of Prince Ludwig of Bavaria—you know, that incredible storybook castle perched on a mountaintop that is the obvious model for every fairy-tale castle in a Disney book or film—but I do know that we hadn't made specific plans to find and visit it. No, but early one morning we were pedaling down the road, heading from Munich to Basel, when high in the mountain mists we made out the outline of the most fantastic castle ever imagined, let alone built. There it was. And we decided, what the heck, maybe we should go up there and see what it was all about. Just a stroke of luck, I guess. Even more remarkably, we had lots of luck like that. Okay, I'm still not willing to concede that such serendipitous finds were anything more than very good luck in a very small part of the world. Traveling slowly and for a long time along the roads of any country of the world, especially a small country like West Germany, I suppose such things would happen.

What we could not have predicted or expected during our travels, however, involved the three people we knew in all of Europe: the other graduate student from the University of Nebraska, Richard, who I knew but not so well that we compared itineraries, let alone planned any rendezvous during the summer; and two young Irish travelers we met in a hostel in northern Germany early in our stay and traveled with for two days afterward. Those three souls were the sum total of all the faces we would have recognized out of the hundreds of millions of people in the countries we visited . . . Germany, Denmark, Norway, the Netherlands, Luxembourg, Belgium, France, Switzerland, Austria, and England.

And we did recognize those three faces when we accidentally met them along the way. In Copenhagen we walked in the front gate of Tivoli Gardens, bought ice cream cones, and saw, sitting on a bench also eating an ice cream cone, Richard. We were so flabbergasted, we couldn't think of anything to say. We said hello, asked him how his trip was going so far, . . . and learned he'd been there three weeks or so, as we also had been. We wished him good fortune, then walked on. Unlike the other surprising circumstances we encountered along the way, this one was profoundly disconcerting. What are the chances of an unplanned encounter with the one person we knew in all of Europe? We didn't know he was going to Denmark, nor did he know we would be there. The encounter was absolutely pure chance. Well, . . . I suppose it was a coincidence, as if that is possible. I imagine that's what I thought at the time. As I say, we were young, and nothing seemed quite so impossible or improbable as it might now in my dotage.

A week or so later we met and came to know two new friends from Ireland. We enjoyed their company and regretted when we separated a few days later, as they moved on their way south and east while we headed west. We presumed we would never see them again unless they came to America or we planned a trip to Ireland. For a few weeks we continued on our way . . . to Holland, Belgium, and back into Germany. We visited the Moselle Valley, Trier and Koblenz, the Ruhr Valley and Essen, and Cologne, where we boarded a boat for one of the few real extravagances of our trip, the fabled tour of castles and vineyards up the Rhine River. I don't remember the exact situation . . . but I know that when we left the boat at Mainz, we had no money, couldn't find a room in a hostel, and wound up sleeping under a Rhine bridge, complete with river rats. But what was remarkable and remains etched in my mind is that at some point not long thereafter . . . perhaps in Stuttgart . . . my wife and I were walking a narrow street of an ancient town left relatively untouched by the destruction of the war, admiring medieval architecture, and probably scouting for a cheap place to eat and sleep when we saw coming toward us . . . our two Irish friends. Again we, all four of us, were so utterly dazzled by the impossibility of this chance meeting that we had nothing more to say that could match our astonishment. So we exchanged greetings, as we had done with our graduate school acquaintance, and moved on. In later correspondence with one of the Irish boys, we compared notes, and he admitted too that they never were able to reconcile with logic and sense how something so bizarre could happen. And in conversation with Richard when we returned, he, like the Irish lads, admitted that what seemed truly incredible about all this is that just as he was one of the only people we knew in all of Europe, we were the only people *he* knew in all of Europe.

At the time I wondered what the hell *that* was all about. Decades later I would figure out that it meant Something Is Going On.

5

Definitions and Distinctions

There are problems in thinking about the mystic experience. Quite a few problems, actually. And even more problems in talking about it with others. We can start with vocabulary. You'd think that as long as I have dealt with this thing, as important as it is to me, as strongly as I feel it could be important to others, as universal an experience as it is, and as gigantic a phenomenon it is to mankind, I'd at least have a word for it. But I don't. I literally don't know what to call this Something that is happening. For decades I referred to it as a vision because the most spectacular instances seem to be similar to the experience Natives sought in the vision quest, a spectacular burst of insight or inspiration obtained through special preparations and self-denial. But that term seems a bit overblown for those daily twinges of coincidence. The word "miracle" is overused (for an upset victory in baseball, for Pete's sake!) and carries a religious connotation that what I am talking about may or may not have. And it again makes the experience seem rare and even archaic, since most Christians think of miracles as having happened thousands of years ago. Should I call it a thrill? Too trivial. An event? Nah, that doesn't seem to work either. High school pep clubs have events. Experiences? Epiphanies? Realizations? Revelations? Maybe I'll call the really big, jarring mystic experiences visions à la Native American traditional descriptions, but what about the less spectacular and yet remarkable day-to-day gifts we are given by the Great Mysterious?

I like using the word visit because it implies some intent and an idea of something special coming by. And yet that obviously is not the right word either. I have sought help from some Native friends, presuming that since they are more familiar with the phenomena, perhaps they would be better equipped to label them. I didn't have a lot of luck there either, however, until Joseph Marshall, a Lakota friend and famous author, wrote me, "There is a Lakota word, 'woableza.' 'Ableza' means to realize or have an awakening. 'Woableza' sort of means to be enlightened or have a perception that is not ordinary to your ordinary experience. To me it's not so much that there is an 'awakening' or a 'realization' though since it's the message with it or behind it that counts."

Not even those most familiar with the occurrence have a linguistic grasp on it! I wonder if that very uncertainty doesn't say a lot about the nature of what we are trying to deal with in these pages. The visions, experiences, awakenings, Wakan Tonka's visits are all so beyond human experience that they also go beyond our linguistic abilities. Perhaps the best word we have in English for such phenomena is so obscure it remains virtually unknown and unused, a reflection of the painful fact that the phenomena themselves are also virtually unknown and unused in our Western culture: "theophany." Or perhaps the problem with that term is that it doesn't quite match what the mystic experience brings with it. *Theophany* is defined as "an appearance of a god to a human, a divine manifestation" in one dictionary and as "a visible (but not necessarily material) manifestation of a deity to a human person" in another. In the examples I provide, the gods as such never really appear but give messages and evidence of their presence. Is that the same thing as theophany? Theophany may then too be a misnomer and misleading.

As I struggle and grope for words that fit what I want to say, I have settled more and more on the term "wonder." As a noun it describes something unimaginably awe inspiring, something truly beyond the normal and the usual type of human experience, and as a verb suggests the confusion and bafflement we feel in the presence of a wonder.

Thing is, we don't have a word for these events because we don't very often recognize the phenomena. We have trouble naming things we don't know. They are like a wrinkle in reality. Maybe that's what I should call them . . . reality wrinkles. Well, for the purposes of expediency, in these pages I will call them events. And occasionally woablezas or visits. My wife, Linda, says there is only a thin line between flexibility and indecision; I like the idea of uncertainty in labeling these phenomena because uncertainty is inherent within them. There are, after all, big events and small events. And we need a word that covers a huge range. A couple times in my life . . . probably in yours too . . . I have picked up the telephone to call someone but didn't get a dial tone. "Hello? Hello?" And a voice comes from the other end of the line . . . belonging precisely to the person I was intending to call. I suppose that could be a coincidence. I imagine someone who knows about statistics and probabilities could come up with a figure about what the chances are of such a thing happening and maybe even some explanations mitigating what seems like an impossibly unlikely coincidence. How many people do we know? How many do we call? How often do we call them? Maybe something that affects or interests us both even makes simultaneous calls probable, even possible.

And yet you know as well as I do that this kind of thing happens when there are no such enabling circumstances. Say you call someone you only talk with by telephone rarely. And you suddenly had the unexplained urge to call them at precisely the same moment they are calling you. What *are* the chances of you both calling at precisely the same instance? And yet it happens. And as unlikely, as improbable, as *impossible* as the phenomenon might be, we still call it a coincidence. The people who really know about such things don't call it a coincidence. Mostly they just nod, smile, and acknowledge the fact that Something Is Going On.

Or we mutually acknowledge (perhaps without words) the agent in such goings-on. My own metaphor of choice for that part of Wakan Tonka is Coyote, the classical folkloric trickster, the Laughing God, the Clever Fool. In chapters 11 and 12 I'll have a lot more to say about Coyote (pronounced KY-oat, never ky-OAT-ee, by the way, for the latter pronunciation is a truly unfortunate, trivializing, and cartoonish mockery).

But you'd be bored if I told you about the small-world experiences we all have and if I tried to use them as examples of the grander workings of a Great Mysterious. So I have told you . . . and will continue to tell you . . . about the most undeniable, most remarkable, most impossible visits, woablezas, or events I have had in my life. That's what most people are interested in learning. And curiously, that's where most people start. This is not a case where you start small and work your way up. The little stuff is too easily dismissed in the beginning, too easily attributed to coincidence. This situation calls for telling you about my being hit in the face by the thirty-ton cream pie that knocked me down two or three times in a lifetime and then about my working my way down to the strawberry tarts that come across the counter every day.

If we hope to recognize Wakan Tonka's visits, one of these mystic experiences, or, as my Lakota friend would have it, an awakening, what should we expect to happen? Well, that is something of an inherent contradiction. The nature of a mystic event is that it is not ordinary. That's a synonym for "not expected." What we must be prepared for then—in fact, the only thing we *can* expect—is the unexpected. I can tell you this: it comes when you least expect it and where it is

most unlikely. Try as you will to prepare yourself, to predict what it is you think you are going to get, to somehow
encourage having one of these wonderful [*sic*!] experiences,
the one thing you can be confident of is . . . it won't be that.

In fact, I have something of a suspicion . . . although I
can't be sure since we can't be sure about anything when it
comes to visits . . . that you can't go out looking for them.
Yes, I know that in traditional, historic Native culture, the
vision was sought for, planned for, hoped for, worked at,
and secured with enormous self-sacrifice. I don't doubt for
a moment that the result was at least one kind of vision in
the Native cosmological system. But I also know it was not
the only kind. I have learned in the Native American Church
that prayer services are understood to be circumstances in
which one simply opens gates and doors and thus invites
visits. Sometimes visions come. And sometimes they don't.
The real value of the tipi meetings is to humble oneself, to
acknowledge subservience to great powers, to express gratitude, to invite blessings. But . . . and here is the important
part . . . when there are visions (and in the case of Native
prayer meetings I feel we can use that word because often,
even with the eyes closed, they are "seen" as visual phenomena nonetheless), they still come as surprises and generous
gifts, remain uninterpreted, and are accepted as individual
experiences rather than as patterns or paradigms that must
be embraced by entire societies or all of mankind.

In my own life these curious and moving events have shown
some common or frequent characteristics. For all I know,
these elements may be simply typical of a visit for me while
for others they are completely different. From descriptions I
have heard from those few people who have shared their experiences with me, however, I am not alone in this impression.

A side note with a story demands telling here. As I write
these words, I am chuckling. Coyote! He never misses a

chance. As I record my feelings about Wakan Tonka's visits and the unlikely explanation of coincidence, I have other things on my mind too. I am having a hard time concentrating because it is a windy day, the tail has broken loose on my windmill, and the fan is spinning madly, rattling with an unholy racket. So I am thinking of an old friend, a windmill repairman who lived not too far from here, just across the border, in Kansas. He got tired of climbing towers like mine in the driving, cold rain, similar to the one falling here now, so he became a dentist and moved to New England, then later back to Kansas. I wish he were here now. I hear from him a few times a year. Wonder what he's doing now. Well, no sense in worrying. I'll call a friend later to come down and help me chain down the windmill fan, and for the moment I'll try to concentrate on the workings of Coyote, the Great Mysterious. Now . . . where was I?

BOING! Hmmm . . . an incoming message sounds on the other computer. Maybe I should see who is trying to reach me. I open my email in-box and laugh again as I do almost every day, it seems. Of course. I should have known. And maybe by now you're catching on too. It's a note from my faraway windmill repairman–cum–dentist friend. He's wondering how I'm doing. Seems he was driving along when a coyote crossed the road in front of him and glanced back over his shoulder, catching my friend's eye for just a moment. For some reason, that experience made my friend think how long it's been since he's written to me. So . . . how are you doing? he asks.

Before we move on, think for a moment about the potential for a coincidence of this magnitude. Okay, so my friend writes often enough each year that a message could come from him any time. And maybe even at a time when my windmill is in collapse, even though the problem has never happened in the sixteen years the windmill has stood here. And of course, almost anytime he wrote, he might have caught me while I was writing since I write for a living. But what would you calculate in your most generous considerations would be the chances of his contacting me precisely at the moment I was writing about Coyote while being distracted by my suicidal windmill? I don't think we human beings have come up with numerical ratios that extravagant.

Okay, getting back to the business of the character and characteristics of Wakan Tonka's visits, I see if I stop this narrative to recount every time a bizarre coincidence comes along in my life, I'll never get anywhere. While we can open our minds to make them receptive to such visits, or to tune our minds to recognizing when such visits happen, it is not at all my impression that we can actively seek them out or encourage their arrival. They seem to me to occur when they are least expected. Even if and when we go out after them, want them, desperately beg for them, they nonetheless come from an unexpected direction, at precisely the least anticipated time, in an utterly unpredicted form.

Next I'm going to tell you a particularly vivid, especially remarkable example of why I think this way. And again I ask you to remember that I am choosing this example because it is vivid and remarkable, not typical or paradigmatic for me, even though it could have happened to anyone at any time with no special character or skill that might invite it. What I want you to gain from the story is not about the form of the experience but about the utter unlikelihood of its occurrence and my complete inability to have anticipated it. The story suggests, therefore, that you are not likely to be able to anticipate whatever mystic experience is headed your way, no matter how hard you try or how assured you are that you have covered every conceivable contingency.

6

The Lesson of the Skulls

When my brother Buddy Gilpin Jr., adopted me into the Omaha Tribe in 1967, as I have told you, he gave me his own tribal name, Tenugagahi (Bull Buffalo Chief), which is an allusion to the historical father of the tribe, the American buffalo. So the bison became something of an icon for me. On the back of my left hand I bear a tattoo of a stylized symbol of my tribal name to remind me of the honor Buddy gave me with his name, of the price he paid for that sacrifice, and of my clan, tribal, and personal obligations connected with that name. Almost immediately after the ceremony I began looking for a bison skull, a traditional altar in Plains Indian rituals, as a center for my own spiritual focus. I knew it wouldn't be easy to find one, but I had no idea how hard it would be. I couldn't find one for sale. I imagine that now it would simply be a matter of going to eBay and choosing the kind of skull and how much I wanted to pay. (To test my point, while writing this passage, I also went online and searched for buffalo skulls on eBay. There were fifteen bison skulls for sale, running around $50 to $100, and two that were ornamented in a Native American style and being bid at closer to $150 to $200. There were also a couple of African water buffalo skulls in the mix!)

I had no options like eBay in the late 1960s and early 1970s. For years I kept my eye open, hoping to find a suitable bison skull to serve as a focus for my home altar. No luck. And so I slowly gave up the notion. After all, I didn't really need it.

And maybe I was somehow being told that it was inappropriate to have a skull of the creature that I had been named after and that was so central to the culture, life, and religion of the people for whom I had so much respect. And certainly, as I learned later, it was inappropriate to *buy* one.

End of that story. Or so it seemed. Whatever the case, the idea of obtaining a bison skull dropped from my mind, and I thought no more about it. One summer day late in the 1970s, however, I was working on my rural land and as usual ended my day by heading for the river to take a bath. My cabin has no running water, but the river fronted by my land is clean and sandy and an excellent place to unwind and clean up. Naked, I slipped into the cool summer water and relaxed, my torso sinking down to the sandy bottom. Whoops. What's this? My bare bottom hit something solid. I don't find solid things in the river, as there isn't any stone anywhere around here. Occasionally I see waterlogged trees or branches, but there aren't many trees nearby either. I could feel with my hands (the water is too filled with fine sand to be transparent) that whatever I had sat on didn't feel like wood. I felt around under the sandy water and grasped the large item, slowly working it loose from the bed of the river. I pulled my find from the water. Hmmmm . . . it was . . . a large cow skull. How neat! I set it on a nearby sandbar until I finished my ablutions and then carried the massive hunk of heavy bone to my cabin, where I could look at it more carefully. I wound up putting the skull on the porch's tin roof to dry. It was after all pretty picturesque. You know . . . cow skull . . . western theme . . . out here in the wilderness . . . a Georgia O'Keefe kind of thing.

A few weeks later I was back at my cabin for the weekend when a farmer friend dropped in for a beer and a visit. He pointed to the skull on the porch roof and asked me what it was. I was a bit surprised because this guy should have already known what it was, with his being an experienced farmer and cattleman at that. "Well, it's a cow skull," I said.

"That's no *cow* skull! I've seen cow skulls, but I've never seen one that looks like that," he said.

Uh-oh. Goose bump time. Could it be . . . ? Nah, it couldn't be. A buffalo skull? Could it be that while naked and digging with my own hands, I had been given the very thing I had been seeking for so long? That would be simply too spectacular a . . . okay, well, . . . a *coincidence*, even for Coyote.

I took the skull to a colleague-scholar at the university, hoping he would confirm my wildest hopes and that I had indeed been given the bison skull I wanted, delivered into my hands by the river I so loved at the land I so loved. (Nah, that would have been just too romantic for words!) And my paleontologist friend indeed confirmed that I had not actually found a skull of the Plains bison, or the *Bison bison*, as the scientists have labeled that magnificent creature after which my Native brother Buddy named me. No, my paleontologist friend said, what I had found was not the skull of a Plains bison.

I knew it. Finding a buffalo skull in such a dramatic way would have been far too good to be true.

"No," he went on, examining the huge skull from side and then the other, "my friend, this is not a *Bison bison*, or modern buffalo. This is a *Bison antiquus*. This is the ancestor of the modern bison we have known on the Plains for fifteen thousand or twenty thousand years. This giant roamed the Plains more than thirty thousand years ago. You have found a rare, complete *Bison antiquus* skull. This guy . . . a bull, I would guess . . . was half again as big as a modern bison. See how his horns curve forward rather than up like the modern bison's? This one was a solitary animal, not a herd animal. You have a real prize here. Scholars search all their lives for a specimen like this."

A truly impossible coincidence, but as I have often said, God is really a very bad writer. God's stories show poor motivation, ragged plot development, questionable character motivation, unlikely conflict, motif disjuncture, ridiculous deus ex machina rationalizations . . . If I were still teaching English writing classes, I'd have to give God's efforts at creative writing a C– at best.

But the story surrounding my bison skull experience gets even more complicated. I forgot to tell you about unnecessary redundancy, which so often is a part of the mystic experience. I mean, read the story again as if it were a sophomore effort in creative writing. It doesn't work, right? Way too melodramatic. The point may be legitimate, but it is stated too broadly, too obviously, too dramatically. There is too little subtlety. So if you were a teacher, you'd probably hand the paper back to the struggling author and suggest a rewrite, hoping for improvement. And if God were your struggling writer-student, you'd be disappointed.

A common characteristic of one of these mystic events, awakenings, or visions is the element of surprise, but an even more common one is a total lack of subtlety. I had now been given in the most dramatic possible way not simply what I wanted . . . a buffalo skull . . . but the very apotheosis of a buffalo skull . . . a thirty-thousand-plus-year-old Pleistocene bison skull. That should be quite enough for a dramatic demonstration to prove to me that Something Is Going On. Again, if this were a novel or a literary drama, when the curtain closes as I stood naked in the river and pull the dripping Pleistocene bison skull from the water, the audience should already have been snorting, giggling, and laughing up its collective sleeve at the utter ridiculousness of the idea and the supercilious melodramatics of it all. But then the curtain would go up again and the play would continue because, as I was to learn, there was yet another act before the final curtain.

Suddenly, as had happened earlier with my receiving the round rocks and copies of the book with Brave Buffalo's speech, I was up to my withers in bison skulls. A friend who worked a dredge in a sandpit near my home came into the local tavern while I was having a beer and said, "Oh, here . . . I found this and thought it would be something nice for your cabin." He handed me an ancient bison skull, one from a *Bison bison*—petrified and ancient but maybe only ten thousand or fifteen thousand years old. And I found another bison skull on a sandbar down at the river during a walk one day. Then a friend brought me another recent, non-petrified bison skull. And the man at the sandpit brought me another.

My best friend in town was at the river with me a couple weeks after some floodwaters receded, and he helped me harvest fence posts and telephone poles that had washed out upstream and found their way down toward my part of the river. I had shown him some of the skulls as they came my way, especially the big *Bison antiquus*. He was tending bar at the town tavern on a couple of the occasions when people had brought skulls into the tavern for me. Believe me, I was neither advertising my interest in bison skulls nor even mentioning my search or my finds. While some people might have been at the tavern when others brought a skull to me, I wasn't soliciting more. For one thing, I hadn't thought my interest and quest was something of public interest, and once the skulls started accumulating, I was afraid people would think I was a liar, a nut, or worse. Each of the skulls came to me without the bearers being aware of the other ones I had. The exception perhaps was the situation with my bartender friend. He knew vaguely about the skulls I had and why I had wanted them and treasured them. But he did not know anything about the uneasy drama that seemed to be developing around them and me.

I suspect, however, that that day he had his suspicions. As we walked along a sandbar in the river, heading upstream with ropes to tie our salvaged posts and poles together as a raft, we talked about a lot of things, and the subject of the buffalo skulls came up. (As ridiculous as it sounds, please believe that I am telling you this story precisely as it happened.) My friend said (and this is almost verbatim), "I've lived here in this town all my life, forty years now, and spent a lot of time at this river, but I've never found any kind of skull, let alone an ancient buffalo skull. Just how do you go about finding a buffalo skull down here? Where do you look? What do you look for?"

And as I should have begun answering his question with some academic and logical answer, such as, "I have no idea how one goes about finding a buffalo skull. It's simply a matter of utter serendipity, a rarity that happens once but never again," I could only say, instead, "Well, it's simply a matter of reaching down and picking one up . . . like this one." And I bent down and picked up . . . yet another bison skull lying at my feet. This time it was a dark black one, a perfect contrast to the bleached white one I had found in almost exactly the same place the week before. It presented a stunning image on the crystal white sand of the shoal. We looked at the skull in amazement. We said nothing more. There was nothing more to say.

And then, precisely as had been the case with the round stones, after the inundation of bison skulls in my possession, there were no more. In a short period of three years, after a decade of looking for a single bison skull, a total of six, spanning an evolutionary period of thirty thousand years, had been delivered into my hands by one means or another. Bad writing or not, the point had been made and written in a bold italic font. And what had started as a drama of seeking and had turned into a melodrama of discovery became in the end a comedic skit about gods toying with human innocence and ignorance.

7

Resistance to the Irresistible

Sometimes a single mystic occurrence, such as those I have already related, is so dramatic that believing Something Is Going On is immediately unavoidable, while at other times the information comes in bit by bit, one piece of the puzzle at a time, until the accumulation presents the unavoidable conclusion. There is no sense, therefore, in looking for or trying to encourage one of these experiences because you may be seeking information that simply isn't there. That seeking is not an uncommon feature of Western culture.

I was once invited to be a head dancer at a tribal event, a profound honor for an adopted Indian. The tribal culture I know best is deductive rather than inductive; that is, one observes, learns, and deduces rather than asking questions or being instructed. A common joke is indeed to suggest that someone take lessons in traditional dance, the reality being that no one gives or takes "lessons"; instead, the only system for learning traditional lore is to observe and follow examples. Questions being considered rude, when a tribal representative called, he didn't *ask* me to be head dancer but only said that the group would *like* me to be head dancer for the event. I expressed my gratitude for the honor . . . and the conversation ended.

The problem for me was that I didn't have any information about when and where this dance was going to be held. And having learned enough about tribal customs to be polite in such matters, I didn't ask. Eventually I got wind of the day when the dance would be held . . . but still nothing about the location or time of day. I finally asked my uncle Frank Sheridan, since he understood all too well the white man's anxiety about such things; he said he would be at his brother Clyde's house for lunch the next day . . . the day before the dance . . . and would let me know. When that day arrived, Frank said he had indeed visited Clyde, but Clyde had never brought up the time or location of the dance. And of course Frank wouldn't ask.

I therefore decided I would simply have to think like an Indian. So the day of the dance I headed toward a park out at the edge of town where such events are frequently held, and en route I met a carload of my Indian friends coming from that direction. Hmmm . . . Well, I guessed the dance wasn't out there then. I went to the next place that might have an occasion like this . . . but no one was there. Finally I arrived at a public building often used by the Indian community, and parked behind some ball field bleachers was Clyde's car. I looked around the bleachers, and there was Clyde and his family, watching a game. Figuring that as long as I had my eye on him I couldn't go far wrong, I greeted my friends and sat down with them and watched the rest of the game.

When the game ended, we stood up, dusted off the seats of our pants, and looked around . . . and behind us in the parking lot were twenty or thirty other Indians' cars. They had seen our cars and were also waiting for the dance. Clyde looked at the assembled group and said, "Well, looks like everyone has wound up here. So we might as well have the dance here. Let's go get things started."

The moral of that story is that I was looking for two facts: when the dance would start and where it would be held. But the reality was that those facts did not exist until Clyde stood up and announced quietly the dance was going to be held there. And at that moment. So it is with the white man, I now find: often we are looking for and insisting on facts that do not yet exist and for that matter may never exist.

We have indeed induced enough fatal flaws into our thinking in America (and to some extent in Europe) that we have made it quite unlikely that we can arrive at the truth even where it does exist. For one thing, we have made ourselves constant victims of the false dichotomy: Better red than dead, love it or leave it, truth or fiction, yes or no, right or wrong, with me or against me . . . The truth is rarely that clear or that clearly and evenly bifurcated. Any time we hear someone proclaim a two-sided conflict, we can, in fact, pretty much automatically presume that the truth lies in neither option. And that point is especially true in religion and politics although it probably pertains just about everywhere in life and reality.

The false dichotomy is especially destructive and particularly common these days in political and religious dialogue, although mutual shouting would describe the exchanges better, I suppose, than the term "dialogue" does. The current fundamentalist view of evolution vis-à-vis creation is based on narrow thinking and small language . . . with the inability for many to express or think about things in ways bigger than their own experience or imagination, thus restricting the notions of God, creation, and miracle to terms and concepts they can grasp and then taking that interpretation literally. Fundamentalists, like the rest of us, cannot possibly grasp the cosmic vastness of Wakan Tonka, and that's normal and understandable; but the problem is that they fail to understand that they do not grasp it and, worse yet, still presume that they do. Their understanding, basically, is that God could not reconcile such a process as evolution and the eons that have gone into it because *they* cannot grasp the concepts. From their point of view, it's not necessary that they do so; but they must accept that they do not understand. That's enough.

Even worse, they accept the false dichotomy of evolution *or* the biblical creation myth. They are touching the fire, as my Native brother put it, when they presume that there is only *one* creation story when there are indeed thousands. When they are confronted by this notion and dismiss it by insisting that actually there is only *one* creation myth sanctioned by God (thus proving that they haven't read their Bible very carefully!), their position segues into the kind of arrogance even their own god specifically warns them against.

So how should we deal with terms and concepts we cannot grasp? How do we grasp what we cannot grasp? By saying and understanding exactly that: these ideas are beyond description and understanding. By understanding just that much, we leap ahead and beyond what many human beings ever come to grips with.

Moreover, we in the Western world too often presume that there is one right answer to a question or problem and one answer only when in reality there may be many valid answers, some overlapping, some completely separate, some perhaps better than the others, and some for all intents and purposes perfectly equal. We don't like that kind of ambiguity, yet we ignore that very real possibility at our peril.

Even where more than two choices are offered, there is always the possibility—maybe even probability—that the valid option isn't in the list. For example, when traditional beliefs—such as folk medicine or folk law—are discussed, one possible explanation for the persistence of such beliefs (and to my mind the most reasonable and likely one) is rarely offered: the belief or practice is true or valid. When authorized—that is to say, "official"—science wonders how laypersons can believe in a nonscientific medical practice or belief system, many reasons may be offered, but two are often omitted: the method or belief works . . . and that it is true. It is a fact that a large part of our sophisticated pharmacopeia has come to us from traditional (for example, herbal) medicines even before we understood the solid scientific foundation of their efficacy. So why do we meticulously avoid the possibility that other traditional beliefs may also have solid, empirical rationale? The day I write this, for example, is a Friday the thirteenth, and the newspapers and broadcast media are full of cute, quaint, condescending stories about the origins of that day's reputation for bad luck. No one has suggested the obvious alternative, however—that is, Friday the thirteenth may be by its very nature unlucky. No statistician or scientist would ever investigate such a possibility that Friday the thirteenth actually is for some reason unlucky because "reputable" scholars firmly believe, without evidence, knowledge, or investigation, that such a prospect just cannot be true. That stance, I submit, is blatant superstition, and, worse, it makes legitimate and honest investigation impossible.

Nowhere is our avoidance of obvious but somehow intellectually unacceptable reasons more true than in our constant attribution of the unlikely to coincidence. The next time you are inclined to say "What a coincidence!" at least slow down and ask yourself honestly how likely this coincidence can be. Is pure chance truly capable of such radical and ridiculous extremes? And even if it is, how often are we to experience coincidences of impossibilities before we have to ask ourselves if our explanations might not be falling short?

Sometimes it is redundancy . . . an absurd repetition of the impossible . . . that brings our doubts in that cure-all of coincidence to the surface. Sometimes it is simply the unsettling extremity of the odds. Once, at a museum in Finland, I saw a painting that enchanted me. In fact, it fascinated me. I studied it at the museum and wondered if I could perhaps buy a postcard or print of the painting, but the people at the museum assured me that it was such an unimportant painting that no one had bothered . . . or would bother . . .

to print copies for sale of something so utterly outside the interest of the general public.

A few days later in another town I took a walk in the public market, where people were selling all manner of items from household goods to food. Eventually I came to a young woman who was sitting on a stairway in the market; she had only one item for sale . . . a copy of that very painting. I bought it, and it hangs on a wall in my home to this day. After I paid the young woman, she pocketed the small amount I had paid for the print and walked away. It was all she had to sell. And it was all I wanted to buy. I have never seen a copy of that painting anywhere else in the thirty years since—not in a book, not in a market, not in a museum, not in a catalog, nowhere. Okay, so encountering the young woman in the market selling her one copy of that picture was a coincidence, and nothing more. That is an explanation. Or at least one possible explanation. Is it the most likely explanation, however? Not in the opinion of my Native advisers. And not in *my* opinion!

The unlikelihood of coincidence becomes all the more obvious in cases of redundancy, such as I had experienced with the bison skulls or the round stones. Wakan Tonka's visits lose all subtlety with their almost comic redundancy. And yet they gain an overwhelming power for the person who is swamped with the cascading events. But there can be no relief from the confusion that results from such an emotional, informational, and sensational (in the meaning "sensation") experience by seeking the counsel of others. Not only is the whole sequence of gifts inherently ridiculous . . . (surely you are experiencing some skepticism as you read these stories and wonder, no matter how much I protest that I am telling you the absolute truth, that they are actually simply too absurd to be true) . . . but even worse, the events of the visits, no matter how repetitious, are always ambiguous. Read again or reconsider the stories I have told you so far in these pages about the stones, Fool Bull and the cedars, and the buffalo skulls.

One of the most peculiar and difficult characteristics to grasp is that as extraordinary as the entirety of each event is, it is perfectly ordinary, even mundane in its individual elements. Each segment of the experience, the appearance of each gift, taken by itself is perfectly normal. Only when they are put together in the mind of the person experiencing the visit—perhaps the single place where they *can* be put together—do they become totally unlikely. Therefore, the events themselves are ambiguous when considered as mystic expressions and experiences. That is, they may be something special . . . but then again, they may not. Not a lot of people find buffalo skulls in the river, but, well, now and then, people have found buffalo skulls in the river . . . and in the soil. It is estimated that there are two thousand prehistoric elephant skeletons per square mile in my part of the Central Plains. No, that is not a misprint . . . two thousand per square mile. If you are building something and dig deep enough, it's altogether possible that you might find an elephant fossil. On the one hand, finding a prehistoric elephant is nothing you can expect, but on the other hand, it's not unheard of. Even more common, people find round stones . . . or more than likely see them but don't pay any attention to them. People cut down trees, people make phone calls, people make flutes. Nothing going on there. Sure, maybe a coincidence or two occur along the line, but it is nothing more than coincidence.

You'd think that it would help identify, explain, or describe such phenomena that each of the visit stories I have told you so far involves objects. You'd think that events involving *things* would be more obviously unremarkable, especially when the things themselves are so ordinary. And most mystic events of the sort I am telling you about do have a material element in them. On the one hand, that fact makes them all the more impressive to the individual who experiences them . . . I was given a thirty-thousand-year-old bison skull, for Pete's sake! And prehistoric grindstones. And not only the cedar trees but then the flute that was made from those cedar trees. On the other hand, that reasoning is no more solid than the narratives themselves. So what? Stones? Trees? Fossils? We certainly can't throw a cosmic fit every time someone finds a round stone, a cedar tree, or a fossil. Once again, just as the circumstances themselves are ambiguous, so too are the items that come as manifest evidence of the experience.

Accounts of the life of the great Lakota warrior chief Crazy Horse inevitably and logically (in conventional thinking) speak of his "vision." In his vision there is an uncertain importance surrounding a small, round, brown stone that he wears behind his ear. But I feel the interpretations, explicit or implied, that he wore the small, round, brown stone because of a sort of instruction he received in his vision is a mistake. I would bet that Crazy Horse didn't dream of a stone and therefore wore one. There is not a doubt in my mind, knowing what I do from my own experience, that he received that specific stone in his vision. It was given to him in his vision. Not the *idea* of the small brown stone but the *actual* small brown stone, which was the physical embodiment of his vision, given to him in the vision.

Crazy Horse's Lakota compatriots had no problem in understanding and appreciating the mystic quality and source of his brown stone. They understood the import of that stone and how he came to have it. Only in later accounts by people who don't understand the nature of visions or visits does it become a symbol of the vision but not necessarily a part and gift of the vision. The stone is an ambiguous element;

Crazy Horse and the mystics around him understood quite well what it was, but we latter-day "coincidentalists" miss that point. It's an easy point to miss . . . it's just a stone, after all! My driveway is covered with small stones, many of them brown. Stones are everywhere. Pick up a stone. There, just as Crazy Horse had a stone, you have a stone too. A stone may be in and of itself ordinary and utterly without meaning. But for the person who has experienced Wakan Tonka's visit, or the woableza, there is not the slightest ambiguity or doubt. The origin, nature, and import of the gift given in a woableza are anything but ambiguous to the person to whom it is given. You may not know what the physical gift means, but you know it is important and have your suspicions about where it came from. And the gift becomes one of the most valuable things you have held in your entire life, even though to those around you it is only a stone. You may have no idea what this gift means other than that it is a mysterious and meaningful gift.

A material gift that comes as a result of Wakan Tonka's visit is not magic. It is not an amulet or talisman with inherent powers of its own (although the one who has been given the gift may carry it as such and attribute powers to it). A gift of this sort is rarely of any value outside its role in an individual's vision or even distinguishable from any other rock, tree, whatever. While round stones, bison skulls, cedar wood, and so on, may have some small inherent value as material objects, the substance of the gift itself is not of enormous value. Even if it does have some trivial value . . . perhaps like a nugget of amber . . . that is not at all the point of its importance to the individual to whom it is given. If the recipient of this gift should die and not leave a narrative of its importance to the recipient, it may indeed become again just an ordinary rock. Or perhaps it only rejoins the earth to wait for another recipient. I don't know how that works, and neither, so far as I know, does anyone else. But I do know that often enough to make a difference, the mystic experience that accompanies a physical object is not in itself remarkable, but in the context of the person's experience of the event, it is powerful beyond an outsider's understanding.

8

The Lesson of the Dolmen

The story of a gift giving—vision, visit, event, mystery—is not particularly important or even interesting to anyone but the person who has had the experience. In fact, as is the case in writing this book, I wonder about the wisdom of even telling you my stories. Since they could have happened to anyone open to receiving them, they are not particularly striking . . . and that factor after all is one of my main points here. While the experiences I am describing to you are of enormous importance to me, they probably strike you as being pretty dull or maybe even downright nutty.

And that might be the case with my next story . . . in spades. You are really going to think I'm crazy when I tell you this one: I heard the voice of the Great Mysterious. Uh-huh . . . that's right . . . God spoke to me. I told you, you'd think I'm wacky.

Actually I am mentally stable to the point of being fairly boring. For one thing, I'm 100 percent German, and Germans are not exactly famous for being emotionally explosive. At least I'm no goofier than your ordinary professor type. I am white, middle class, state school educated, married with kids, and live in a Middle America, rural small town . . . I have had my share of eccentricities in my life, I guess . . . I went to Grand Prix racing school in California, I solo climbed some of Colorado's Fourteeners (mountains taller than fourteen thousand feet altitude), and I left a good job at a state university (where I taught English and anthropology, having previously taught languages at other institutions of higher education) to live and write here in the middle of nowhere . . . I have a tree farm, I have some success and reputation as a mechanic, and my children are no more or less difficult than anyone's children. My closest friends are a housewife, a government bureaucrat, an auto body repairman, a car mechanic, a historian, a retired industrialist, a brick mason, a computer programmer, a school janitor, a distiller, and another mechanic . . . I don't own a suit; I am usually recognized by the overalls I habitually wear. I am fat (*author's note*: Linda wants to corrects this to "sturdy"), gray haired, and seventy-eight years old. I have done some media work on a state and occasionally even a national level, but I have not dealt with the subject of this book previously.

All of which is to say, if anything at all I am a splendid example of a pretty plain guy, not the least bit inclined to the eccentric or to fits, seizures, spasms, conniptions, collywobbles, swoons, comas, spells, fantods, vapors, or possessions. I don't see things . . . in fact, if you ask my wife, she'd probably tell you that I am more likely inclined to miss the obvious. In short, I am the last guy in the world you would expect to have a mystic experience. For damn sure, I didn't expect the following to happen to me.

I was overseas at a professional conference in about 1976 or 1977. The international group convened at a splendid country estate in the Welsh countryside that catered to professional and academic meetings like ours. Our days were spent reading and hearing presentations on academic papers about research, and our evenings were often devoted to further research in our topic. It was a particularly pleasurable occasion because many friends I see only rarely were also at the meeting. Generally speaking, I was comfortable, happy, relaxed, having a good time. The last thing I expected was to have a mystic experience that would jar me to my very roots.

This particular day went according to plan . . . nothing

special about it. Along with our professional obligations of hearing reports and discussing our professional work, we had a short bus tour of the surrounding countryside and through the nearby city and did the usual touristy kinds of sightseeing, including a stop and short walk across an open field to a dolmen, a gigantic prehistoric (probably Iron Age) tomb consisting of a gigantic stone slab—the capstone—perched atop anywhere from three to six vertically set rock pylons. Not much is known about these structures except that they are very old; they were probably tombs, worship altars, or death monuments; they were major building accomplishments for a people with few tools; and the English, Scottish, Irish, and Welsh countryside is pretty much blistered all over with them. It was an interesting feature of our tour but nothing particularly striking since in my travels I had seen plenty of dolmens before.

After the day's work and the tour and some time to rest and clean up, we took the bus into the city, where we had an elegant dinner at a great castle. Yes, I'll admit I probably ate more than I should have and drank more than was good for me, but believe me, I was not drunk. Whatever effect the alcohol might have had on me was quickly swept aside by the events that were to follow. I have had too much to drink in my life, more than once. A lot more than once. I know how it feels, and this event was not a case of having had too much to drink. And I had laughed and talked more in a few hours than I normally do in a week out here in America's rural countryside. When we returned to the estate, the bus stopped, and we all disembarked and started through a light mist toward the estate's dormitory-style building where our sleeping rooms were.

But not me. I was suddenly taken by the inexorable need to walk. My friends were surprised . . . it was late, dark, not a good night for a walk. But they read instantly that I was not going to be talked out of what I needed to do and that I needed to do it alone. At the time I was confused too because I had no idea of where I was going or why. I just knew that I was being led as if by a strong hand away from the estate and back down the rural country road. This walk was not without considerable trepidation on my part. I'm not the sort that takes well to being led. Ask my wife. I didn't know the area's roads or the countryside in the least. It was not the kind of night to go out exploring unfamiliar rough country. But I had no choice. I was being almost forced into the night and into the pitch-black, moonless countryside.

I have no idea how long or far I walked, but I do know that I had no idea where I was until I came to the gate of the pasture where earlier that day our bus had stopped and a guide had led us to the dolmen. I was not at all eager now to leave the road and start off across the empty, rocky, pitch-black pasture. If I didn't know my way on the road, I most assuredly did not know anything about the open countryside I was about to enter on foot. I went through the iron gate and into the rock-strewn field. I was worried about stumbling, but I figured that whatever was moving me into the field was going to have to be responsible. (By the way, I am not suggesting that I was somehow teleporting, floating, or being carried along without moving my legs. I was simply walking, but I was not walking of my own volition. But believe me, I am about to tell you something even more unlikely than teleportation, so . . .)

If I hadn't known something was going on in this adventure to this point, it was now about to sock me in the face because whatever uncertainty I had about my path through the countryside was set aside when I saw through the dark night two echelons of perhaps twenty horses, facing each other and with their heads turned toward me, forming a long, open aisle. It was clear that I was to walk between them, and I did.

I am not at all fond of horses. They are beautiful animals, but they really don't like me. Over the years I have been bitten, kicked, stepped on, bucked off, run under trees and doorways, banged into gates and fences, pooped and peed on by horses. Everything a horse can do to inflict damage or indignity on a human being one horse or another has done to me. And for no apparent reason.

I was once doing a research project on barns and a farmer told me I was welcome to go into his barn and take some measurements and photographs. "Don't worry about the two horses in there," he said. "They're friendly." As I walked by those horses, minding my own business, one of them reached out casually, grabbed my shoulder in his mouth, and shook me, damn near dismantling me on the spot. I'm a big guy . . . more than 250 pounds . . . but that horse made the decision to work me around like a rag doll. Then when he was done, he went back to eating hay. Nothing personal, he seemed to be saying . . . "We horses just don't like you."

Please be clear on this point: the Welsh horses were not specters in the night, not visions or dream horses. They were real horses, behaving in very un-horselike ways.

I was shaken by the behavior of these horses, lined up as they were like an honor guard, but that alone was enough to convince me they were a part of whatever was going on. I had no choice in participating and accepting what they were clearly telling me: "This way . . ." Now when I think back on it, I am a little surprised I wasn't frightened. The horses were light colored and almost spectral in the darkness. And they didn't make a sound. They just stood and watched me walk down the aisle they had formed.

As I exited their double ranks I found myself at the foot of the dolmen I had visited earlier that day. By following the same guiding force that had led me there, I climbed up onto the top of the sloped stone "roof," or capstone, of the dolmen. And lay down on my back. I had no idea what I was doing or why, but I knew that was what I was supposed to do. I have no idea how long I lay there in silence but probably not longer than a few minutes, just long enough to catch my breath and wonder what was next. I was not frightened or even, as I recall, uneasy. I was simply mystified, in the most specific sense of that word.

It turned out that what was "next" was a voice. I recognized at once it was the voice of the dolmen. There was no actual sound, nothing hitting my eardrums, and yet the voice was loud and deeply resonant. It came up from the surface of the dolmen's capstone and up through my spine. And it asked quite simply, "How often do you imagine I can do . . . this?" And almost like a point of punctuation, I felt a flake of stone about the size of a computer mouse spring off and up suddenly from the huge monument and, gently but firmly, into my left hand. It was not a loose stone that I now held but a piece that had broken from the solid and massive stone suddenly and soundlessly and was thrust firmly into my hand. And then there was nothing but deep, heavy silence, although my head and body still resonated with the voice I had heard, unlike any other sound has ever touched me.

I lay there a while longer . . . although again I have no idea how long. At some point I brought my hand in front of my face to see what I had been given. I could tell from the feel that it was a piece of stone. And that's all it was. A plain piece of stone. It could have come from anywhere, but the fact of the matter is it had sprung from the gigantic monolith on which I was lying prostrate and into my open hand of its own accord. Once the astonishing reality of this soaked in and I regained some composure, I thought about the question I had been asked: "How often do you imagine I can do this?" What the hell could *that* mean? Or did it perhaps mean nothing more than what it said?

The dolmen's capstone was huge. One of the puzzles of these prehistoric monuments in fact is how the people with their primitive technology managed to move such gigantic slabs. And yet as large as it might be, like any earthly entity, that stone is finite. I suppose(d) that over the length of many millennia it could do what it had just done for me many thousands of times without totally disappearing. And yet it could *only* do it thousands of times before it would be gone. The gift of that flake of stone that seemed so small and insignificant a portion of the gigantic whole was indeed a small and insignificant portion, but it was also an irreplaceable part of a diminishing and limited supply of such gifts. What I had in my hand was at the same time utterly ordinary and insignificant . . . and yet a gift so gigantic it was beyond calculation. The stone's gift of a piece of itself could be, and perhaps had been, made many times over endless times, but the bottom line remained that it could give only a limited amount of itself. And *I* had just received a piece. Could there be a more precious stone on the face of the earth? Not to the dolmen. Not to me. This great, venerable, and venerated monument had given me a piece of itself, and it had apparently done so of its own volition. It told me that itself. To this moment, nearly forty years later, I sit here flummoxed by my own memories.

What was the voice I had heard or, perhaps more precisely, felt? Had the huge stone of the dolmen spoken to me? Or was it some kind of spirit? If so, was it within the dolmen? Under the dolmen? An unearthly power using the dolmen for an earthly presence? And why had this entity chosen to speak to me here, so far from ground familiar to me, so far from any of my customary chthonic or spiritual connections? And why me? Perhaps because I was just as ordinary as the stone flake I was holding in my hand? Perhaps because the stone somehow knew that I certainly was one person who would recognize and appreciate the gift?

To this day I have no answers to the questions. At the time, after taking a moment to gather my senses again, I did ask into the dark, open night above me, "What was this all about? Who spoke to me? Was I was supposed to do something with the gift that had been given me in the stone flake?" But there was only silence and the clear impression that all had been said that was going to be said that night in Wales. Nothing more has been revealed to me about this event because, I suspect, there is nothing more to reveal. The meaning of the experience is almost certainly the meaning I have derived over and over again from the visits and gifts: Something Is Going On. I am grateful to have been told that much, especially in this uncommon way, in this uncommon place. And I do after all have the flake of stone, which I still treasure, and I hope to be buried with it.

Does anyone believe my story? I certainly wouldn't believe it if someone related the story to me. Well, what does it matter if anyone else believes it? I was there, and I certainly have no questions about what happened to me that night. As you can imagine, the events of that night are as clear to me at this moment as they were nearly forty years ago. I walked out of the pasture and to the road . . . there was no sign of the horses that had guided me through the field to the dolmen . . . then down the road in the direction from which I had come. Eventually I saw the lights of the conference center and found my way to the dormitory, where some of my friends were still awake, talking, and wondering where I had gone. I have no idea what they recall of that night or what my condition was when I returned. I am reluctant to ask them, but I will. I told them some of what I had experienced but was uneasy about saying too much about it (especially having heard the voice of the dolmen) for fear of giving them concern about my sanity. I wouldn't have blamed them, after all.

I believe there are holy sites, places that are somehow sanctified in and of themselves, and totally apart from any attributions of holiness by man. Like all gifts of visits and visions, we are not likely to know why such places are sacred and have power, but we know they are sacred and do have power. They simply are sanctified places. Often we mistakenly ascribe holiness to places built by man's hand . . . a cathedral, a temple, a monument, a pyramid, a tomb, a dolmen . . . but I suspect that the opposite is likelier to be true: the site is not holy because of what mankind has construed or constructed; rather, the manmade construction exists because someone has had the sense to realize that the *place* is holy. Tourists often stand on the crest of the village of Acoma, New Mexico; look across the wide landscape toward the sacred mountain in the distance; and presume that the people who first settled there at some point decided almost arbitrarily that the peak was sacred because they too had stood here and looked across the valley at it, ever in view. My bet is that the truth is the reverse . . . that the early people who were open to such knowledge learned that the mountain was sacred and, in order to be near it and to keep it in their minds and sight, built their village nearby and within their constant field of vision.

So perhaps it was not simply the dolmen that had spoken to me but that the voice sprang from the *reason* the dolmen was placed there in the first place, something that far smarter and more sensitive people than we are had recognized long ago. Is Stonehenge a sacred location because of the monument, or was the monument built there because it is a sacred location? A 2010 NOVA television documentary about the Bahamas' blue hole cenotes stated that early inhabitants of the Bahamas thought the water-filled cenotes were sacred.

That is a misstatement. Those early Native people *recognized* that they are sacred. It was not an artificial theory but a realization of an undeniable truth.

Similarly, as suggested by thinkers and seekers like Brave Buffalo, the dolmen stone has a life of its own. It has the capacity to teach and give.

In the case of the gift from the dolmen, the agent of delivery—the dolmen—was in and of itself the gift. But that is not always the case. Sometimes humans are used to deliver visits, visions, or gifts, and their role in the process is as much a surprise to them as it is to the recipient of the gift. Perhaps a better word than "surprise" would be "confusion," because if the recipient of a vision gift somehow understands that something very remarkable is happening, the messenger, or the involuntary and innocent deliverer of the gift, still may have no idea at all of the nature of his errand. He is only an agent, neither a giver nor a recipient.

When my scientist friend John delivered that round grindstone to me, for example, we had little to say to each other because, as he admitted, he had no idea why he was bringing me the rock. It seemed to me at the time that my educated, non-romantic, coolly scientific friend was if anything a little embarrassed by his confusion, by what obviously seemed to him like a bizarre bit of behavior on his part. I was in no position to explain anything to him about the mystery that was going on and why I was so stunned, and not simply surprised, by his unlikely appearance at my door and his remarkable delivery. When the antique dealer and the taxidermist gave me their round stones, they were puzzled why they were doing it but not so struck by their action that they questioned it or gave it much thought. They did it, as strange as it seemed to them, and . . . well, then it was done. The most common attitude of someone who is not acquainted with the whole process of visions, visits, and mystic gifts is momentary and minor confusion that is quickly dismissed as nothing of particular importance. The usual introduction to the delivery of the gift is "I have no idea why I am doing this, but . . ."; "I can't imagine why I'm here, but . . ,"; "This is really silly but I had this feeling . . ."; or "Excuse me for bothering you, but for some reason . . ."

The recipient of the gift may be surprised, stunned, amazed, puzzled, awed; whatever the transfer's meaning, it may not be immediately clear. But the recipient does know something important is happening, even if it is unexplained. The messenger knows only that he is being moved by an unexplained motivation outside his control.

Author's note: I am grateful to my old friend and colleague Jay Anderson, who had traveled with me to the conference, for providing further information about my experiences with the Welsh dolmen that night. For example, I had forgotten that when I returned (to the place we were staying . . . perhaps to life!), the stone fragment I had been given was wrapped in an oak leaf. Jay writes in a private communication:

"The next morning I breakfasted with two eminent folklorists. One was a Scot so I told him Roger's story. He smiled understandingly. 'Oh, sometimes they talk to believers.' Then he turned to the other famous folklorist, a Welshman, and he asked, 'When did they last talk around here?' [The second scholar] thought for a moment and [then] said, 'Around 1770. Yes, that was the time. They talked to a brewer—just a humble ale brewer, but well regarded hereabouts.'

"After 200 years the Druid's stones had finally spoken again."

9

A Lesson from the Pipe

Nowhere is the whole subject of mysterious delivery dealt with better than it is by Kurt Vonnegut in his novel *The Sirens of Titan*. Vonnegut makes it clear in his book that he gave a lot of thought to how such things work, and he does it in such a way that I can't help but wonder if he had direct and personal experience with such remarkable events. It's hard to imagine his having such insight without direct involvement in the processes of the mystic vision.

Briefly, in Vonnegut's story his hero—or perhaps more precisely his antihero—Malachi Constant, has a long series of adventures as an innocent adventurer, uncertain of what is going on around him in a futuristic world and of what his role in all of it might be. Nor do we readers understand much through the first 300 pages of a 325-page narrative. In the final scene, however, Constant winds up stranded on Titan, the largest moon of Saturn. There he meets a space traveler from Tralfamadore, a distant planet. The traveler has been crossing the galaxy for hundreds of thousands of years . . . or more precisely he was on a cross-galaxy trip to another civilization when he was stranded on Titan after his spaceship malfunctioned and needed a part to repair his spaceship.

Delivering a spare part for a disabled spaceship across endless space and time takes a good deal of fancy work, of course; so the traveler's mother civilization set about the task with what resources it could gather most quickly. The process involved the development of a civilization on a nearby planet . . . namely, mankind. On Earth. And the good luck amulet we have occasionally noticed on a cord around Malachi's neck during the long narrative turns out to be the part the space traveler needs to repair his ship. With only a few pages left in our reading of Vonnegut's book, we are kicked in the stomach with his science-fiction fantasy that the entire development, history, and course of mankind have been to serve one purpose—to deliver a spare part to a stranded spaceship on Saturn's moon Titan. We are nothing but a delivery system and have never been anything else. That is our meaning and purpose . . . to deliver a spare part for a broken piece of space machinery.

While the reader is still reeling from this crushing idea, Vonnegut sideswipes us from yet another direction, finishing off whatever arrogance the brief history of hominids might have given us. Okay, so we have fulfilled our destiny and brought the part to the space messenger so he can complete his journey to deliver the Tralfamadorian message across the galaxy. Now that we are at the end of Vonnegut's narrative, now that the replacement part for the disabled Tralfamadorian spaceship has been delivered (futilely, as Vonnegut and Coyote would have it), what could the message possibly be that brought about the existence and thus the meaning of mankind? When the message the space traveler is carrying across the universe is opened (contrary to the fundamental and strict requirements of the messenger and his assignment), Malachi Constant learns that it is . . . a sheet of metal with a single dot on it.

•

And that is it. A dot. Vonnegut tells us that in Tralfamadorian, a single dot is the symbol for the word "greetings"! Thus the entire meaning of mankind and its works has been to deliver a part to repair a spaceship that had been sent across the galaxy millions of years earlier to deliver a message consisting of the single word "greetings." And as if that weren't enough, now the errand is a futile one because even that modest message is not going to be delivered.

What can be said of such grand futility? Well, Malachi Constant perhaps says it best: "Oh my—life is funny when you stop to think of it." And of course, it is. Not to forget, Vonnegut's *Sirens of Titan* is fiction. However, one thing I have learned (and learned and learned and learned and learned) in a lifetime of writing is that fiction is not the antithesis of fact except that "fact" is an elusive thing indeed, shifting from time to time and place to place. As any creative writer, and even some scholarly and scientific writers, will tell you, fiction is the place where you can tell the truth. If you want to know what's really going on, avoid the nonfiction section of your library or bookstore and settle down instead in the fiction aisle. We are prepared to set aside our disbelief when we are told that what we are reading (or seeing in the case of drama and life) is an invention of the human spirit, but when we are told something is factual, we expect it to be believable. Nothing could be further from the, well, . . . the fact! The truth is often too preposterous for our senses of reason and logic to accept. Fiction is a way to mitigate fact to make it believable. If I had couched all my stories in these pages as snippets of fiction to be enjoyed but . . . hahaha- haha! . . . certainly not to be accepted as anything close to the truth, you wouldn't at this point be looking at me with that funny look in your eye and I wouldn't have to scramble to convince you that I am being straight with you here and am actually quite sane.

At least twice in my life I have been an instrument of delivery for someone else's mystic gift. There may have been more such occasions, maybe even many more such occasions, but how would I know? About the only sign we have that we have just been a part of insanely improbable things as delivering a mystic gift for someone else is an expression of surprise on the part of the recipient, and that depends on our being there at the time and on the recipient's being the sort who is surprised. Richard Fool Bull, after all, was not at all surprised to find that I had the red cedar heartwood he had sought. As he said, that was after all why he had come to me. So why should he have been surprised?

It was only by chance that I learned of another occasion when I had been instrumental in such a gift delivery. That too was with a Native. It follows that if the only sign one has that something extraordinary has happened is from the recipient's reaction but the recipient lives in a cultural matrix where such events are not seen as extraordinary and therefore expresses *no* surprise, your participation in the process is also accepted as unremarkable.

As I have noted before, during my life I have now and then garnered a modest amount of recognition and what passes for fame in Middle America. Through my writing, teaching, speaking, and working in broadcast media, I became known by a fairly large public. As a result I receive some fan mail, about a half dozen to a dozen pieces a week. My public persona hasn't been far from my real self . . . a pretty ordinary guy in a pretty ordinary place interested in really ordinary things. I have received all sorts of letters, mostly saying nice things, some a little on the nasty side. People have sent me things, mostly out of the goodness of their hearts, out of their generosity, or because something I had said on their television sets fired their memories or imagination. But I don't think anyone ever sent me anything quite as valuable or remarkable, however, as one fellow in Colorado did—a beautifully made and ornamented red pipestone pipe constructed in the Indian style.

I suppose I shouldn't have accepted the gift . . . I think there are rules to the effect that only people above assistant

vice president of the corporation were permitted to participate in graft and bribery. But I wasn't really in the profession
of journalism, the gift was not impossibly lavish, no favor
was asked, and I didn't want to be rude, so I accepted the
pipe with thanks. I had no particular use for it, and it wasn't
even clear why this person I didn't know—I can't even show
him the courtesy of remembering his name!—had sent it to
me. In fact, he didn't know why, either, and said as much. In
a note accompanying the pipe he just said he had seen me
on television talking about something or another and had
the feeling that the pipe was something I should have. So
he sent it to me. And I leaned it in a corner of our hearth,
where it gathered dust for ten years. I never moved it from
that spot, probably only touching it to move it out of the way
when I moved something else. It was a very attractive piece
and would have served as a decoration if the clutter of our
hearth didn't pretty much hide it from view during most of
its tenure in the household.

Then one day I was lying in the hammock and reading one of
my weekly news magazines when I had a sudden, clear internal signal that I should take that pipe, clean it off, and send
it to my tribal son Jeff Gilpin. No particular reason . . . I just
suddenly felt that he should have it. I hadn't even thought about
that pipe for years, but I packaged it up and sent it off to Jeff.

I didn't hear anything more about it. I really didn't expect
to hear anything, because in the tribal tradition the benefits of
giving fall to the donor, not the donee . . . very much in the biblical tradition of it being more blessed to give than receive. So
in the system of tribal thought, I already had my reward for
the generosity and really didn't need any thanks in return.
Many months later I happened to be on the tribal reservation at the same time as Jeff and his family were. Jeff's wife, Colleen, mentioned to me that he had received the pipe, and it had
arrived in fact "just in time." Just in time? Just in time for what?

"He hasn't told you about why he needed it?"

"No, I haven't heard a thing."

"Oh, I'll remind him to tell you . . ."

Later, when Jeff told me what had actually happened, I was chilled to learn that I had apparently been a part of a mystic gifting process, for all the world like Kurt Vonnegut's fictional character Malachi Constant. Jeff was learning songs, rituals, and information in regard to his sacred "fireplace," his ordination, and his "church" within the Native American Church from another tribe's spiritual leader who knew and understood the intricacies of this particular expression of the church. Jeff knew that a gift was in order, but he wasn't sure what would be appropriate. He conferred with some elders in his own tribe, and the consensus was that he should give the spiritual leader–elder from the other tribe a pipe. That gift, apparently, was not only appropriate but also traditional.

But Jeff didn't have a pipe and furthermore didn't have access to pipestone, which is considered a sacred material in many Plains tribes for many thousands of years and to this day quarried and worked by Natives at its only source near Pipestone, Minnesota. He asked around the reservation, among tribal and family members, and while no pipe was available, someone did recall that a piece or two of pipestone had been obtained many decades before and buried to keep it soft for later working. But as that time had never come, the stone remained buried and had been pretty much forgotten by all but a few elders. Jeff went to the site with some tribal elders who vaguely remembered where it had been buried, and they dug and probed but . . . well, landmarks had changed, memories had faded, and they could not find the cached pipestone.

Jeff returned to his home in a large city about an hour away from the reservation to find . . . you guessed it . . . a package from his adoptive dad, me. Jeff wondered what the package might contain; a tribal uncle visiting in Jeff's home opined without any particular gravity or wonderment that, well, it probably was that pipe he needed. Jeff opened the package and was pleased but not stunned (as we who are unfamiliar with the true workings of the world might have been) to find the pipe I had sent. He told me that it was a bit more ornate than his tribal tradition recommended, but once he removed some of the beads, feathers, and doodads, it filled the bill quite nicely.

I couldn't resist. I asked him if he didn't find it rather remarkable that he needed a pipe, that I had a pipe (sent to me many years earlier, as it so happened, also in a curious, even mysterious context), and that I happened to send it at precisely the moment he needed it . . . No, he did not find it remarkable at all. He figured that his biological father, my adopted tribal brother Buddy, knew of his need, presumed that I as surrogate father was obligated to meet that need, and that he as an extra-human observer did what he needed to do to facilitate the matter: so Buddy told me, without my knowing I was being "told," that I should send the pipe, which another unlikely exchange had put in my hands earlier, to Jeff. It was all very logical to Jeff, who was thinking in tribal ways. In short Buddy had told me to send the pipe to Jeff. And years before, Wakonda had told the man in Colorado to send it to me. Because Wakonda knows such things.

What makes such a natural and normal process seem unusual are our own human limitations. Not understanding the magnificence of the ways of the Great Mysterious, I was doomed to perceive of what is easy for Wakonda as impossibly unlikely . . . because it would be impossibly unlikely for a mortal like me. Especially unthinkable is that I, a mere mortal, would somehow be part of an impossibly enormous, complex, arcane system for delivering a sacred gift.

10

The Lesson of the Feather

Of enormous interest to me throughout my considerations of the gift events are my recollections, impressions, and feelings about them as they happened. That is, in retrospect, I try to reconstruct my feelings and perceptions as they were when I experienced the mystic process in hopes of better understanding them. This introspection was particularly important to me as I struggled to protect my firmly and dearly held skepticism about such things while my stronghold was smashed and pushed out of the way by the irresistible forces of evident truth—which is to say, Something Is Going On. My obvious first reaction to the undeniable things I insisted on denying was astonishment; it is the nature of Coyote to express himself using surprise and humor, and often it is the Coyote manifestation of Wakan Tonka that brings us gifts and visions. There was (and is, since I continue to experience these phenomena) also awe and confusion not only because of the mysterious nature of the visions and gifts but also because, of all people, I am the one who has been visited. The first question I might ask is, "What the hell is this?" It is almost immediately followed by another: "Why the hell is it me?!" The long, thoughtful afterglow of what my Lakota friend has called woableza, or awakening, has to be an enormous satisfaction in the ultimate meaning of it all: Something *Is* Going On.

On another occasion when I discovered I was being used as a messenger, the process of delivering a sacred gift was also a gift and vision for me; that is, while my assignment was to deliver a material item as part of someone else's mystic experience—or woableza—it was as moving an experience for me as for the recipient of the gift. I was spending some winter days grading papers in the quiet solitude of my century-old log house, deep in the woods along a Plains river. One day I snowshoed into town through deep drifts, visited with some friends, had a couple drinks at the tavern, picked up my mail at the post office, and snowshoed back to the cabin. One of the letters in the packet was from a dear old friend who had also spent a lot of his time among Native peoples, so we both felt we could talk with each other about mysterious but revealed things others might not understand. He told me in his letter that he had had an occasion when he was moved to give away something very precious to him, an eagle feather. As if an eagle feather were not powerful enough a gift, a special friend had given this one to him, and it had a powerful history behind it. But an irresistible feeling had arisen within him that he was to give the precious feather away to another person, who was also special to him. With enormous reluctance and perhaps even some pain, he therefore gave away one of the most precious things he owned . . . that very special bald eagle feather.

But my friend wasn't telling me this story just to share it. He said he was troubled by a question that arose while transferring that feather. "How," he asked in his letter, "does one get back something as powerful as an eagle feather when you give it away? Once given a gift so sacred, so unique, so personally and spiritually important, how can you ever recover the loss if you then give it to someone else?" Wow. I was the wrong person to ask. At that point in my life I had not been "feathered," or given a sacred eagle feather as a very special Native recognition. Eagles were very rare at that time in my part of the world, although they have become wonderfully abundant since. I had seen a golden eagle up close once in western Nebraska many years before. I had seen an occasional bald eagle along the river by my cabin but only rarely, the first time being only a year or so earlier. I knew a lot of things about a lot of things . . . but absolutely nothing about how one winds up being honored with the gift of an eagle feather.

Of course, my friend's question was about much more than a surrendered feather. He was asking how one gets back something—anything—enormous in his life if he gives it away? When a treasure is somehow won, why should it ever be surrendered? And why was he suddenly moved to give away this precious gift? It made no sense. The feather was not something to be given away. It was something to be treasured, held, protected, because once it is gone, he could never obtain one like it again. It was not simply another eagle feather; it had come to him as a gift from a very special friend.

Yes, the person to whom he had given his feather was very important in his life too, as were so many others. I was important in this man's life, but he had never felt moved to give me an eagle feather yet with this eagle feather . . . So . . . why? Why this person, this gift, at this time? And what was he to think of this huge emptiness in his life now that he had given the feather away? Could the Great Mysterious possibly have seen it as disrespectful that he had now so easily given away something that had been so potent and important? Had he made a mistake? How, indeed, once something so valuable has been given away, does one get that power back?

I gave a lot of serious thought that day to my friend's question, not simply because I wanted to help him but also because his question struck me as worth thinking about in my own life, about gifts, about friends. I pulled on some warm clothes, waded out from the cabin through the snow, and headed down toward the frozen river to clear my mind and reflect further on what he had asked me. I stopped, looked across the ice of the river, and listened to the water rustling and growling under it. I walked through the juniper trees and the now-naked sumac spikes. I looked at the deer, coyote, turkey, and rabbit trails in the snow. I walked under a huge, old cottonwood tree that leaned out over the ice. And there at my feet was . . . a large, perfect, bald eagle tail feather. I don't know how long I stood there in amazement. I had never before and have never since found a bald eagle feather. And yet precisely on the day I read my friend's letter with his question, at the very moment I was out walking and thinking about how indeed one ever regains value after passing along a gift as precious as an eagle feather, there the answer was: the way you get an eagle feather . . . is to give away an eagle feather. It's not a matter of something ending and then beginning anew. It's a flow and eddy, deep and wide. It involves adjectives, maybe verbs, but not nouns. There is only process and meaning, not cause and effect.

I picked the feather up from the river's ice and snow with reverence. I had tears in my eyes as I realized that Wakan Tonka, the Great Mysterious, had just touched me. I had just been spoken to by what some people call God. I had been given a very deep and difficult philosophical and theological question to contemplate and then just as astonishingly been given the answer . . . and not just in words or an idea but with the proof of a clear, bluntly obvious, actual physical item of undeniable evidence. I had been assigned an errand, to send the feather to my friend and tell him, "*This* is how you get an eagle feather once you have given one away."

And I had received a lesson too . . . the same one, of course, along with a very clear instruction: sometimes we are not simply given answers by the Great Mysterious but also, even more important, given the *question*. My friend had been moved to give his feather away so he would ask me the question; I was given the feather to send to him as

an answer. Both of us were taught the lesson . . . or, more precisely, lessons. How many lessons after all were taught and
learned in that short day between the moment I read my
friend's letter and my walk to town to send him my answer?
There were lessons of humility in how little we know and
instructions in listening for the forces that swirl around us
and tell us what to do if we pay attention. There was that
central point about giving and receiving. In that I had just
been a party to a massive demonstration of power and awe,
there was the laughter of a force that knows so well how to
joke with mortals. (I mean, really, how much more absurd
could a "coincidence" be?)

I now shared my friend's experience . . . giving away a treasure . . . the only eagle feather I have ever found . . . and his
question was now mine. And yet his answer was also mine:
first, you receive by giving; and second, no doubt about it,
Something *Is* Going On.

11

The Dubious Eye of Coyote

find myself consciously resisting to this day the temptation of taking comfort in the idea that I am somehow special because I receive and recognize remarkable gifts. First, they happen in every life so it would be silly to feel my own experiences are in anyway special other than their import to me. Second, I'm not at all sure that it's good to be the focus of such attention. As with so much of what I am telling you, that unease reflects an old idea. In many cultures and for much of man's history, even saying the name of God has not been advisable for fear of calling attention to yourself. That's why we call God, God—similar to calling a cat Cat or a dog Dog—rather than calling Him by His proper name.

In our Western culture, perhaps from Judaic origins, we avoid using the personal name of God and instead use the generic term "god." Or perhaps we simply struggle to find a term appropriate to the gigantic concept of . . . well, whatever "it" is. My experience with Plains Indian cultures has led me to the Lakotas' Wakan Tonka, the Great Mysterious, and the Omaha-Ponca variant Wakonda, but I am also taken by the archaic Pawnee term "Tawadahat" (This Immensity). (Modern Pawnees use Ateus Tawada, or "The Creator of All.")

That hesitancy in invoking the name of unpredictable powers and calling their attention to me is especially true regarding the element of the divine paradigm I think of as Coyote. With his perverse sense of humor, his utterly unpredictable nature, his peculiar notion of how everything fits together, it is sometimes . . . maybe even often . . . best not to call attention to yourself when dealing with Coyote. I provide more thoughts about that when I talk about Coyote the Trickster in detail.

As noted previously, Kurt Vonnegut's Malachi Constant is an adventurer and a pilgrim. He is an innocent victim of all that goes on around him. Throughout Vonnegut's novel, Constant has no idea where he is going or what he is doing. He is lost and stumbling through unfamiliar surroundings in the dark. Those of us who have some capacity for honesty realize that the same can be said of all of us. No, that's not quite right: it's not what *can* be said about all of us, it's what *must* be said of all of us.

Vonnegut is obviously not the first person to think of such things, and as with so many before him who have thought most critically about our clueless seeking of truth, he has a sense of amusement about our bewilderment despite that this frustration continues to be a constant worry of mankind. Life is *funny*, a curious word that can mean either laughable or peculiar and unpredictable. Both definitions fit mankind and life in general but most certainly fit the mystic phenomena that are discussed in these pages specifically. Despite our best efforts and most insistent arrogance, we don't know what we are here for or what we are doing or where we are going. And we most assuredly cannot claim responsibility or even knowledge of such things . . . especially when we find ourselves as a kind of mystical delivery mechanism for a special gift from Wakan Tonka to someone else, even though we don't know who is sending us on the errand or what the message is that we are carrying. Or when we deliver it, what the message means.

Many, understandably, find the prospect of being manipulated into serving as helpless agents depressing, if not downright terrifying. People, especially Europeans and Americans, want to be in control, particularly of their own lives. We are told, you are responsible for yourself and your fate. Be what you want to be. There are no limits to the possibilities. In America anyone can aspire to the presidency after all. That is, at any rate, the great American myth.

As if the thought that we aren't in complete control of our destinies weren't unsettling enough, there are the additional worries that whoever is in charge is unpredictable, is perhaps not even operating at our own human level of reason and reality, or worse, has no apparent design at all. My own impression that, at least within the confusion, there is a wonderful sense of humor may not be a comfort to others.

We have major disadvantages in the narrow scope of our horizon. Even when we can perhaps see a larger pattern, we tend all too often to think in terms of what is immediate. Again and again in my own life, I have experienced very painful losses, failures, disasters, pain, disappointment . . . Continue the list as long as you want. But looking back I am again and again surprised at how often the apparent pain hasn't just faded or gone away but has turned out to be actually a prelude to something quite positive and almost always a complete surprise. No one who knows me would ever accuse me of being a Pollyanna or even an optimist, but as with my reluctant conclusion that Something Is Going On, I have to go even further, still with enormous unease, and say, well, damn it, . . . Something *Is* Going On.

I've told the story already in these pages, but let me repeat it briefly and in another context. I bought a small parcel of ground in a beautiful setting, behind Pike's Peak, but was disappointed to find that my intentions to build a retreat there stopped by a change in zoning regulations, lowered speed limits, and more expensive gasoline. So I sold it and bought a piece of ground instead in central Nebraska. I immediately came to love this ground but in a divorce almost lost it. The very painful divorce also left me rudderless and empty, when out of nowhere came Linda, with whom I found a love and security I was sure I would never know again. I enjoyed some academic successes and thought despite my personal setbacks I seemed to be advancing professionally. Being elected then to a seat on the board of the Nebraska Sate Historical Society was as high an aspiration as I had, but out of nowhere a contingent of Indians, mostly Pawnees, appeared before the board, requesting the return of the remains of their ancestors from the society's shelves. Appalled at the way the board received and rejected the Indians, I resigned from that coveted seat and joined instead with the Indians, a path that also generated trouble for me in my academic position. With my tribal associations, I found a renewed satisfaction, far exceeding anything I had felt in either my academic or professional situations. This realization then led to my surrender . . . one might say "loss," but there was not so much a sense of loss as one of gain.

Of course many of the setbacks in that abbreviated narrative were of my own volition, but the same cannot be said of the whiplash reversals that again set me on a positive track. It seemed that every time I suffered what seemed like a crushing defeat, something from nowhere came along to yank me back from the cliff. And *that* has almost never been of my own doing.

I could cite strings of events when serendipity pulled me back from despair. Nonetheless, I fear the consequences of the hubris of suggesting that there is something benevolent in This Immensity. Nor am I ready to presume that whenever everything seems to fall apart that there will always be this safety net. I cringe when I suggest this idea to friends and family as they suffer their own inevitable life problems. When I tell them some form of my story, that what may seem as though a total disaster has had a way of turning out to be if not as terrible as it seems and perhaps even a blessing, I know how crazy it sounds. And as often as not their skepticism, as they thank me for my encouragement, makes it clear that they see no mystic power coming along to rescue them from their fix, whether they have brought it on themselves or it has been inflicted on them by something outside their control.

I don't want to suggest to Coyote for a moment that I'm counting on him to pull me out of my next jam or that everything is going fine in my life, because all the traditional stories of Coyote and my own experience with him make it clear that such attitudes are similar to giving straight lines to a stand-up comedian: it's the perfect opportunity for delivering a punch line, with some "punches" coming harder than others.

I take hardship as reluctantly as anyone, but when I can, perhaps only after the unexpected and sometimes wonderful reversals come along that clearly show how small the setbacks are and how grand the advances, then I pay Coyote the best tribute I can think of, considering his perverse ways: I laugh at his joke.

12

A Lesson from Poop

t strikes me as strange, and probably would seem to some to be closer to madness, but I consider one of the most persuasive arguments for the actual presence, character, and living nature of Coyote as one face of Wakan Tanka, or perhaps even the central nature of Wakan Tanka, to have been shown to me in the unlikely form of . . . poop. Blasphemous? Maybe it is in some understandings of what the powers are that swirl around us but not if, like me, you see the workings of those forces in Coyote!

For many years I have asked my hunting friends to drop off the spare parts of their quarry . . . goose remains, deer guts, even pheasant and buffalo carcasses, and now and then the offal from butchering operations . . . down in our river bottoms. It doesn't take the coyotes, foxes, buzzards, crows, eagles, and occasionally mountain lions(?) long to clean up the discarded intestines and skins completely. From our household, we save and discard in the same area trimmings from our meats or freezer-burned, outdated food, especially meat.

Over these same years, I have grown accustomed to finding "messages" from Mr. Coyote—that is, excrement in the road leading down to our river bottoms. How do I know it's coyote poop? There's not much doubt about what is coyote poop and what is not. Living in the country and spending time in the wild, one comes to recognize various forms of excrement just as surely as one knows the song of a cardinal from the squawk of a cock pheasant. You can't confuse coyote poop with deer, turkey, or raccoon poop any more than you would confuse a deer, turkey, or raccoon with a coyote. I have dismantled a lot of coyote poop too, but it's not something I would recommend doing because animal excrement, especially that of predators and carnivores, carries disease and parasites that can be picked up by inhaling the dust from the poop or even by handling it. (Raccoon poop is particularly toxic and dangerous.) Coyote poop provides evidence of the animal's diet, which is omnivorous in the extreme. There is apparently nothing a coyote won't eat. In any sample of coyote poop, one finds tiny teeth and bones, feathers, insect wings, grass, hair, grains . . . amazing. Coyote poop is, in fact, more hair, teeth, plant matter, insects, grains, and so forth, it seems, than . . . well . . . poop!

The curiosity about this subject, however, is based not on the fact that coyotes poop . . . that seems obvious enough . . . but on *where* coyotes poop. I have only rarely in the past thirty-five years found coyote poop anywhere on my sixty acres but in the middle of that road leading to the river bottom. Not in the tall grass or in the woods, but on that road. We have also found poop close to our house, always near the gate or the paths we travel. I am still and always the skeptic so my first thought was and is that coyotes don't like to squat and put their rear ends down into the tall grass or, more perilous yet, above the dreadful cactus that infects this land of ours. The only place where the grass and other plant growth are beaten down on these acres is that road. So perhaps the coyote simply and wisely relieves himself where it is most comfortable. Or perhaps simply the scat piles are more visible to me on the road than they might be in a meadow or woods.

But as a folklorist and storyteller, I like to think of ancient Coyote stories so common to so many American Indian tribes, so I imagine Coyote enjoying a good meal of venison or goat remains or perhaps some freezer-burned chicken thighs from our leavings in the river bottom below our house, and with his belly full for a change, he trots down the road toward the nearby creek to get a drink. And Mr. Coyote stops. He thinks, "I shouldn't be rude [as if Mr. Coyote could be anything *but* rude!]. I really should acknowledge this gift food somehow. Let's see . . . what do I have that I could leave by way of a thank-you present? I don't own anything. I don't carry anything with me as I do my rounds along the river. So . . . what? Oh, wait a minute—I *do* have something I could leave . . . What was that again? I know it's here somewhere . . . oh, wait a minute. Here it is, right behind me! Right under my tail! Yes, there it is. And what a lovely present it is. And nicely placed right in the road where my benefactor will easily find it. This will be the perfect thank-you gift for my generous friend!" And having proven himself to be socially responsible, Mr. Coyote goes on his way to the creek quite satisfied with his good manners.

No, that kind of thinking is childish. Just a silly story. It must just be a coincidence, a matter of the easiest place for a song dog to poop, as well as the most likely place for the casual hiker to spot a pile of scat. My confidence in that theory has been shaken, however, by recent experiences. Coyote's interaction with us seems to be more deliberate, more meaningful, more clearly expressive than we might think. The first major reburial of Pawnee remains here was high on a hill overlooking the Middle Loup River Valley. Friends and I felt strongly that we should not use machinery to dig the huge, round grave . . . approximately fourteen feet in diameter, six feet deep . . . so we did the work over a period of weeks with shovels. We threw the sand . . . and the soil here is nothing but sand . . . onto a pile at the edge of the grave so we could more easily replace it after the remains were in place. A day before the reburial ceremonies, my wife, Linda, and I went up the hill to make sure the excavation was still ready to receive the remains, and we were astonished to find clear tracks of two coyote visitors in the soft sand of the pile at the grave's edge. Two coyotes had walked up the pile of loose sand overlooking the open grave and stood there. Looking into the grave? Over the grave? What were they doing there? Was it simply their curiosity that brought them to that place? And why on that particular day? Coincidence? Perhaps.

Ambiguity was chipped away when two days after the reburial weekend we again went to check everything was still in order and found that the grave had been circled again and again by canine, turkey, and deer tracks, as if . . . I know this sounds insane . . . as if they had moved in a traditional dance circle around the bison skull that had been placed on the center mound of the grave. Were they there simply out of curiosity about the grave's naked sand cover and the bison skull? If that is the case, why then have we again and again over the years found the same pattern of animal tracks at the grave?

My modern, Western mind wants to discount this occurrence as a coincidence or to find a logical explanation, but there is always the temptation too to turn to mystic interpretations. I have found that inevitably in such situations, empirical evidence increasingly swings even the most logical mind to the alternative conclusion: Something Is Going On that is beyond logic and reason. It's hard to deny the obvious and visible, especially when it is part of a personal experience.

For example, a woman from Denver had asked to bring remains from a desecrated Pawnee grave to this burial site and, by way of atonement, to plant a plum tree near the grave. It was traditional for the Pawnees to plant plum brush near their hilltop burial sites along this same valley centuries ago, and as we have followed that procedure here too over the years, the woman's intentions were easy enough to accommodate. Her plum tree made it through the first summer relatively well, considering this normally dry climate suffered even more severe drought during these months, and through a very hard, cold winter. Because of our own personal and health problems, we didn't visit the gravesite as much as we wanted during the tree's first winter, but eventually when spring came we made our way up the hill. Deer had severely pruned the plum tree, but it was still alive. Since fewer than half of our other plum plantings had survived, we considered ourselves lucky to have the tree with us yet.

Even more surprising, however, was a deposit of coyote poop at the immediate base of the six-foot tree. The uplands around the grave are open, empty acres of native grass prairie with only a few trees: some willows in a wet low spot, a few chokecherry bushes, scattered and isolated scrub junipers, and the one plum tree. And yet a coyote had chosen this very place to relieve himself. I chuckled as I saw coyote's gift, but as I looked at the arrangement, I realized it had not been the result of a wild dog merely taking a shit. Somewhere. Anywhere. In no way was its location a coincidence. That coyote simply could not have been strolling along and decided on a whim or on internal recommendation to stop a moment to poop. The only way the coyote could have placed his turdly gift at the very base of that plum tree was to back up to it. He was not backing up to get somewhere or to move away from a skunk or to find a way out of a tight spot; instead, he deliberately backed up to that small tree with only one intention, to drop a load of shit right there and only there. We can only speculate what exactly he was thinking when he did it, but we are left with no alternative to the single possible conclusion that he backed up to that tree in order to leave his turd at that spot. Burglars notoriously defecate in homes they rob and psychologists argue that it isn't done out of a physiological urge or even a desire to further insult the victim but because of some sort of deep-seated [sic!] trait of human nature. Why don't I see Coyote's defecations as an insult or rebuff? Because we are talking here of *Coyote*, ever the Trickster! And this is what he does.

Can anyone continue believing it might be coincidence after coincidence with coyote tracks there by that grave on the hill? Simply random acts of a wild dog? Luck of the poop? Well, recently Linda and I went up again to check the plums and start considerations for the location of yet another mass grave. To our astonishment, and my glee, there it was—a coyote turd. And not just anywhere. No, this time Coyote the Trickster, the blasphemer, the irreverent, the Heyoka contrary, the disrespectful, the arrogant, the obscene had really done it up . . . well, "done it up brown." We had placed at the west edge of the main grave a flat rock, perhaps six inches by nine inches, on which we had set the cast-iron pan of glowing coals for the cedaring ceremonies that blessed the grave and the ground. The fire hazard is such that we couldn't set the pan on the ground, and the rock also marked the position in a Pawnee lodge or tipi where the traditional altar would have been placed for similar sacred observances over the centuries. And now here was our stone, dedicated to holy services, sporting a hair-filled turd. A sacrificial gift from Mr. Coyote? "Let's see. I really should leave some sort of gift here on the altar. But I don't own anything. I don't carry anything with me as I lope over these hills. Oh . . . wait a minute! There is something I could leave. And, why, . . . here it is!"

There is no coincidence that is that cynical, ironic, ridiculous, irreverent, and, most important of all, funny. Was Coyote insulting us? Making fun of us? Reminding us that life may be short, but it is also funny? Telling us that he still wanders these hills and makes his jokes after all these millennia of appearing in Native folktales and religion? It surely wasn't an accident that he pooped right there, on the only rock anywhere around on sixty acres of sand, on an altar dedicated to holy uses right at the grave's edge, on a spot where we wouldn't miss seeing it. He knew what he was doing. That we don't know what he was doing has no bearing on anything other than reminding us that we don't know very damn much when it gets right down to it. Not even when it's a joke. Not even when the joke is on us.

Not in my long life of considering the nature of God have I ever had clearer information. Coyote the Spirit is here. He moves among and around us. He has a remarkable sense of humor. He is utterly unpredictable. But mostly . . . he is here. He is Coyote. After all these years, after all the changes, after all the warfare on his human, animal, and spiritual manifestations, he is here. And he is not only here, he not only prevails, but he prospers. And shits. I suppose it speaks to my own perversity, but a god that takes a shit now and then delights me.

13

The Pilgrim

On one occasion some Native friends called me to ask if I might be driving up to the reservation. They had planned on taking a bus, but "the bus had left without them." It was not a matter of their having shown up late and missed the bus; that would be an activist's interpretation of what happened. No, the bus had left without them. How a society would come to a point of view such as this one over centuries of convincing evidence is understandable: For countless thousands of years before Europeans came to these shores, either it rained and the corn grew, or it didn't. The bison appeared, or they didn't. One lived, or one died. It would be foolish to consider oneself a prime determinant of life's events in a context where that quite evidently is not the case.

Now to be sure and to be honest, there are some things we can determine for ourselves, responsibilities we must assume, and actions that only we ourselves must decide . . . but with equal certainty and honesty, there are also many we cannot. And there are situations where the issue of control is difficult, maybe impossible, to sort out, times when we think we are making decisions for ourselves when we are in reality functioning within a greater framework so large, so mysterious, so confusing that we cannot see it or, because of our arrogance, that we refuse to acknowledge it. This theme has been a favorite of thoughtful writers and thinkers for a long time.

About the time the Pilgrims were entering into their own adventure at Plimoth Plantation on Cape Cod on the North American continent, Hans Jakob Christoffel von Grimmelshausen was writing his master work, *The Adventures of a Simpleton: Simplicius Simplicissimus*, with *Simplicissimus* being a Latin variant for the "the simplest of them all." More precisely, Simplex Simplicius Simplicissimus—even more naive than you can put into one word: dumb, dumber, dumbest, *and* dumberest!—is a character of sublime innocence. He stumbled through the horrendous chaos of war-torn Europe, which was engaged in the most idiotic of all pursuits—namely, a civil war that massacred huge numbers of neighbors and kin—in what is most assuredly the most insane of man's manifold insanities, a struggle to the death to determine whose version of Christianity was true. Grimmelshausen's "hero" drifts from hopeless situation to hopeless situation during the Thirty Years' War, sampling a wide variety of depravities and excesses, the highs and lows of which man is capable, but never understands the meaning of what is going on around him or what his role in the entire disaster of man might be. Grimmelshausen's story, in short, depicts what each of our lives ultimately is, whether we like it or not.

In our own time Hermann Hesse has given us much the same story in his genius work, *Siddhartha*, a story of the Guatama Buddha. It tells the same narrative, but this time it is not with a soldier-peasant but with a figure who eventually would be revered as a representative of the godliest among us. Siddhartha leaves his village home to venture through the world. Like Simplicissimus, he devotes his life to the military sciences. And to wealth and opulence, to sex, then to the life of the aesthete, or the monk, in a pursuit of knowledge, business and commerce, politics and influence. But in the end he returns to the place where truth lies . . . his home village, where he becomes the ferryman on the same boat that once took him across the river for his adventures in the first place. Ultimately the meaning, the lesson, of it all is precisely where we are, where we begin, in the humblest of stations we will know. The answer, . . . perhaps all answers, . . . lies in the truth, rhythm, and persistent cycle of the river.

Remarkably, and perhaps unself-consciously, the latest and most modern of efforts to tell this same story is in the unlikely form of Steve Martin's film *The Jerk*. It tells exactly the same story as that of Simplex or Siddhartha and reaches precisely the same conclusion but in the form Martin knows best, that of an absurdist storytelling for the modern age, and in a format that is the most appropriate for discussing theological considerations, the comedy. In Martin's farce, as with Hesse's Siddhartha, an innocent soul—eager to know the world and find a place in it—leaves a secure but wretched home, as the fairy-tale phrase goes, "to seek his fortune." In his life's journey, he looks for comfort and truth in wealth, power, sex, luxury, self-denial, education, danger, but nowhere does he find the inner comfort he seeks. While the pilgrim of Hesse's classic work suffers pain, hunger, disappointment, and danger along his way, Martin follows his own muse, allowing his audience to laugh at his antihero's bumbling while at the same time generating sympathy for his honest search. In the end, as with the Gautama Buddha, Martin's Jerk finds all that he seeks right back where he started, at home with family . . . as unlikely as that family is . . . with his being a white adoptee in a poor, southern black family. (I don't know how to find out, and perhaps no one ever will, but I can't help but wonder if in making this film Steve Martin isn't serving as one of the sacred vision-gift bearers to his movie audience just as Malachi Constant does in Vonnegut's work or as I myself did in "The Lesson of the

Feather.") I would love to have the opportunity to ask Martin if his work is an unlikely coincidence or, as I suspect, a deliberate homage to an eternal motif.

At another time I realized that the movie *Joe Dirt* starring David Spade is the same story. Spade too approaches the theme of the innocent pilgrim adventuring into the world with humor, but his story is essentially the same as Hesse's and Martin's—a poor boob stumbling off to "find his fortune" without the slightest clue of where he is going, what he is doing, or what he is looking for. Joe Dirt, so named because the base for his search is his occupation of school janitor, experiences much the same range of experiences other literary pilgrim endure (or enjoy!): sex, wealth, pain, disappointment, deprivation, danger, power, asceticism. As with the other seekers, he too finds what he sought only when he returns to his original, humble home. In fact, now I see the same story appearing again and again with very little variation. Is this idea so universal that it is an example of polygenesis, the same idea recurring over and over again? Or is there some connective thread, a writer or a producer or even an actor who knows the Siddhartha theme and consciously mirrors it in art? Beats me. I'd sure like to know. I sure would like to find someone to ask.

I've never understood why in the Western world our theologies are so grim and humorless. (To return to a thought in chapter 12, why do our gods never poop? If Jesus has at least a third of his manifestation as a man, then why . . . ?) If man is indeed created in God's image—or as is more likely, the other way around—shouldn't God also have a sense of humor? There are not a lot of laughs in the Bible. I have been told by biblical scholars that the laughs were there and that our culture's Trickster figure, or Coyote, was once Jesus, but all of the texts reflecting that side of His character have been purged because some found laughter to be inappropriate to such matters as morality, cosmology, and divinity. I believe it should be exactly the other way around, and to my way of thinking and to that of many other peoples of the world, that is indeed the case. In most of the world's religions, now and historically, God has had a distinct and active sense of humor, and in a pantheon of gods showing various faces of the divine, at least one member is a prankster, fornicator, deceiver, practical joker, and wag.

To me that makes sense. I distrust a religion whose god does not laugh. Only the most evil of men and their creations do not laugh often and innocently. Isn't there indeed humor in the excess of round stones and buffalo skulls that have been a part of my own exposure to the Something Going On? As frantic as the sorcerer's apprentice might be when the magic goes awry, our reaction has to be laughter at his discomfiture. At least in the 1940 Walt Disney depiction.

When Wakan Tonka actually does speak to us, really does present us with a gift, truly leaves us with a new question, or deftly uses us as Malachi Constant was to make a delivery to someone else, why is our reaction never pride? Aren't we in this process brought closer to the Great Powers that move mystically across the landscape? Shouldn't we feel . . . well . . . *chosen*? I don't think so. In fact, once again it is almost precisely the opposite of what we expect that is true. Those who are so touched are reluctant to speak about it, much less crow. If there is any reaction appropriate to experiencing such woableza other than surprise or awe, it must be laughter.

(You can't imagine how uneasy I am as I write all this down. I wouldn't be surprised or disappointed if this book winds up lies neglected, bug and mouse eaten in an attic somewhere, and known to the family as "The Old Man's Crazy Rantings.")

And conversely, anyone who loudly proclaims enlightenment, salvation, or special status as one of Wakan Tonka's chosen is almost assuredly not that. In fact, the more certain someone is that he possesses the absolute truth, the less likely that is to be the case. The more loudly people proclaim that they have the truth, the more of a waste of time it is to listen to them. There is an absolute and inverse correlation between genuine wisdom and an insistence on having that wisdom. That fact is part of the moral of the stories of the innocent pilgrims, from Simplicissimus to the Jerk, who bumble through the world. Only the innocent and ignorant can possess the greatest truths. Isn't that the way Coyote would have it? Isn't that the way Coyote himself is? The mad fool? The divine heretic? The wise naïf?

But don't for a moment confuse innocence with stupidity! They are not the same thing at all. Stupidity implies that information is available but ignored or rejected. We see this foolishness constantly around us as clear and obvious facts about religion, politics, education, and so on, are systematically shuffled into the brain's holding rooms while equally obvious . . . and dishonest . . . substitutes are mouthed instead. Sometimes liars do it to convince themselves of their justifications for their lies, but sometimes they do so with the hope (or arrogance) that being so much smarter than everyone else, only they will note the contradiction and can make it simply go away by ignoring it. This kind of stupidity becomes a parody of itself, an embarrassment not so much for the person who is stupid as it is for those who have to watch the sorry performance.

Recently I set in motion a remarkable explosion of self-induced (or perhaps maintained) ignorance by saying, in all honesty and candor, that I increasingly have trouble justifying activities (often called sports, as if they were games) in which one of the participants doesn't want to be there. Hunting, for example. Which is to say, recreational killing. I invite you just once to utter those two words—"recreational killing"—to a hunter and stand back for the reaction. In my case, the hunter's first manic reaction was to accuse me of being "politically correct." What? The greatest gesture toward political correctness is to express approval, or an outright obsession, with hunting. Or the peculiar aversion its advocates have, no matter how ardent they may be, to call it what it is. It is recreational killing. If you disagree, explain to me why it isn't. It would be political suicide for any aspiring politician to be honest enough to make the mistake of mouthing this truth or so much as expressing a disinterest in, let alone distaste for, hunting. If you don't endorse recreational killing, are not photographed in hunter's orange and toting a long gun, or don't at least go through the motions of being an enthusiastic hunter, you can forget being elected to public office. But political correctness is one of the many empty bumper-sticker condemnations common in today's America and is thrown around with mindless abandon. Remarkably the accepted way to condemn what is clearly the unpopular point of view is to suggest it is the opposite—that is, politically correct!

After I was accused of political correctness, which was precisely the opposite of the case, suddenly, frantically indignant gun-totin' patriots spewed the usual (and ridiculously silly) rationalizations for recreational killing. They attacked me with the usual, laughable, specious nonsense.

1. "Hunting fees support wildlife habitat, science, conservation, education, and recreation." Okay. But why couldn't the same amount of money be sent in to the Game and Parks Commission without the follow-up of . . . recreational killing? Or since I don't hunt but do enjoy wildlife, why not spread the costs through tax levies and let all of us support the worthy causes such as wildlife conservation . . . again, without recreational killing?

Then if I dismiss that inevitable first silly stab at rationalization, the arm-waving loonies standing in front of me shift their focus to the next patently silly one:

2. "I hunt because I love nature." So do I. I walk the same ground the hunters do. But I skip the part about lugging around a gun and killing the nature I declare I love so ardently.

So . . . now what? Well, uuuh . . .

3. "My hunting puts food on the family's table." The hunter could afford pâté, lobster, prime rib, and caviar on a daily basis for what he or she spends on transportation, firearms, time, ammunition, guides, land access, licenses, and permits. Come on. Just for a moment, try being honest about this, okay?

4. "Well, er, I eat what I shoot." I eat what I *don't* shoot. How does it follow that the joy of killing is somehow validated by then eating the dead?

5. "So are you a vegetarian or something?" Okay, I respect vegetarians and figure that what they eat or don't eat is their own business. I am an omnivore. I eat everything. I have even done my own butchering. I understand that what we eat is dead. But I still don't understand the pleasure hunters take in killing.

6. "Oh, so you're one of them antigun nuts!" No, quite the contrary. I own more long guns and handguns than most hunters I know. I think guns are fascinating mechanisms, and I enjoy shooting. The difference is that I don't need to see a beautiful, living creature in the sights to enjoy shooting.

7. "If it weren't for hunters thinning out the populations of various forms of wildlife, we'd be overrun by deer, turkeys, quail, pheasants, doves, coyotes, and more." Curiously, I see the very same people who are enthusiastic about trimming the overpopulation of deer in Nebraska lobbying for the obliteration of wolves, coyotes, and mountain lions, or the natural controllers of overpopulation. Again, come on. When you're up there in your tree stand at dawn, there is not the slightest hint of this noble intent to improve the deer gene pool. How many hunters make a point of taking the first and weakest of a population and refining the gene pool? Not one.

8. "Hunting is a tradition. It's a way of life. It's in our blood." So is fratricide, anti-Semitism, slavery, and war. (Read that Bible that you thump so vigorously during other debates in which you have no rational position.) Pooping six paces from our cave entrance is a natural inclination, but I have some hope for the cultural improvement of our species, don't you?

9. "I resent you calling my hobby recreational killing." That's okay. I resent you thinking you can fool me by referring to what you do as sport, harvesting, taking, bagging, or anything other than what it is. Why is honesty so offensive to hunters if the activity is so noble and rational? Be true at least to yourself. Hunters hunt because they enjoy it and for no other honest reason. It is recreation. And it *is* killing. See? It isn't that hard to say. Try it. Just once. "Recreational killing." Now, isn't the taste of honesty in your mouth less bitter than the poison of mendacity?

If your antagonist has stood still long enough to reach this point in the discussion, it is not likely he or she will try to present many more ridiculous, hollow rationalizations. Hunting is recreational killing, plain and simple. But should the same argument be restarted moments later with another debater, I guarantee you the new "sportsman" will start a rundown of the very same catalog of inconsistencies and inanities without any hesitation or a scintilla of self-doubt. In fact, the next time the hunter you first argued with is confronted with the term "recreational killing," he or she likely will put forth the very same arguments, regardless of having already been confronted with their ridiculousness. Logic, sense, honesty, truth, and fact—they all wither away in the face of devoted self-justification. The fraud endures.

As I said, the ignorance, or conscious dissembling, of such people can be so painfully stupid that it embarrasses anyone who likes to think of our species as being Homo *sapi-*

ens (meaning "wise"). That is the difference between stupid and innocent.

When God has spoken through someone, no one is less confident of what has just happened than that person himself. The words "God's will," even in so contracted and apparently innocent a form as "amen," are sure signals of false prophesy. Someone who has truly had a vision or has been an agent of one is far more likely to say, "What the hell was *that*?!" Think for a moment of Malachi Constant's reaction upon learning that he is at the pinnacle of the meaning of human life, that he is the ultimate bearer of cosmic intervention, and that the message for which it has all been put together is a dot meaning greetings. He said, "Oh my—life is funny when you stop to think of it." That's pretty close to "what the hell was *that*?!"

I am in fact so reluctant to try to manipulate the Great Powers, as Native tribes refer to them, that I don't even like to ask for anything in my prayers. Yes, the main reason why is that I figure I've been far too lucky as things already stand and it would be downright greedy to ask for anything more, but a second, less obvious agenda is that I just don't want to call attention to myself. Cosmic, mystic powers are unpredictable . . . or at least that's what it seems to those of us who do not now and never will understand the grand scheme. More precisely, if I am correct in my assessment (a conclusion shared by billions of other humans throughout time and around the world, I might add, despite what Western religions seem to think) and these Great Powers around us have a sense of humor, what could be more natural than to make the butt of any cosmic jokes the most arrogant, ignorant, clumsy, unsympathetic living creatures on the face of the earth . . . that is, us? And what could be more arrogant (and thus offer an obvious invitation to a cosmic slap down) than trying to tell the Great Powers what they should do?

Thank you, but I prefer simply to offer my thanks and keep a low profile when it comes to dealing with things too enormous and complicated for me even to come close to understanding. Awe, submission, gratitude, humility, and anonymity appear to be not only the appropriate course when dealing with realizations that Something Is Going On but also the safest.

14

Establishing a Cosmic Buffer Zone

One of the many interesting features of Brave Buffalo's text as published in McLuhan's *Touch the Earth*, where my whole narrative started, is that he refers to his round stones as intercessors. In his enormous wisdom about and experience with such things, the Lakota holy man has placed them between himself and the Great Powers that might easily, even mistakenly crush him as they go about their regular chores. That's not a bad idea. Why not let your allies, the round stones, carry your messages so you can remain relatively anonymous while nonetheless conveying what you have to say? I feel especially strongly about this kind of safety margin because of the nature of Wakan Tonka that I find most clear to me . . . Coyote the Trickster. While I respect Coyote enormously, offer regular gratitude to Coyote, laugh at his pranks, and am awed by what seems to be his awareness of my existence, I really don't want to call any more attention to my presence than absolutely necessary. I enjoy watching a good hockey game or boxing match, but I would just as soon not be standing right in the middle of the action between the players and combatants.

I suspect that's why Christianity uses Jesus or even Jesus's mother as a means for communicating with a power way too enormous to approach too closely. An intercessor doesn't have to be anything or anyone in particular because in the end they are all metaphors we can grasp and represent concepts that we can't ultimately understand. During a visit to Mayan holy sites on the Yucatán Peninsula, I found I had a strong attraction to Chaacmool, or simply Chaac, the ancient Mayan rain god and messenger. Two Indian tribes have detected a connection in my nature with the sky, rain, storm, wind, and lightning; could the affinity I have for Chaac derive from this part of my person? I have asked that Chaac, or whatever he is or represents, to help me out in my timidity and fear and carry my prayers of gratitude to those larger powers like Coyote or Wakan Tonka, and I find myself comfortable with that arrangement. Do I believe in Chaac? I believe in the idea of Chaac, and that's about as close as I can come to understanding the relationship at this point.

My general experience . . . and admittedly my experience is very limited but seems to be wider than the experience of most others I know in my white culture . . . has been that visits, visions, guests, and gifts have been enormously benevolent in my life. I find that downright flattering, but I keep ducking my head waiting for the consequences of all this generosity. I'm uneasy not only about dealing with such enormous, even fearsome forces but all the more so about possibly catching their attention in the process. In this case I would prefer to be anonymous, thank you very much.

During my 1967 conversation while sitting on the curb with my new Native brother Buddy Gilpin, an exchange I mention in chapter 2, he filled me in on the new obligations I had as a result of having become his brother, having been given a new name, and having thus become a full-blood Omaha. It turns out that as a member of his KonCe (Wind) Clan, I could no longer eat shellfish, a totemic taboo (as perverse as it may seem, these water creatures are totems of the sky, wind, and weather clan), or touch verdigris (sky material), for example. It has been hard these forty-seven years not to enjoy lobster, shrimp, clams, oysters, mussels—foods that were once favorites of mine—but when it comes right down to it, observing that taboo is relatively easy to do simply by watching listings on menus and food packages. Avoiding verdigris, the blue-green corrosion that appears on copper, is surprisingly a good deal harder. Every so often, after all, a bad penny encrusted with verdigris does show up. But I have carefully observed those clan prohibitions.

Why would a grown, educated man embrace something so silly as ancient tribal taboos? Well, I'll tell you why. For one, I do it out of respect for Alfred "Buddy" Gilpin Jr., who took some considerable risk in taking me as his brother, in bringing me into his tribe and clan, and in giving me his own name. But there is more. That night I asked Buddy Gilpin what the nature of the Wind Clan prohibitions is. I asked him if it is perhaps similar to Catholics (at that time) not eating meat on Fridays? And Jews not eating pork? And white people not eating dog? Buddy thought about my questions for a few minutes; it was clear that the answer was not easy to express. Even then I guessed that the matter was probably more complicated than I might have initially guessed. Finally he said, "It's like touching the fire. You know, you reach for something and accidentally touch a live coal. Or a spark jumps onto someone's clothing, and you try to brush it away. No matter how accidental it might be, no matter how good and honest your intentions are, when you touch the fire . . ."

He didn't have to complete his explanation. When you touch the fire, for whatever reason, you can expect to suffer the consequences: you get burned. Go ahead and challenge the ancient understandings of your new name and the Wind Clan if you feel it is all nonsense. But understand that there will be inevitable consequences. So it is when you touch the greatest, hottest fire of all, the essence of all that is, the Great Mysterious, Wakan Tonka. Touch the fire if you must . . . but know what may follow.

If it's all the same to you, I would just as soon not touch

the fire until there is absolutely no other alternative. Until then I will watch the fire from a distance, where it provides only warmth and heat, not pain. I will approach it with instruments that insulate me from the full consequences, as clumsy as that move sometimes might be. When it comes to forces so much greater than I understand, I prefer the passive, deductive processes of Native culture to the blatant hubris of the white man's arrogance. Something Is Going On, but if it's all the same to you, I'll keep my distance from the Great Powers and other forces around us and be grateful to be aware of them, receptive to them, touched by them, and even interact with and be used by them. And if it's all the same to you, don't mention my name when the Great Powers come around asking.

15

A Lesson from Touching the Fire

have had a couple bad experiences with this cosmic notion that Something's Going On. I don't know for sure how rebuffs fit into the scheme of the other mysteries. I suppose if anything they have taught me that you can learn just about as much from mistakes as you can from good fortune. And there is as little doubt about when the Something That Is Going On is turning badly as there is when it goes well.

For example, my wife, Linda, and I once had many problems for a year or so. Little (and, Linda reminds me, big) things went wrong in our lives and around the house, and we had a constant uneasy feeling, a sense of something being out of place. And one day, out of the blue, it hit me what the problem was. I immediately went to my lovely and spiritually sympathetic wife Linda and said, "Hon, I've been thinking about all our recent difficulties, and I think I know what the problem is, why everything seems to be out of synch around here."

"That's strange," she said. "I've been thinking about it too, and I was just coming out to tell you that a few minutes ago, I got the feeling I know what the problem is. What did you come up with?"

Neither of us wanted to speak the words first because we had the really uneasy feeling that we were thinking precisely the same thing at precisely the same moment without having discussed the matter at all. I said, "Okay . . . three . . . two . . . one," whereupon we both said at precisely the same moment, "The rocks." And we both looked in the same direction across our backyard toward a small pile of water-worn (but not round!) stones at the base of a tree. Yeah, right . . . our having both struck independently on precisely the same totally illogical source of our problems was just a coincidence! But here's the background story. The summer before all this happened, I had taught some classes in Wyoming and during my stay was directed by a researcher-historian friend to a remarkable Native campsite defined by dozens of tipi rings, or circles of stones that had been used to hold down the edges of skin tipis where it would have been difficult to drive stakes into the ground. I wandered around the site, trying to imagine how it appeared when it was occupied. I won't go into detail, but I assure you that the physical, geological setting is clearly striking enough that the camp was not located here simply because it was close to water and wood; it is in a sacred site. I have camped on Lakota ground at sun dances where I was the only white man in attendance, so I know the magic of light coming through tipi walls and smoke rising through a smoke hole. Those times made it easy to imagine how the people must have lived in this encampment before the white man poisoned the water, killed the bison, and "broke the circle."

I thought I would take some of the magic of the site back home with Linda and me, so I picked up a dozen or so of the rocks from one of the rings and put them on the floor of the backseat of my car. Yes, I know that as a professor of anthropology I should have known better than to disturb a site. But I rationalized that it was one of those situations where the site was threatened anyway by constant traffic. Isn't it better that someone who appreciates such things as rocks should have some of the thousands of stones and pay them appropriate homage than for some passing idiot simply to help himself to rocks for his suburban garden, probably without so much as noticing that they were arranged in circles, circles, circles across the narrow plain? Logic would certainly tell us that, right? And if knowing better hadn't reminded us of the protocol against tampering with archeological sites, let alone sacred sites, then our car's breakdown on the way down from the site and our having to call friends to rescue us and drag our vehicle and its load of rocks back from the mountains should have.

Well, apparently at the time we weren't in a receiver mode. Linda and I were told silently by some inner-outer voice on that afternoon, a long distance from where the rocks belonged and a long time after we had taken them, that we had made a mistake in taking them and that we were paying for that mistake. As dumb as I felt for taking the rocks, I felt even dumber boxing them up, taking them to the post office, sending them to a friend near the site, and asking her to ignore the wackiness of it all and without asking any questions to take the box out to the campsite and put the rocks back where they belonged. Our friend was wise and knew me well enough not to question why I was sending her a box of rocks and asking her to do something so utterly bizarre as to take them out to the country and replace them in the tipi ring. She simply did what I asked . . . whereupon our long and constant series of tribulations stopped.

So what does that all mean? I suppose it means that you can't presume a gift where one is not offered. I suppose it means that some things (for example, rocks!) belong right where they are. I suppose it means that sometimes mysteries are about giving things and not receiving them. I suppose it means . . . well, the same old thing I have been saying to you over and over again in these pages: Something Is Going On. Since that experience I have become very cautious about moving rocks. Rocks are where they are for a reason, and I am increasingly uneasy about displacing them.

Once when I was a boy, a best friend moved to Hawaii. I

asked him to find and send me a lava bomb. I had read about the fist-size rocks of molten lava that are hurled from active volcanoes on the islands, cool in the air, and then fall to the ground as grotesque, jagged examples of the living nature of the earth. I thought it would be neat to have a fragment of ejecta from one of the many volcanoes on the islands. But he informed me that he really couldn't do that because, first, it's illegal to take lava bombs from their geologic matrix. Second, Hawaiians strongly believe that the goddess Pele curses such geological shoplifting. It is widely acknowledged that such Native "curses" of Pele are sometimes the creation of tour guides, taxi drivers, and park officials who use the device to discourage the casual theft of geologic treasures. But even if there were occasional modern fabrications, would that diminish the truth and force of such curses where they are legitimate and ancient? Isn't one possible explanation for even the most colloquial Native beliefs and customs that they are true? Even if they are delivered not by burning bushes, talking stones, earthquakes, and volcanoes but by tour guides, taxi drivers, and park officials? I think so. In fact, my experience suggests precisely that: the more ordinary, humble, and less official the agency of a mystic delivery is, the more likely it is that we will find truth in its message.

It is one thing for mysteries to be visited on us, it is quite another to go out after them, tamper with them, try to manipulate them, or manage them. Especially, I have come to believe, rocks! It is dangerous business. It is very risky business to presume to guide the designs of the Great Mysterious or even predict them. To begin with, the chances of your success in such endeavors are next to zero; for another, things might go quite wrong and somebody could get hurt. I cringe when I hear someone say, "I'm just doing God's will" or "God must have something in mind for me" or "God must have been looking over us." And I do so even when I hear someone's "Praise Jesus!" in response to what is perceived to be good fortune or, for gods' sakes, when I see some dim bulb drop to his knees and thank Jesus for a successful touchdown reception.

All too often, for one thing, the good fortune being celebrated is only for the person who sees God's will in his or her good luck while ignoring what that good luck may mean for others. For instance, when people win the lottery and presume it is God smiling on them, they are somehow missing the point that millions of other people have spent their money—in some cases money they can hardly afford—to enrich them. Or some folks emerge from the basement of their destroyed homes, look around their tornado-devastated neighborhood, and thank God for saving *their* lives. One team's touchdown is just what it might take to end another player's contract and chance for a decent living. That is an unsettling hubris to my mind. And it is downright stupid to attribute all "good" events to God and ignore all the "bad" things that are part of the same complex of circumstances. It is presumptuous to guess the will of the Great Mysterious and downright obnoxious to arrogate it to one's own welfare. We human beings are simply not equipped to make such judgments. We just don't know such things. We can't know such things. All we can do is stand in awe and be grateful for what little we know and for what little we see.

We see exercises of this kind of arrogance on an almost daily basis as various disasters, man-made and natural, are reported on television. A reporter often talks with a survivor in front of a scene of total destruction where dozens, maybe hundreds, maybe even thousands have died. The survivor praises God and says something really stupid, such as, "We were blessed by God. Only three quarters of the population of our town died in this disaster." Well, uh, yeah . . . It's nice that there are survivors, and that may indeed be a result of

God's will, but I don't think it's up to a victim, survivor, or bystander to guess what the message might be.

I understand why the survivor is still dazed and most certainly why the survivor is grateful to whatever it is that resulted in his or her being the one on camera instead of in the numerous body bags. But then comes the ultimate and inevitable expression of arrogance: "I guess God was looking over me. All I can figure is that He has a plan for me." Aside from the implication that God was apparently *not* looking over all those who died, now the survivor feels somehow anointed as a special favorite of God's and is therefore endowed with a mission, which this person will now almost certainly divine. And you can bet that new purpose is almost exactly what that selfsame person would have wanted to do anyway.

For all I know, from much of what I see and sense, Coyote-Tawadahat-Wakonda-Wakan Tonka does indeed have a plan. But as for what the plan is, as John Kay of Steppenwolf sang, "if all of this should have a reason / we would be the last to know."

16

Lessons from the Zealot

My friend Todd is a God-drenched zealot who accompanies most of his pronouncements with such phrases as "according to God's will," which turns out almost inevitably to be precisely the same as Todd's will. People who talk this way are immediately recognizable as the last souls in this world who are likely to know, understand, or obey "God's will." Impossible fools such as Pat Robertson, the telepreacher who not only interprets natural disasters as curses against those he hates but has the gall to call down God's wrath on them too, are beyond contempt. Robertson sees a city destroyed by flood, fire, or storm and immediately concludes by virtue of his special relationship with God that the devastation is a result of the moral failings of those city's residents who disagree with him (meaning Robertson, not God!). He never once considers that just as many people who *do* embrace his looniness might have died and that perhaps the disaster is instead a comment on his own hubris. Nor does he ever declare disasters that strike his own followers to be God's judgment but rather to be "Satan's work."

I always wonder if it ever crosses the mind of the survivor who feels blessed by God when others have apparently been cursed and destroyed that maybe the design God has in mind for that survivor is fifty years of miserable suffering, culminating in a painful death? I imagine that happens more often than would be likely by pure chance, knowing how Coyote deals with this kind of arrogance!

It is not easy for the rational person to deal with, but True Believers can look at an exploding volcano not three miles away, rivers of lava pouring out, pillars of smoke filling the sky ten miles high, seismic tremors visibly rippling the earth, buildings and cliffs falling, pyroclastic flows sweeping everything away before them, blazing forests, avalanches tearing away half mountains, rivers flowing with boiling mud, a roar so deafening it blots out even one's own thoughts . . . and insist calmly and confidently that they see nothing. Nothing at all. True Believers see nothing at odds with what the panel of old men ruling their church tell its flock to see. Further, the True Believers read and accept sacred texts without wonder or question. When all illogic, evasion, and manipulation fail zealots such as Todd, however, they simply deny the existence of the competing evidence and plead blindness.

Zealots are not driven by conviction but by fear and uncertainty. Those who have had mystic experiences are sublimely, calmly, and supremely confident of what they know and, far more important, of what they don't know. The zealots frantically flail about as they try to convince others by whatever means they can conjure of what they themselves are not at all sure. The True Believers' approach seems to be that if only they can bring others to believe what they think might be true, or what they hope might be true, then the zealots gain reassurance that maybe they aren't as wrong as they privately fear.

The result of such mental gymnastics is often, sadly, more comic than convincing. My friend Todd maintains that he has read the Bible several times and has yet to find a single contradiction or inconsistency in it. His assertion is, of course, absurd. It is possible to examine apparent problems in time, logic, morality, philosophy, and so on, in the Bible from directions of history, culture, interpretation, or language. To dismiss them as nonexistent diminishes not only this zealot's insistence that he is a believer but also puts the very credibility of his religion—or, for that matter, religion in general—in question. Most of all, it sadly reveals the insecurity of my old friend, the evangelical: unable to convince himself of what he wants to believe, he turns his attention instead to someone who perhaps has more faith or less sense . . . and he further presumes that person to be . . . a church authority.

This attitude has been in fact the final straw in destroying my affection for my old friend Todd. I have not only a general acceptance but even an affection for those folks who demonstrate innocence-cum-ignorance and confusion or even those who are confused or are the victim of spiritual deception. But once the zealot crosses the line from innocent acceptance to deliberate, naked deception designed to mislead others—that is, knowingly and cynically betraying a trust while presuming an ignorance on the others' part—then my willingness to share that trust disappears like a wisp of smoke.

Purposely disingenuous lying is a confession of a weak spirit. For example, Todd whines about being persecuted. He bemoans that the True Christian—namely, of course, himself (a follower of the mini-sect the Lutheran Church–Missouri Synod, by the way, one of the most dogmatic and benighted of the myriad Protestant Christian offshoots)—has lost all freedom to practice his faith in the United States of America. What he means, obviously, is that he is still thwarted (although, I fear as of this writing, not for long) to inflict his own faith on others, to dominate religious thought and expression, to crush infidels, and to march all of us to the river at the point of a sword for a full-immersion baptism not simply in the name of Jesus but also in the name of the very small, narrow cult that he believes has an exclusive possession of the so-called Truth.

Todd is so unsure of the power and truth of the Great Powers swirling around us that he figures he has to invent the grandeur, vision, and "miracle"—something he is incapable of doing to any degree close to the actual spectacle—and somehow sell an interpretation that those of us who do see the wonders constantly swirling around us are heretics while he himself is a martyr for faith! I once told Todd that I was surprised to hear of his persecution, because my own beliefs seem even further from the mainstream than his are and yet in my life I have never found the slightest problem in believing what I believe, praying as I wish any time I want, or practicing procedures I believe speak to my faith. So I wondered aloud if he could give me an example or two of circumstances in which his own faith and practice had been thwarted, assaulted, or even so much as in any way at all condemned. He couldn't think of a single example. Not one.

Nothing is more certain than the ignorance of those who are most certain of their rectitude. It seems to be a law of human nature that those who insist they know everything there is to know and who believe their understanding is complete, without error or gap, and perhaps too that what others know is therefore without any validity at all are most likely to be devoid of anything to offer by way of knowledge. Zealotry is in and of itself a confession of ignorance but, sadly, an ignorance without the redemptive virtue of innocence. The loss of my respect for Todd was in large part my embarrassment for his inability to doubt his own infallibility.

17

Lessons from Real Shock and Awe

don't know what to make of one of the mysteries I have experienced. I simply don't know what it was about even though other people I trust have offered interpretations and warnings, because they read it as a cautionary experience for an accidental or even well-intentioned action on my part . . . In chapter 15 I told you about the hazards of touching the fire; good intentions don't make much difference when you touch the fire. I also shared the example of the consequences when I wrenched stones from their context and moved them to an unaccustomed and inauspicious new home, but I have encountered other examples too.

One spring I was camped in an idyllic place with my best friend, Mick. We had worked hard all day, it was a beautiful evening, and we had pitched our tents at the edge of a placid pond far from any disturbances of civilization. In fact, we had to drive through a running creek to get to our campsite, so we knew we were well beyond the reach of any interruption. We had had a nice meal cooked over our campfire and were sitting back to smoke a good cigar, drink a glass of good whiskey, and go to sleep because just as it had been a long day, we knew the next one was going to be even longer. Moreover, while Mick was accustomed to hard physical work—he's a bricklayer—this tired old professor was not.

Our mission was in itself a remarkable one. It's a long story . . . too long to tell in detail here . . . but briefly, I had been on the board of governors of the Nebraska State Historical Society when a Native tribe that had originally occupied most of the area asked the society to return the remains of their ancestors that were stored on the museum shelves. For a century Pawnee graves (as well as those of many other tribes, of course) had been robbed for artifacts and human remains. They had been taken allegedly for study but were only rarely researched, with work being often redundant, and in my own experience, treated with glaring and embarrassing disrespect. The tribe's request was delivered to the society respectfully and seemed to me to make total sense. The petitioners stressed that no one has more to gain from collective knowledge of their history than the people whose ancestors were being studied and that they of all people wanted to encourage research. All they asked was that those grave goods and human remains that were clearly theirs should be returned to them for reinterment. That request made perfect sense to me, not only out of decent humanity, but also clearly because there would be no particular loss to archeological research commensurate with the enormous inappropriateness of keeping the human remains and burial goods in cardboard boxes on storage shelves.

But the petitioners' discussion with the society's staff and governing board was not conducted on any level of scholarship, common sense, or humanity; instead, it was a cruel volley of insult, contempt, arrogance, and insensitivity from the unanimously white, rich, influential members of the board. I was stunned by the behavior of people I had considered to be decent human beings. I worked for some time with the society and in my official role to change policies and attitudes regarding human remains and burial goods through established, official channels but to absolutely no avail. If anything, the situation deteriorated. Even while the original tribal petitioners (and now other tribes) struggled to maintain some dignity in the negotiations, the historical society and its representatives sank even lower in their unprofessional and inhumane ethical standards. I finally resigned from the board and joined the tribal representatives in their struggle. After a long and ugly public, private, legislative, and legal debate, the Indians won their case, and arrangements were made for transferring the grave goods and remains—hundreds of human remains—that were going to be surrendered to them. To my enormous honor and gratitude, the tribe asked me to serve as an agent at the physical transfer and as a pallbearer for the reinterment.

My family and I offered the Pawnee Nation space at our farm for the reburial—it is their ancestral home ground— and a contingent of elders came from their reservation lands in Oklahoma to consider this ground, as well as some other lands around the state, as the site for the reburial. The tribe eventually settled on and accepted an offer of land from the small nearby town of Genoa, Nebraska, at its cemetery, which was the site of a huge, traditional Native village prior to their inhabitants' removal from their homeland in the mid-nineteenth century. There was a snag in making the final arrangements, and I learned from some of the tribal elders that the problem was the cost of building the vault to hold the enormous volume of human remains, which were packaged in fiber and cardboard boxes for transfer and transport . . . enough to fill a very large moving van, as it turned out. The Pawnees, having no physical presence in Nebraska any longer, had to negotiate long distance for digging the huge grave and constructing the concrete vault, and it was not going well. The bids for the construction were coming in above the estimates, which alone were nearly $12,000 . . . a lot of money for a tribe that barely has funds to meet its own contemporary social requirements, let alone its historical obligations.

I had no experience in construction and its costs, so I turned to Mick, who has worked in construction all his life and did in fact build my home on the farm. I gave him the tribe's specifications, and he did further research. Mick decided that the materials and labor should run considerably less—thousands of dollars less—than the estimates from local contractors ran. He offered to pursue matters on the site of the planned vault, some distance from his home and from mine. As he made more and more contacts, he found more and more people of goodwill who offered deeply discounted rates for materials and some of the work itself—such as the machinery and time for digging the large grave—as donations, gifts, and volunteer work. And then Mick contributed his own time, labor, and skill in the construction of the vault itself. I said I would do what I could to help. Keeping in mind my own inexperience, he said all he needed was someone to carry block and cement to him. I said that I thought I was intellectually up to those tasks. So during a long week, we gathered our materials and worked with other contributors and volunteers to dig the grave and organize our project. With more friends, we set about building a huge, concrete burial vault.

When we were camped at the pond's edge, we'd spent the day moving and cementing the blocks and the reinforcement steel in the excavation. It had been a beautiful day for the work, and Mick and I had enjoyed each other's company. As we worked we considered the importance of what we were doing and of our responsibility not only to atone for the insults to the tribe but also for the irreverence that had been shown to their ancestors over the years. We were also aware that in the graveyard, on the site of a historical tribal village, we were on ground that was already sacred even before it had been designated as a site for the reburial. We had evidence and indications of that . . . I am to this day too uneasy about the events to discuss them publicly. I am already telling more about my spiritual experiences than I ever thought I would reveal to people outside my family and direct circle of friends.

So that evening as we settled down around our campfire at a serene site not far from the cemetery, we were tired, accomplished, and happy that we had finished our tasks and fulfilled our promises. We were eager for the next day when we would retrieve the Pawnee remains from the Nebraska State Historical Society and assume the honor of being pallbearers for the hundreds of remains we would rebury. We were also aware of the profound solemnity of the entire process.

My own tribal relatives (not, I should note, the same tribe whose repatriated remains we were reburying) had strongly advised me not to participate in this process. They felt that any contact with the dead is ill-advised, and in this case the implications were even more significant because the dead tribespeople we were about to rebury had been obscenely disturbed and violated over the decades. The argument of my adopted Omaha tribal family seemed to be that all spirits are dangerous and should be avoided. The spirits of these violated tribespeople were almost surely even angrier and therefore even more dangerous. Finally as they were a potential danger to everyone everywhere, we were really taking an enormous risk by putting ourselves in proximity of the remains by handling them, transporting them, and reburying them. Yes, we were only trying to atone for past atrocities of others; yes, our intentions were only good; and yes, we would have a cedaring purification ceremony performed after the reburial to mitigate the potential dangers . . . but still . . . there is that lesson about touching the fire.

Mick and I had discussed the potential consequences, however. And we decided that we were willing to take the necessary risks to apologize to decent people for the ill manners of our white kinsmen and to compensate insofar as would be possible for the centuries of abuse those long-dead tribespeople had endured. But nonetheless, we also knew we were touching the fire, philosophically and realistically. We sensed that we were already involved in an auspicious historical moment and a spiritual activity with potentially unknown consequences. At this point in my life, now at the age of seventy-eight, I have served as a pallbearer many times . . . and carried more than two thousand Native people to a safe resting place; life just doesn't get much more momentous than that. But at that time I had no idea what would happen at this new reburial, despite my own feelings of the enormity of the event and the warnings of my adopted tribal family and friends.

Mick and I settled down at the fire for about as pleasant an evening as one can imagine, in about as good company as one can enjoy. As we talked in the silence of the approaching night, however, I saw something that first puzzled me, then confused me . . . and then frightened me. A yellowish light, brighter than any star, appeared in the eastern sky just over Mick's shoulder as he continued the conversation. Was it a plane? I know airplanes very well . . . I've watched them all my life . . . and it was not an airplane. It moved erratically, making lateral movements no airplane makes. A star or planet? No, the movement alone was enough to remove that from consideration, not to mention the intensity and color of the light. Although it moved a bit from side to side, the curious thing was that it was also clearly coming closer to us . . . in fact, directly toward us and fast.

Without turning, Mick said, "You see something, don't you?"

Later he told me that the look on my face was so dramatic that clearly I had seen something completely out of the ordinary and that I was startled and even frightened. The look on my face was so strange, he didn't want to turn to see it himself. I couldn't think of words to say. I continued to stare at the apparition, one I had never seen before. Mick then turned, and he too was stunned by the intensity and utterly unexpected and inexplicable movement of the light.

Now please note that in my life I have spent hundreds of nights sleeping outdoors. I so love sleeping outdoors that I never even use a tent unless the weather, modesty, or bugs give me no alternative and sometimes not even then. I like to wake up seeing the stars. I sleep with my feet toward Polaris and note the time as I crawl into my sleeping bag; that way whenever I wake up I can judge what time it is by comparing the position of the Big Dipper with where it was in the sky when I turned in. I wrote a book about the glories of sleeping under the open skies. Believe me, I know the night sky.

Mick is even more of an outdoorsman than I am. There is nothing in the night sky he hasn't seen before. But he had never seen anything like this light. Mick is a former Marine, a fit and strong laborer . . . and a mason and blocklayer, as I have already noted. He is not a man given to hallucinations, panic, hysteria, or fear. But the moment the yellow light flashed to the side and disappeared from the sky and we compared our impressions, we both admitted to astonishment and a touch of uneasiness about what we had just witnessed. Neither of us had any idea what it was. We knew what it was *not*, but we couldn't even guess what it was.

When the light suddenly disappeared, not turning or retreating but fading to nothingness, we turned to each other in amazement. We talked about what we had just seen, compared our impressions. Our heartbeats slowed down, and we tried to regain our composure. Yes, it was just a light in the sky, but it was not like any light either of us had ever seen before. We presumed we would never see anything like it again, as it was so totally unusual. We sat at our fire, stunned and baffled.

And perhaps ten or fifteen minutes later . . . "Oh my God!" I said. "Here it comes again!" And this time from the south-southeast, perhaps at an angle of forty-five degrees from our first sighting, the yellow light reappeared, coming at us much faster and more directly. Mick, much smarter about such things than I am, dropped to his knees and tried to sight the light along a fence post to get some idea of its elevation and establish a stable reference to determine its movement. It approached quickly enough and directly toward us that it unsettled us both even more. This time when it disappeared, I no longer cared what it was or what its implications or consequences might be . . . I just didn't want to be watching the sky if and when it came back. The light, its nature, and its behavior were that disconcerting. I was not afraid; I was in awe. Those two emotions are similar, but they are not the same.

I retreated to my sleeping bag . . . not much of a protection, I'll admit, but I wanted to close my eyes and hope for some refuge in sleep from what was quickly becoming an uncomfortable anxiety. Something wasn't right. Something Was Going On, and I wasn't comfortable with it. The night passed without further disturbance. Mick stayed awake a while, hoping to see the light again and perhaps learn more, but it didn't reappear. He was as much relieved as disappointed.

The next day the reburial and associated ceremonies went as planned. The ceremonies to reinter the dead were moving. It was a moment of both triumph and humiliation for the tribal members in attendance and of comfort and shame for those of us who are not Native. We moved the boxes containing the human remains and burial goods from a huge moving van down into the vault Mick and I had built, shoveled tons of sand onto the boxes, and directed the pouring of a cement cap over the boxes and the vault. Soil would be placed over the vault once the concrete cured and hardened. There was a funeral feast near the site and a cedaring ceremony at the feast to purify those of us who had participated in the reburial and had come in contact even though indirectly with the dead. The cedaring was reassuring. Mick, I suspect, and I still felt a sense of jeopardy since we had already had some indications of the power and risk inherent in what we were doing.

Still we had no idea of all the implications, resonances, results, and consequences of the day. The Great Mysterious was not done with us; more was going on than we knew or suspected.

A few days later Mick called me. His father had died while we were at the campsite. The man had been in fine health. His death was sudden and totally unexpected—sort of. When he left work late Friday, while Mick and I were settling into our campsite seventy-five miles away, his coworkers had wished him a happy weekend and said they would see him at work again Monday. "No, I won't be here," he told them incongruously.

Puzzled, they asked why they wouldn't be seeing him as usual on Monday. "Because I'll be dead," he said without particular emotion. And then he went home and died. Believe me, the first thing I wondered was if it had somehow been a self-inflicted fate, but no, it was a natural death. Mick's father just went home, sat down, turned on his television, and died . . . about the time we were seeing the yellow light in the sky.

I immediately asked a roadman ("ordained" practitioner) from the Native American Church to go to Mick's home and conduct another, focused cedaring, which he did. And for months I waited for and expected (or perhaps feared, although "awe" is closer to the mark than "fear") the second shoe to drop, for something momentous to happen in my own family. Not much time had passed when Linda was driving home with Antonia, our daughter, and Mick's daughter, Liz, and a mysterious, unsettling light appeared in the sky just after dusk. It began speeding toward the car from the right. As Linda accelerated, so did the light, apparently coming within reach of the car. She gripped the steering wheel and accelerated even more. The girls in the backseat were oblivious to the light and Linda's concern. The experience was so unnerving, she decided not to alarm the children by calling their attention to the light. There was no sound other than that of the automobile's engine and the wind around the car.

As was the case with Mick and me, Linda knew at once that this light did not come from an ordinary thing. Not an airplane, star, or planet. Not a sun dog, moon dog, or reflection of city lights on clouds. It rushed on beside the car and then suddenly retreated in the same direction from which it had come, back across the empty fields, much as it did when Mick and I experienced it. The events were troubling enough that Linda told me about it and has felt uneasy about the experience since it happened.

I have made every effort throughout this book to be as accurate as I can be in my narratives. I also asked Mick to go over the events of that night before the burials and the following week so I could be sure of what I remember, but Mick has . . . probably wisely . . . declined, saying that he does not want to revisit those events. Like me, he would not change what we did for the offended tribe (and for ourselves). Everything was as it had to be. Neither of us is comfortable drawing conclusions about the separate events or even speculating about them. What is simply *is*. About the most either of us is comfortable in saying about everything that happened then and there is . . . the same old thing . . . Something Was Going On. And once again, that's enough.

18

Lessons of Hubris

f it is a big mistake to touch the fire accidentally or innocently, it is utter madness to reach into it with a false sense
of impunity or vanity. Yet that is precisely what so many
people do, especially when it comes to matters of the spirit. To
presume to know anything at all about God's will is impossibly prideful; to presume absolute infallibility in such pursuits,
as some people and official churches do as a matter of course,
displays an arrogance beyond contempt. But this righteous-
ness is the very foundation of what many people express as
a fundamental principle of their faith . . . that they alone are
right in all things and that all others are wrong—certainly
at those points where they disagree.

As I have noted, I had a dear friend, one of my oldest
friends in this now long life, who is a prime example of this
sort of terrifying arrogance. Todd is a bright enough fellow
and fairly well educated. He is well traveled and has more
than average talent. And he is honest . . . insofar as his absolutely ridiculous religious arrogance allows him to be honest.
The problem is that his church demands that its adherents
presume absolute rectitude in all things theological, at least
as long as they embrace the directives of the church's man-
made and man-based structure and government. And since
the churchgoers must embrace all directives of the church's
government and since the church is always correct, then
those who mindlessly obey must be correct too.

This acquiescence requires followers to perform some

truly amazing intellectual gymnastics. They must accept, for example, the Bible as the absolute word of God and the church's interpretation of that word as the absolute truth, without conflict or contradiction. Even where the conflict or contradiction is evident in the Bible . . . the word of God itself. I love my friend dearly in spite of our disagreements and his contempt for any religious or theological thought other than what he is told to believe (and therefore magically, wonderfully, and immediately truly *does* believe, to my amazement). I am fascinated by our discussions and therefore welcome them simply to see the immense armory and armor of illogic, distortion, doublethink, sophistry, and solipsism he draws on to deal with his own inevitable internal struggle in having to believe the unbelievable.

Please do note that I am not denying here the validity of faith or the acceptance of what defies reason and logic. The problems for me arise when a person argues with himself or with his own proofs or embraces and insists on what is evidently not true in any context . . . for example, the infallibility of theological reasoning, especially when it is based on what are essentially political decisions made by a man or a panel of men. The church's adherents consider humanism their worst enemy even while they insist they themselves are the ultimate practicing humanists, contending that human judgment is the ultimate determinant of all things . . . even of the nature and will of the divine.

Aye, there's the rub! When examined closely, most fundamentalist religious expressions are not "fundamentally" related to any sort of power or expression but are in essence based on—brace yourself!—humanism. That's right; my friend Todd's faith is actually precisely what he says he has the most contempt for—humanism! His entire theological holdings are based not on any personal experiences with the Great Mysterious, and to be honest not even on traditional reports of such experiences by others (for example, in the Bible), but on what the human authorities of the secular, political organization of his church say those experiences are and what they mean. Further they are subject to change, reinterpretation, addition, and removal by those same human authorities and *only* by those authorities.

The remarkable reality is that the sincerest form of worship is doubt. Doubt is a prerequisite to wonder and awe, a virtual antenna for knowledge, an open door with a glow-in-the-dark welcome mat for the Great Mysterious. If the genuine truth seeker, the honest pilgrim, is not an *empty* vessel, he can at the very minimum be a *receptive* one.

The issue is complicated by Todd's genuine sincerity, gentility, and deep piety. A mutual friend of ours was surprised when I suggested that meek and gentle Todd is hopelessly arrogant. "How could such a quiet, sweet, gentle guy be arrogant?" Well, isn't feeling, saying, and insisting that one is absolutely right, without any possibility of error, by definition arrogance? How about his insisting then that not only does he have a corner on the truth but also everyone else who has even the slightest difference of opinion with him and what he has been told to believe is wrong and doomed to hell for the error? Isn't that a form of arrogance? Does it really matter if such absurd assertions are made quietly, gently, and with pity for the alleged error?

I don't think so. It's arrogance, plain and simple. And an arrogance shot through with transparent silliness. First, Todd is a great guy and no dummy, but no one who knows him is going to accept his self-labeling as a chosen recipient of all the knowledge of the universe. Second, the "immutable and absolute" knowledge Todd possesses has been spoon-fed to him by human authorities who simply claim it is the truth. Moreover, they are authorities who now and again change their minds and occasionally meet to decide what, at that point, constitutes the new immutable and absolute truth. Doesn't the most basic logic suggest that anything dependent on human decision and majority vote and subject to occasional revision is *not* immutable and absolute? The rationalization is the church's governing body may be a collection of goofy, narrow, antiquated, old fools—not innocent but ignorant—but their decisions are guided by *God*! Case closed.

The system of logic (or perhaps more precisely, illogic) that Todd applies is a common one in religiosity, a kind of commercial religionism intended largely for public show and self-satisfaction. It is a solipsistic form of mental gymnastics: "I believe what I believe because it is God's word. I know it is God's word because it's in the Bible. The Bible is God's word because that's what God tells us. God tells us that in the Bible." Todd has never wondered that he just happened to be born not only into the one true religion but, even better, the one true denomination of the one true religion. In fact, he just happened to be born into the one true congregation of the one true sliver of the one true church of the one true denomination of the one true faith. Todd is one lucky guy, I guess.

A stunning array of remarkable weapons is made available to True Believers to divert any challenge: "That is Old Covenant and now we have the New Covenant." This contention is followed almost immediately by an insistence that God never changes His mind—as blatant a contradiction as possible, sometimes within the same sentence! It is a remarkable admission that God changes His mind from time to time even while insisting He never does. "That is parable . . . that is literal . . . that is a metaphor . . . but that part is absolute word-for-word truth." Could the conflict stem from translation or historical transmission? "No, God has also guided the translations and transmissions, so there can be no error. At least not within the acceptable translations and transmissions." And which would those be? "The ones the men of my church have approved." And why should we trust their human, and therefore flawed, judgment? "Because they are guided by God."

Circles, circles, circles, circles . . .

My friend Todd has accumulated a lifetime's worth of rhetorical devices, like the tools in a mechanic's box. On the rare occasions when they seem about to fail him, Todd is perfectly capable of launching his own attacks . . . He says I deny the truth (that is, whatever he believes is the truth) because I deny Jesus, the Bible, and even God Himself. Of course, that is not the case; in fact, it's precisely the opposite. My only intent as a true pilgrim in the spirit of Simplicius Simplicissimus, the Jerk, and Siddhartha is to find out what the truth is and to clear away whatever fog I can for my own understanding and satisfaction. And Todd is a veritable fog machine, as is his church.

Todd insists that his churchmen have the answers; I counter that they are not even capable of understanding the questions much less arriving at the answers. I am not asserting that the Bible is false testimony or that Jesus is not what He said He was or even that Jesus is not what others claim Him to be. I suppose it's even possible (although not immediately evident, at least to me) that the humanistic systems developed as church organizations might not have a lot of the truth in their studies and teachings. Further, I really do doubt their contention that they have *all* of it while no one else has *any* of it. There is almost certainly some truth in something as venerable and durable as the Bible, but I don't see a lot of evidence that organized, structured, mainstream, accepted, human-based churches are the best mechanism to investigate, understand, disseminate, interpret, or preserve that truth.

There are signs of unconscious doubt in Todd's adamancy. When he asks, "How can one have a faith that is not absolute?" he tacitly exposes the flaw in his own absolutism. The real question is, how can one have a faith that *is* absolute, when doubt is everywhere, unavoidable, natural, and powerful? The answer is that doubt *is* faith. Doubt is a human expression and admission of the helplessness that is reality, one that we *must* feel in the face of the enormity of the Great Mysterious and of Something Going On. It's the only reasonable and worshipful calculus. Insisting that one knows everything there is to know reveals blatant disrespect for the wonder of it all. Confessing non-understanding, however, is the ultimate reverence, the one true prayer.

19

Lessons from Mother Corn
and Father Buffalo

Tribes such as the Omahas and Pawnees combined what
are often seen as diametrically opposed worldviews,
those of the farmer and the hunter. They lived in semi-
permanent large villages in substantial houses or lodges and
left the settlements twice a year, summer and winter, to go
on annual buffalo hunts. In these cultures the story of Abel
and Cain makes no sense because the Omahas and Pawnees
saw no conflict in their two cultural bases.

Moreover, this traditional system brought together another
two concepts we think of as opposites in mainstream Western
culture, animals and plants. And still another . . . mankind
and those other worlds. For the Native, plants and animals are
not considered separate and apart but as kin and coopera-
tive partners in a complex, synergistic relationship. When
Natives speak to animals and plants, it is on an equal level.
And they have a reciprocal relationship: you feed us, and we
will feed you. We thank you for what you do for us, and we
accept your thanks for our part in helping you fulfill your
role in this circle. To this day prayers are sent to the four
directions, to Mother Earth, and to the Powers of the Sky,
and blessings are sought not only for the "two-leggeds"—that
would be you and me—but also for the "four-leggeds" . . .
and those that fly above us, the insects and birds, and those
that swim in the waters and creep beneath the earth.

Within Pawnee cosmogony the workings of the earth,

including the weather, animals, plants, cosmic events, and man, lie not in man's power but depend on the decisions of the Nahurac, or the spirit animal council that meets in deep caves in the earth at sacred places such as the Pahuk site near Fremont and Fullerton, Nebraska. (When I tell non-Natives of this view of the world's workings, I usually note that I would far rather have such decisions made by the spirits of owl, coyote, buffalo, mountain lion, eagle, crow, beaver, and so on, than by a far less wise group of humans like our Congress.)

I am not a vegetarian. I am an omnivore. I understand full well that when I eat, something dies. My understanding, however, extends beyond animals and their flesh. I realize the obvious: when I eat, plants as well as animals die. I also understand all too well that death is inevitable for plants, animals, and human beings, so it doesn't make much sense to lament or even avoid that inevitability. I am not distressed therefore for the animals that hunters kill; instead, I worry about the hunters and a mankind that kills for fun. I would be equally troubled to learn that the wielder of the killing tool on a slaughterhouse kill floor showed glee as he fired the fatal nail into the brain of the animal before or beneath him. I would accept a workmanlike indifference in such slaughter but would find a greater hope for mankind in general if the man or woman delivering the deathblows felt a sense of gratitude and humility toward those creatures that die to nurture mankind. I do.

But I feel the same way about the barley that goes into my beer, the wheat in my bread, the corn in my soup, and the cotton in my clothing. I intend to return the favor by doing what I can to ensure that my own remains will go as quickly as possible back into the cycle of life . . . and death. I am troubled that so many human beings struggle against the natural process of "From dust ye came, to dust ye shall return" and inter themselves in concrete and stone after being embalmed with poisonous fluids, squandering fortunes on boxes and monuments, and denying the very real inevitability of death. And let's face it, life!

Indians had, and to some degree still have, a reverence for corn and buffalo not simply as a specific, remarkable plant and an animal; they regard Mother Corn and Father Buffalo as representative symbols of *all* plants and *all* animals. And of the relationship between those two groups of beings and mankind. And of the relationship between all of us—animal, plant, and man together—with the Great Mysterious. And more. If rocks have life and can instruct us, what then might we learn from plants and animals? More than we suspect. Certainly more than I suspect. And what I think of when I consider a lesson from corn and buffalo is that I don't know nearly as much as I think (or more precisely hope) that I know.

I do not understand the idea of boredom. How could anyone be bored in a world so full of magic and mystery? I cannot imagine. This past year I have taken on a new interest in crows. Not the Northern Plains Indian tribe but the black-robed corvid, the loud and raucous bird that wakes me up far too early every morning. And the surprises have come almost every day as I have tried to talk with the family of crows, our neighbors down by the river, as I watch their awareness of my family and me, as they consider my food offerings, and as they find enormous amusement in my efforts to imitate their calls and to establish a relationship with them. Increasingly I find that crows are not simply smarter than I thought, not only smarter than other birds and animals, but certainly smarter than I am. I find that discovery not only interesting but also amusing and inspiring. I am less comfortable with the obvious truth that crows know more about us than we know about them.

And some people shoot crows. For fun. Now which one is wiser, the crow or man? Not a doubt in my mind.

The question in my mind regarding plants and animals is the same as the one I have about rocks: what do they know— especially, what do they know beyond what mankind knows or can know? Without any doubt in my mind, the only answer is a lot. To illustrate this I will share two stories of my own ignorance. It's not something I enjoy doing, but I hope that by confessing my own unawareness I can recommend that the reader reexamine his or her own.

First, a brief story about a momentary (I hope) lapse in my consideration of what plants are about. In particular, corn. Corn is an unusual plant in that it relies entirely on man, just as man relies on it. Scientists may have found proto-corn in the wild—that is, the ancient plant from which corn came millennia ago—but there is no such thing as "wild corn" in America. Only domesticated corn. Corn and man are inextricably bound together in a synergistic, or mutually dependent, and effective relationship. No wonder so many Indian tribes thought of corn as the very mother of mankind. But how many people think of corn as a divine gift or a partner in life when they down a cola or a beer, let alone an ear of sweet corn? I think a lot about corn, but not even I can maintain an attitude of constant awareness of the remarkable position that plant occupies in our society and in our lives.

One of my personal habits is the making and distribution of prayer packets. I make small leather pouches and I put the following items into each one:

a small, round stone that I have found that has struck me as meaningful;
a tuft of buffalo hair;
a pinch of dirt from an anthill on this blessed ground where Linda and I live;

a few white cedar needles;
a few leaves of prairie sage;
a cottonwood leaf; and . . .
a pinch of cornmeal that was blessed and given to me long
ago by a woman who had received it in turn from a spiritual leader in New Mexico.

While all of these inclusions have a meaning for me and seem to me to be special in a spiritual sense, the bundles are only my prayer in a tangible form. I do not think of them as magical, powerful, sacred, or even special. They are simply a physical manifestation of a prayer. I give these parcels to friends, especially when they are facing some sort of important, dangerous, or troubling time. I also leave them in places where I want to deliver a prayer . . . graves that are significant to me or simply places that move me to prayer, especially when I want to express gratitude.

When I was given the blessed cornmeal in New Mexico thirty-five years ago, I was told that it was obviously a small amount and would inevitably be depleted, but I could extend my supply with other cornmeal, especially cornmeal that had been blessed by someone or some event or cornmeal from particularly significant corn, such as the blue corn of the Omahas that is issued in services of the Native American Church and is therefore considered blessed. I have been reluctant to add any other cornmeal at all, but I have made a special effort to extend my supply only with cornmeal that carries implications equivalent to those of what I had received originally. With that in mind, I recently asked the Pawnee Chiefs Council, the Nasharo, and the Corn Sisters of the Pawnees—women who have taken on the nurturing of ancient corn varieties as their special role in life—if I could have four ears of ancient and now revived Pawnee eagle corn to grind and add to my cornmeal supply.

I was surprised by their response, but I shouldn't have been. I should have known that the Pawnees' reverence for corn, even if only culturally vestigial, is still strong and complex. The Nasharo requested more information about how I intended to use the eagle corn. I explained the prayer packets and added that I sometimes "feed" the buffalo skulls I have at my hearth and at nearby Pawnee reburial sites. I gave a list of the contents of the packets, much as I listed here for you. They then told me that it is not something the Pawnees do, and it would therefore not be an appropriate use for the eagle corn.

I came away with several thoughts from this process. First, I was impressed by the depth and breadth of thought the Nasharo and Corn Sisters had given my request. What they told me, and what I should have considered, is that we are not just dealing with *corn* here but also its use in religious contexts. And the contexts themselves. To my Pawnee friends, this corn is not just a grain but a grain that in and of itself requires special consideration; moreover, where and how it is to be used is also a concern that must be considered when dealing with it. I was impressed that the corn is held in such regard, but even more, I was pleased, even while being a bit disappointed, that the tribe is being very cautious in potential uses of the eagle corn. I would rather they were overly careful about who gets the corn and for what applications than their being excessively generous in handing it out. The lesson for me was that corn can and should be considered to be more than grain. Or even a symbol. It carries with it meaning—not just symbolically but in actuality. The eagle corn is in and of itself sacred.

Next, at the same time, I was made aware of and became marginally involved in another tribe's efforts to renew ancient and "lost" corn varieties. And please do note that the Pawnees and other tribes maintained many different genetic corn strains for different applications: soup, green corn (or what is generally known in the mainstream as roasting ears or sweet corn), popcorn, storage corn, and so forth. Well-meaning, non-Native scientists are working to regenerate lost Native corn varieties ostensibly to benefit the tribes that hold in reverence those strains and depended on them at one time for their people's very survival and because the more genetic varieties that can be rescued, the greater the inventory available for modern agriculture.

Because of my experience with the Nasharo and Corn Sisters, I had a new understanding of what I was seeing in the scientists' genetic work: they view corn as a plant . . . a foodstuff, an archaeological curiosity, a laboratory challenge, a fond memory of past times. But they clearly do not consider the cultural, religious, spiritual, and inherent nonbiological content of the plant. That is, corn is not simply a biological, historical, and anthropological entity. Corn may have a cultural and spiritual content, and that content may be far more important than an outsider realizes, beyond and more important than nutritional, historical, aesthetic, or scientific considerations. There may be clan prohibitions with certain strains of corn, for example, or gender issues to consider. Can only women handle a particular variety? Is it forbidden to some clans? Can it be eaten or used only at certain times of the year—for example, during a moon phase, on a particular day, or in a ceremony? Is it reserved for specific ceremonies? Considerations of that sort may not be of concern to non-Native scientists, but what of the people to whom the corn belongs? Indeed, it may no longer be of concern even to Native peoples or to members of the tribe who originally used it, but what if the corn has its own agenda and protocol? Is it not possible that the corn itself may have a voice in how it is grown and used? And how would we know . . . if we don't listen to the corn?

The culture(s) I grew up in—midwestern, small town, American, Protestant, white immigrant—considers mankind to be something separate and not a part of the larger world except insofar as it is available for our use when, where, and how we want to deal with it. The idea of giving consideration to how these things might feel about the arrangement would be considered peculiar at best. But in the Native world, we are within a much larger community of beings that also need our consideration. It is not at all unusual in Native conversations—and sometimes prayers, which are after all only conversations with the Great Powers—to address many other elements of the world we see around us: plants, animals, physical features, hills, rivers, rocks, even the weather. Prayers asking for and bestowing blessings include "those all two-leggeds, four-leggeds, those that fly above us, creep below us, swim in the waters, spirits around us, those who have gone ahead and those who will follow, these plants and creatures that feed us, those who are our companions." Recent news reports (for example, Reuters, "Oklahoma Native Americans Tame Twisters with Ancient Rituals," June 20, 2014), describe conversations between tribal elders and tornadoes, with the former requesting the understanding and mercy of the weather phenomena regarding problems they might cause people with whom they have no argument. Civil, rational conversation is the means, it is felt, toward avoiding unfavorable consequences.

If that idea sounds . . . well, . . . nutty to you, consider my next story. And whatever you may think to the contrary, the following story is true. But it is also long and complicated. Be patient!

Dawn, a friend of mine, once found herself in a very difficult situation. Her lease on a large parcel of land was being recalled, and she had to find a new place to live for herself, her resident "friends," and all her possessions. Okay, that kind

of thing happens, but in this case it was a bit more complicated because some of her friends were her buffalo. In fact,
she had a herd of buffalo. (And you think you had a hard
time finding a rental property that would take *pets!*) She
turned to me for help. I did what I could to find her a tem-
porary or even permanent foster home for her bison herd (as
I recall, somewhere around a dozen head). I tried ranchers
in the area, a nearby (four hundred miles away!) tribe in the
same state with its own buffalo herd, a private herd owner
(in fact, Ted Turner's land manager and his enormous land
and bison holdings), haulers, anyone who could help. Nothing. I would have taken the animals on my sixty acres, but
buffalo require substantial fencing and I have none. Not to
mention that this land is too fragile for any livestock, much
less a herd of buffalo, and we occupy a home and buildings
that would have been very difficult to isolate from the herd.

Other issues in dealing with this situation complicated
the matter: the buffalo were on rugged canyon country land,
which was virtually impossible for herding with horses, let
alone vehicles. The buffalo also had little contact with human
beings and were therefore not likely to take well to being handled. Finally, there were no loading pens, ramps, or docks
in the event that we did find a hauler willing to move them.

Buffalo do not take well to hauling in any event. Another
friend and neighbor of mine had a small bison herd near our
home ten or fifteen years ago, and even approaching them
had to be done with caution. I watched his huge bull tear up
cedar trees just for fun and once shred a tire with his horns
because it was nice exercise for his neck muscles. When my
neighbor sold his herd to a breeder several hours away, I was
disappointed because I would have liked to have had the bull
at least for meat. I enjoy cuts of buffalo that few other people
bother with—liver, heart, tongue, gut—and it would have
been very convenient simply to dress out the animal so close

to my home. So I called the buyer and offered him ten cents a pound more for the bull than he had paid for it . . . a handsome profit for which he wouldn't have to do a thing. And it would save him from trying to truck the bull. The man turned me down, laughing at my offer and boasting that he was going to haul the buffalo bull to join his herd in Lincoln. He did get the huge bull loaded into his stock truck, almost, whereupon the bull completely dismantled the vehicle. The buyer then had to butcher the bull right there in the field to save what was left of his truck. Buffalo, and especially bull buffalo, do not take well to being pushed around.

I knew therefore that moving my friend's buffalo herd would not be easy under the best of circumstances, even if I had found someone to round them up, load them, and move them. But I hadn't. Time dragged on, my friend grew ever more desperate. I was frustrated again and again in my efforts to help her, and even people who had joined the effort failed in their search for a new home for even one, several, or all of my friends' friends. And so she faced the prospect of abandoning her animals to a less-than-auspicious fate with the venal white man who was ending her lease and who knew full well the difficult position he was putting her in. I wonder to this day if he wasn't looking avariciously at the herd she was pretty much doomed to leave behind.

The last possible day of removal came and went, and I gave up hope. Days went by and I moped around, lamenting the fate of the buffalo and my own powerlessness. Eventually I sent my friend an email and expressed my condolences and wondered what had been done with the herd. She replied, "Didn't Jimmy talk with you? I thought you'd know by now."

Know what? Jimmy who?! And she told me the damnedest story I have heard, and I have heard a lot of stories in my time.

Dawn had talked with Jimmy Horn, a Pawnee friend with

whom I had corresponded about my friend's bison dilemma. Jimmy explained that as if he didn't feel bad enough about my friend's situation and letting me down, he really was pained by the situation of the buffalo. They exchanged information, and he said he was going to do something to help. She was dubious, but on the last day of her tenure on the land, he and a Comanche friend of his, who not only had a semi-trailer rig but also kept a buffalo herd for another tribe in Oklahoma, arrived. There they were, ready to load up and move the buffalo. Wow.

And hmmmm . . . There remained that little problem with what the buffalo would have to say about this relocation. How would they get the animals down from the canyons? How would they get them loaded in the truck? How would they move them six hundred miles? The problem was not even close to being solved. I would have given generous odds that it was indeed an unsolvable problem.

But no one had yet bothered to talk with the buffalo. And I know from many conversations with my tribal brother Louie LaRose, longtime keeper of the Winnebago Tribe's herd, that one simply cannot discount the wisdom of these mighty and spiritually powerful animals. And I was reminded of that fact as my friend Dawn went on with her story . . . Jimmy and his friend backed up the truck and opened the trailer, dropping a loading ramp to the ground. The buffalo herd, under the leadership of a very large and very daunting bull, approached this curiosity—not a common sight in their experience—and watched the proceedings with suspicion. Jimmy's friend, as it turns out, didn't just know *about* buffalo . . . he *knew* buffalo. He walked toward the herd and sat on the ground . . . at best a dangerous situation to put himself in. He calmly drew out a pipe, tamped it with consecrated tobacco, and lit it. As is proper, he blew smoke in the four directions and to

Mother Earth and the Power of the Sky. He said his prayers and spoke to the Great Powers. The buffalo herd stood behind their bull leader and watched all this quietly.

Then Jimmy's friend turned his attention to the herd, especially the bull standing so close to him and in front of his herd. The man seated on the ground explained to the buffalo why he was there. He prayed, apologized to the buffalo for his intrusion in their lives, and explained that there would be more discomfort to come for them. He explained why they were moving the herd and where they would be going, that he and Jimmy would do everything they could to make the long trip as comfortable as they could, and that this bull and his herd would soon be joining other relatives on new pastures, where they would again be safe and comfortable. The man refilled and relit his pipe. He explained the procedures of what they hoped to do: the loading onto the truck, the travel, the stops for water and feed, the arrival on the new ground, the unloading, and the integration of herds.

And then the man asked the bull and his herd for their help. He asked. He didn't tell . . . he asked. He prayed for their help. He made it clear that all he hoped for could not happen without the help of Father Buffalo and his herd. It was all up to that bull. The two men and a woman would be helpless without the leadership . . . not just the help but the leadership . . . of the herd leader and the understanding of his family. And the man then rose and walked back to the truck. The humans stood there in a posture of supplication. And the bull and his herd began to move. Toward the truck. And up the ramp, something they had never seen or walked on before. In the truck they settled down for the long trip, and they cooperated fully during watering, rest, and feeding stops (and a couple of blown tires resulting from the massive load in the trailer!).

On arrival at the new grazing ground, the buffalo easily unloaded and were greeted by their kin. They joined the old herd comfortably and quickly and relatively easily established a new hierarchy. And there they and their many progeny live to this day. Happily ever after.

What *do* animals know that we do not? What *could* we learn from them if we bothered to ask and listen? I suspect it would be a lot more than we will ever gain from killing them with little or no respect or understanding.

20

Lessons from the Nahurac

Traditional Native understandings of how the world works depend in very large part on the mutual relationships between animals, plants, nature in general, and man. Here we find one of the most profound differences between the Native American and mainstream America. The history of America and its frontier mentality remind us again and again that nature is our enemy, that it is something to be conquered, subdued, tamed, brought to its knees. All life is here for our purposes and ends. Animals are here not for their own sake but for ours . . . to kill and eat. Or not to eat, just to kill. For personal amusement, if nothing else. Religious zealots are insulted at the suggestion that they are somehow . . . anyhow(!) . . . related biologically to other life forms. They argue that we humans have the spark of the divine within us. I counter, Dogs don't go to heaven? Please! Anyone who has known a dog at all closely knows that while there may be questions about which humans go to heaven, most dogs deserve that elevation.

For that matter, anyone who spends any time at all interacting with animals or observing their behavior in the wild knows that they are far wiser and more clever than the non-observer might think. As mentioned in chapter 19, I devote a lot of time and energy to studying the ways of crows . . . the birds, not the Indians. They are incredibly smart, among the very smartest creatures of the animal world. I read as many studies of crows as I can find, and every day I observe them as I carry our table scraps and even some purchased food items to them down on our river road. I am thrilled with what little bits of progress I make, learning something new about them, finding out they're more complicated than I thought, finding I was wrong, finding that I only know a part of what is going on. And then they utterly baffle me and do something that totally negates huge amounts of what I thought I had learned. The bottom line for me, I guess, is that to my mind my experience with crows is a terrific metaphor for my relationship with Wakan Tonka, Wakonda, Tawadahat, the Great Mysterious—whatever this power is that swirls around us. Serious researchers (I am not!) have found that crows can count, that they not only use tools but also *make* tools, and what is even more astonishing, that they *save* what they have made for later use! They recognize and differentiate human faces (how many crow faces do *you* recognize?) and quickly learn to imitate with unsettling accuracy the sounds of such things as doorbells and car horns, a dog's bark, and the human voice. How is it possible not to be surprised by the remarkable intelligence of these common creatures?

When I started trying to establish a conversation with the family of crows that occupies the area where I live, I bought, practiced, and tried using artificial crow calls. They worked once. Then the crows just laughed at my pathetic efforts to imitate their calls. Then I learned to be myself, simply yelling that I was on my way to their feeding area with table scraps, and they respected and responded to my honesty. (So do others of the wild world, apparently. As of this writing, I find that when I yell out to my crows, I now get a screaming response from a red-tailed hawk that sits in a tall cottonwood, waiting for the same food. Sometimes the crows scold and harass the hawk; sometimes they apparently think it's not worth the trouble, allow him to take what he needs, then clean up what's left.)

Linda has noticed that it takes only moments from the time she fills her bird feeders for the birds to appear . . . Inevitably a row of wild turkeys comes running up over the hill at the end of our yard, ready to clean out what Linda intends for her cardinals, jays, finches, and flickers. If she throws out cracked corn, deer appear almost instantly. It is clear that they don't just stumble on the bounty. Nor are they checking regularly to see if food appears. They watch. From somewhere down in the woods, they watch and know within moments when she puts out food or water. That is, from whatever casual observations we make of them, clearly they are making very careful observations and notes about *our* behavior. I have been warned again and again from people who have befriended crows that I should keep the scrap drop well away from the house. If the crows figure out where that food is kept before the two-legged walks it down to the river road, they will start reminding me about their requirements and even scolding me for my lack of keeping a reliable schedule by knocking on my windows to hurry the process along!

If you have a dog, you know that that creature's senses are well beyond basic. He or she knows when you are even *thinking* about heading out or going for a walk or digging out the food dishes. We have tried again and again to figure out what clues we give when we are about to leave the house and go to town, but we cannot detect what in our behavior signals to our two dogs that something is about to happen . . . not in our preparations, not in our conversations, not in our slightest behavior. The dogs simply know, and we can't figure out how they know.

If Linda goes to town for groceries, returning on no particular schedule, the dogs know when her truck is approaching the bridge a quarter mile away. Inside the house or lounging in the sun in the backyard, they become alert and show by looking, smelling, or listening that they know Linda is near and getting nearer. Many minutes later I hear the gravel crunching in the yard, and then and only then do I know that Linda has arrived.

Can anyone possibly experience such things and not acknowledge that animals know things we do not? And that that sensory superiority might be useful? Respected? Even honored? Can anyone in modern twenty-first-century America doubt that Indians who live in much more intimate contact with nature and the animal world could have failed to realize the same thing? To my mind, there are then other questions with a less certain answer: Why do we continue to ignore that wisdom ourselves? Why does the modern American have so little regard for the ancient and (to my mind) undeniable wisdom of the animal world?

I imagine the problem is that to some degree it is easy to ignore the animal world today, especially in our increasingly urban contexts. Here in the rural outback, along a free-flowing river, in the heart of the Great Plains, and constantly in contact with Native American sensitivities, perhaps it is simply easier for us to observe and acknowledge our connections (or inadequate connections) with the animal world. Nor are these interactions based merely on natural animal behavior. There seems to be something more, something along the lines of the woableza, a bit of remarkable, even mystic consciousness. Based on my observations, animals don't just act in accordance with their basic needs of finding shelter and food, rearing their young, and dealing with the rest of nature. Some, perhaps many, maybe even *all* animals seem to understand that they have a relationship with man even if man has forgotten or ignores his relationship with them. They take the initiative. They start the conversation. They are the ones who seem to have something to communicate.

I first saw a bald eagle about 1978. I was sitting at the big window in my ancient log house down by the river, grading papers from one of my university classes. I looked up and not fifty feet away, at eye level, a gorgeous eagle cruised down the swale just outside the window. To say the least, I was stunned. I jumped from my chair and ran down to the river, hoping to get another look at this gorgeous creature. As I came through a dip in the path and around an edge of forest, I saw this huge . . . what? . . . "thing" in a tree not far away. I stopped. I gaped. My mind simply couldn't grasp what my eyes were seeing. There he was . . . hook billed, piercing eyes, incredibly beautiful and proud. And I just stood there. Only someone who encounters an eagle in the wild knows that feeling.

Another time, Linda had a similar experience. She was carrying water out to our chicken house, and halfway across the yard, her eye suddenly caught sight of that same impossibly large being. Something that appeared to be six feet tall, as unlikely as that was, was sitting on a fence post at her eye level. She stopped. She stared. And then the eagle turned its head and looked directly at her and our dogs, which were accompanying her. She told me later that she set the bucket down, slowly backed away, turned, and walked into the house. The dogs did too, without so much as a single bark. They were not frightened but instead intimidated by the bird's steely gaze. An eagle close at hand does that to a soul. Stops you in your tracks, makes you set your bucket down, and walk slowly away, your own spirit unable to rise to an equivalence of what you see.

Now those are chance encounters, and we have plenty of them here . . . eagles flying the river looking for prey, sitting in trees overhanging the river bank, circling higher and higher, pretty much minding their own business, and not particularly paying any interest to our business. And there are occasions when an eagle's appearance strikes one as being particularly fortuitous. At the first reburial of Pawnee remains on our land, we were surprised and pleased when an eagle appeared over the river as if in recognition of what we were doing here on the ground. Well, that's a grand stroke of luck, we thought.

What then are we to make of eagles appearing at almost *every* reburial event? Can that possibly be mere coincidence? Imagine a group of young Native Americans visiting this place and volunteering to finish a grave of nearly five hundred repatriated remains. The larger reburial was done, but as the grave settled, it needed to be dressed, finished, reseeded, and raked. It was definitely a task for young people, not only because of the physical demands of the work, but also because of the opportunity the occasion presented for them to pay their respects, to remember their history, to understand the injustice of the desecrations, and to learn the location of this relatively unmarked and secret site. We were standing in the parking area at our house, organizing our tools and preparing to start our walk up the hill, when one of the older Natives in our group nodded in the direction of the river and looked with obvious intensity past the house. And there he was, an eagle, headed right for us from the river, flying at very low altitude (perhaps thirty-five feet). He tipped a bit to acknowledge our presence and, with a couple powerful sweeps of his long wings, glided over us. And over the grave.

Serendipity starts to fail as an explanation. And then it happens again and again. At a much smaller reburial just weeks before this writing, four of us were standing at the new grave, having burned cedar, having said our prayers, having apologized to the offended elders, and having offered our thanks to the four directions, to all the creatures, and to Tawadahat. We stood there silently. Then we all saw it, that unsettlingly large spot up the river, moving in our direction in huge, overlapping circles. We stood and gaped. And as the eagle reached a point on the river just below us, he detoured and looped over us, tipping to acknowledge our presence. All we could do is nod and thank him for his benediction. And he went back to the river and continued on his way. Once maybe. But not again and again and again and again . . . Native Americans saw (and to a large degree still see) the animal world as directly connected with our own species here on this earth. To me it only makes sense. Tribes often had animal identities . . . the Crows, Sac Fox, or Wolf Pawnees, which is a redundancy since *pani* means "wolf." Even more repetitive is the Wolf Pawnee Skidi . . . *three* words meaning "wolf." Or an identity was recognized through a totemic association or clan or family relationships. Within the Omaha Tribe, my name, Bull Buffalo Chief, places me within the KonCe (Wind) Clan, which is understood to be associated with creatures that came to earth from the sky . . . that is, shellfish. My sister-in-law Naomi's name put her in the Bear Clan, and I know Omahas in the Buffalo, Deer, and Turtle Clans. Many Plains Indians speak of the animal coyote as "Little Brother." The Pawnees once had many societies, many of which were associated with specific animals: Crow Lance, Society of Crows, Crazy Horse, Brave Raven, Wolf, Big Horse, Young Dog, Bear, Buffalo, and Deer. Within the Lakota Oglala Tribe, my name associates me with Coyote, both the animal and the spirit Trickster. Historical names are familiar to all—Standing Bear, Crazy Horse, Black Elk, Blackbird—but even in my own life are friends with names such as Dog Chief, Fool Bull, Leading Fox, Bird, Echo-Hawk, Bear Eagle, Meadowlark Woman, Spotted Horse Chief, Horse Capture, Good Eagle, Crow Dog, American Horse, and so on.

Animals in Native societies are understood to be kin and on equal footing with those of us who are two-leggeds. The feeling is that we are all in this together, no matter how many legs we walk on. Animals are not resources to be exploited but partners in the great cycles of life. Is it surprising then that animals play a central role in many Native mystic experiences, visions, dreams? As spectral appearances, gifts, conversations and instruction, tales and legends?

How then do we reconcile the obvious fact that these people who felt kinship or even revered and honored these animals also kill and eat them? To some degree, as I have mentioned earlier, various taboos do indeed prohibit the eating of one's kin animals. Or parts of them. It would not have been easy for my old friend John Turner's family to survive without eating buffalo, but then his clan prohibition applied only to eating or touching head parts of the buffalo. Those taboos are not casual, self-imposed dietary restrictions. As I explain in my book *Embracing Fry Bread: Confessions of a Wannabe* and in my novel *Touching the Fire*, the natural consequences of violating clan totemic taboos are severe, even fatal. It's a matter of touching the fire. Whether intentional or accidental, if you touch the fire, you are burned.

But what of Father Buffalo? Or any of the vast panoply of highly revered animals that were used as a part of the regular or ritual processes of tribal life? How was the taking of those lives rationalized? Easy enough. I have already explained how the relationships work: we are on an equal footing. A *really* equal footing. And we are all in this together—not in some sort of abstract, theoretical way but in an absolute, ironbound union. As a hunter killed a buffalo, he thanked the buffalo for dying to contribute to the welfare and survival of his family, his clan, his tribe, and himself; but—and here is the very important difference—he also accepted the gratitude of the buffalo, which that animal extended to the hunter because the relationship was a closed circle in which each played his own clear role. The respect was mutual, and that respect was the essential element. Again, I ask what hunters today, who kill as often as not simply for the thrill of killing, extend that same kind of respect? Is it respectful to kill a beautiful creature like a deer, turkey, or mountain lion and, while another person takes your photo, then mock its death by propping it up while you kneel proudly, grinning and holding your gun as if you had actually accomplished something heroic? Maybe have the corpse stuffed so you can have it as a trophy? Really? That's not respect in any form I know. Even if something short of contempt is shown in mocking the dead body of the slain animal, what consideration does the modern hunter give to the spirit of the animal he has killed?

In some tribes, the Natives' respect of the animal world extended to the degree that it was understood that not man but animals ruled the earth, making the decisions of fate and future. In *Indians of the Plains* (University of Nebraska Press, 1982), Robert H. Lowie writes, "The supernatural beings who befriend man vary enormously in character. Animals were very frequent visitants of Plains Indians; buffalo, elk, bears, eagles . . . and sparrow hawks . . . also quite lowly beasts such as dogs and rabbits. . . . A Pawnee boy gets supernatural aid from mice. . . . Celestial patrons are also frequent, stars figuring prominently among the Pawnee" (159).

Animals, as well as rocks, trees, storms, rivers, stars, planets, the sun, and the moon—all of these natural environmental elements were (and to a large degree, still are) seen in the Native cosmogony as being in constant interchange with that one other, equal element . . . humankind. Mainstream non-Indian culture sees itself apart and even at war with these elements, in part as a result of a general cultural context but also as a consequence of a religious system that places mankind as separate and completely different from and superior to all of nature. Again Lowie writes, "The first thing that strikes an observer of most primitive peoples is the way in which supernaturalism pervades every sphere of social life. . . . In short, for the Plains Indian, supernaturalism was not the equivalent of churchgoing on a Sunday, but something that profoundly affected his daily life and offered an explanation of extraordinary occurrences."

Lowie could just as easily and correctly have constructed his sentences in the present tense. Moreover, I am reminded of Richard Fool Bull's observation that it is not so much a peculiarity of Native senses but a natural understanding that the white man is educated out of. Sadly. I believe there is still some chance to rebuild those associations with considerable positive return for anyone who makes the effort.

Author's note: The week I was proofreading these pages, a full year after writing them, a friend of ours who lives nearby told me about his experience with an eagle. He and his wife were driving down a country road and came over a small rise and around a corner to find a huge golden eagle sitting on the roadside, feasting on some road kill. The sudden appearance was so stunning, so sudden, that my friend slammed on his brakes and slid to a stop. As with us, his eyes could not accept the huge size of the bird; he shrank back in his seat as the eagle's gaze pierced him. As the bird spread its magnificent wings and took to flight, he and his wife could only sit there in startled wonder, uncertain of whether what they had seen was real or spectral.

21

Where Lessons Are Lost

My impression is that throughout human history many people have sensed the Great Mysterious, much as I have. In fact, the phenomenon really isn't at all unusual in the human experience. I suspect that almost anyone can have a woableza, an awakening or realization, if they only listen. This position is simply is not possible, though, for those who insist that they already know everything and need no more information than what they already have . . . a posture that pretty much describes the basis of any organized church's political structure.

It is not hard to imagine how churches and their apparently inevitable schisms have come to be. I imagine that some individuals within the formal, conventional church structures or within a context where there is *no* church structure have had a genuine mystic insight and found the courage (or foolishness) to tell others or perhaps friends or family members. Perhaps the story of a mystic experience takes on a separate life from the person who first felt it and becomes a narrative passed beyond the initial circles of the person involved. A group of believers or disciples develop, then around them builds a movement—a congregation. Leaders carry the narrative of the original mystery and are entrusted with keeping it safe and pure; then we have priests. And soon an organization and structure develop to collect resources, maintain property, enforce regularity, ensure authenticity . . . and man has taken over and totally distorted what began as a simple contact for a person who felt the Great Mysterious.

Sadly, the intervening structure then considerably complicates and obstructs the potential for its adherents also to experience such mysteries . . . because they aren't official and sanctified by the proper authorities. Not being part of the original narrative, the new revelations are not a part of the codified structure so they are not considered legitimate. The new church has successfully taken the truth and converted it into precisely the opposite, an anathema to discovery and the mystic experience.

Imagine that a man is given a round rock in a context that suggests that the rock is far, far more than simply a rock. Coincidence piles on coincidence, import on import. There is, he begins to feel, a message. Something Is Going On. He tells some other friends, who tell their friends, and they too are moved by his experience. But not having had this experience themselves, they direct their attention not toward the message but instead at the round rock that came with the mystic insight since it is of divine origins. Then by way of spreading the gospel, not just *his* round rock but all round rocks become objects of veneration. There is some grumbling, and one or several dissenting groups diverge, one insisting that the rock has to be not only round but also pure white to be legitimate, and then later that the rock has to be white but only more or less round. Another few miles down the valley some people say no, their black rock . . . which is perfectly round, by the way . . . carries the true power. Then along come the Square Rock people, a truly heretical group that has made a fake rock out of painted wood so they can more easily move it from camp to camp.

From a genuinely meaningful mystic event, the idea has been transformed into a symbol, then a reproduction of that symbol. Finally, all that really matters in the humanistic "church" structure is the human structure and debate, which have nothing whatsoever to do with the true meaning of the original experience; in fact, it works contrary to it. What's worse, it blurs the eyes and minds of anybody who might otherwise have been open to yet another visit from the Great Mysterious. So gradually the original meaning and power of the round rock are forgotten. Thus an experience based on a mystery and knowledge that Something Is Going On has degenerated into a rigid dogma of enforced ignorance, denying and forbidding precisely that mystery and knowledge.

My argument here isn't really with opposition or aversion to official church structures. My concern is that their policies, dogma, and rigidity get in the way of people who might otherwise have regular contacts with the Great Mysterious and genuinely understand the wonder of the mystic, which lies more clearly in questions than answers. Once again, as Richard Fool Bull instructs us, the white man has been educated out of seeing and identifying the mystic experience and thus out of a whole world of new knowledge.

Therein lie the key and secret. Look for yourself. What does any belief system offer you? Answers or questions? It is an almost absolute that the more surely a system believes it has the incontrovertible truth, the further the system is from it. Yes, we may *want* answers, but the bottom line is that the real answers are in the questions. Can it really be . . . dare I say it? . . . a coincidence that by at least one report Jesus's last words were a question? If anyone should have been able to draw down the curtain by providing all of the ultimate answers, shouldn't it have been Jesus? But no, He perhaps was showing us the way to truth by asking yet another question even as He died.

Confusion increases. Transforming the mystic experience into a symbol of something else is not in and of itself a bad thing to do. Symbols are enormously important. They provide a shorthand that permits us to talk about very complicated things more easily. They are metaphors that mitigate the blunt trauma of truth. The problem comes along when we forget that the symbol *is* a symbol and in the process forget the concept that it represents. Right-wing zealots forget that the American flag is a symbol, a representation of our Constitution. And that Constitution ensures freedom of expression. Including . . . maybe even especially . . . destroying symbols. Like the flag. To forbid destroying a symbol, such as the flag, is to weaken the reality that the symbol represents. Destroying the *symbol* has no effect whatsoever . . . except perhaps reinforcing the principles for which it stands.

I have tried therefore to exercise some caution in my own life. I do not worship round rocks or buffalo skulls. They are metaphors. They are only symbols. As with languages or flags, they are important symbols to *me*, but they have come to me only to tell me or remind me that Something Is Going On. Something Going On will persist even if and when the skull and rock gifts have been lost, destroyed, or forgotten. It will continue even if their only message is, "Greetings!" The point is to heed the message and not the medium . . . I know that's not an original idea, but it is still a valid one.

I once commented to Mr. Fool Bull that he should take on some apprentices to learn all he knew about Native spiritualism and especially plants, about which he knew immense amounts. He laughed quietly at my innocence. He explained that it really didn't matter whether he taught anyone what he knew about plants. It's not as if when he died, the power of the plants would die too . . . only his knowledge of them would cease. The truth would live on just as it has for eons *before* he knew it. "Truth never dies," he said.

Moreover, a claim of absolute knowledge, or even superior knowledge (for example, the infallibility claimed by zealots or churches that pander to zealots), is not only an arrogance that gets in the way of any possible real, genuine religious experience for the individual but also a *dangerous* hubris. Hubris was a device of Greek drama. A fatal and obvious pride, it served as a kind of signal to the audience of a stage play that an ugly twist was about to come up in the performance. I have always found hubris to be a weak device in both drama and life, because the action of pride and its inevitable consequences are obvious enough that they don't need a signal. Everyone knows what is coming. Everyone sees it coming. Only the densest idiot doesn't know when it's headed his or her way. We knock on wood to negate perceived hubris. We know when we have committed even the smallest act of hubris, we know what the jeopardy is, and we worry about what we have done. We attempt to avert or mitigate it by acknowledging what we have done and admit we are embarrassed, troubled, or rueful about our error.

Take these scenarios:

We are really making good time. I'd say we have a good chance of getting there a good half hour early.

I aced that exam. Nailed it. I studied just the right parts of the book and wrote perfect answers. I just cinched a place for myself on the Dean's List this year.

No doubt about it, that babe is going to wind up in bed with me tonight. I have my lines down pat, I am wearing the right aftershave, and this outfit I'm wearing tonight is going to knock her out. In fact, my bet is that she won't even want to stick around for the second half of the Monster Truck Rally, even after I treat her to chili dogs with extra sauce. I bought brand-new earplugs since we're in the front row and got a new blue tarp we can wear in case the trucks start throwing mud. And it won't hurt my chances at all that my buddies Marv and Durward are coming along and bringing a case of beer to drink before we go in!

That's how dumb and blatant hubris is. In each of these scenarios you know exactly what the conclusion is going to be. Case #1: If the flat tire doesn't make them late, then a blown transmission will. Case #2: The idiot missed the questions on the *back* of each page of the exam. Case #3: Well, you know this numskull wound up going to the Monster Truck Rally alone; he and his buddies drank the beer and went to the show without female supervision. And he was picked up for driving under the influence on the way home. He lives alone to this day. In a river cabin. Without plumbing.

Similarly, the wisest path to spiritual development is to realize and admit one's cosmic ignorance. Anything else is stupid . . . and dangerous. A claim to universal or even superior spiritual knowledge is an incredible arrogance . . . and I use the adjective "incredible" here with careful consideration. Anyone who claims to know all the answers, or even most of the answers (in fact, in my opinion, *any* of the answers), is not credible . . . that is, is not to be believed. Pity would be an appropriate emotion, in fact, because this person is headed for a fall, perhaps in a big way.

Spiritual pride is a thin and wobbly tightrope, after all. And the greater the pride, the thinner the wire becomes. If a person insists, as my friend Todd does, that he and his support system know everything, without error, it takes only the slightest crack in the shell, some small but undeniable fault, for it to collapse. If people such as Todd begin to realize they are wrong about anything at all, then they see the possibility they might be wrong about a lot of things. Or everything. Their solution almost always is not to admit fallibility, however, but to shut off all incoming information that might contradict what they already "know." (We have seen this behavior recently in American politics too, and the consequences of deliberately imposed ignorance have impacted our entire nation and history adversely.) Perhaps the biggest task for followers of conventional, contemporary, organized religions is to convince themselves, not others, because their theses are utterly ludicrous.

Who knows better that he is *not* infallible than oneself, after all? Who is most likely to know the limitations of one's own knowledge and capabilities than oneself? (Although I'll have to admit that to an astonishing degree some people seem remarkably capable of avoiding any honest self-appraisal. A stunning example is former president George W. Bush, a tragicomedy character in two acts, who, when asked at a press conference in 2004, was unable to think of a single mistake he had made since the attacks of September 11, 2001.) An even greater leap than convincing oneself that the most incredible of impossibilities are coincidences has to be avoiding the brutal obviousness of one's own limitations while presuming that one has absolute knowledge! The ability to maintain two totally contradictory bits of information or opinion at the same time without the two ever encountering each other in the same cerebral cortex is perhaps one of the greatest mental feats of mankind, being simultaneously a necessary tool for mental survival and the poisonous draught of self-delusion.

I once suffered from an association with a woman who baffled me with her ability to jump from one ethical standard to another (or more precisely, one unethical standard to another) with scarcely a moment's interval between making a 180-degree reversal. But then I realized her capacities were even more dramatic than I was supposing: she was not changing from one position to another with unbelievable rapidity but actually holding both contradictory ideas simultaneously! She could hold two diametrically opposed arguments in her mind at the same time without the two crashing headlong into each other no matter how narrow the space and time between them. For her, ethical and logical contradictions were not just superimposed but thoroughly collaged and integrated.

Even while I was horrified and battered by this madness, I couldn't help but be fascinated too. As ridiculous as it might seem, without this ability, it is impossible for anyone to embrace modern, evangelical fervor, for this near madness is its very most basic premise: "I will use the ignorance, impotence, and confusion of my own life as a platform from which I will direct others how to live their lives."

From my discussions with my friend Todd, I have learned at least one way he manages such mental contortions. At some point during our discussions over the past sixty years(!), I began to wonder if he had ever noticed or was at all interested in the fact that no opinions, behavior, beliefs, and so forth, of his ever conflicted with those he ascribed to his God. He never once had to change an opinion or behavior because his God forbade it. It just worked out in such a way . . . that everything he believed is precisely what God would want!

Such a coincidence in my own life would make me a trifle uneasy and cause me to reexamine the validity of my conclusions. I guessed that I would begin to wonder just a little who was actually running the show. Is God's will Todd's will, or is Todd's will God's will? On several occasions I have asked him if it doesn't strike him as remarkable that he disapproves of precisely what God disapproves of and that his preferences are exactly God's preferences. Doesn't it seem a bit unlikely that things have worked out so well, especially since a lot of the biblical points could be interpreted in any of several ways—and as it just so happens, every correct interpretation of God's judgment and will (that is, the view sanctioned by himself and the ruling committee of his church) coincides precisely with his own?

He has never answered my question. He can't. Even a consideration of what seems obvious here—that he is simply passing off his own opinions as God's will—would jeopardize the fragile construct on which his cosmogony is built. If he should ever even suspect that he is doing nothing more in discovering God's will than exercising his own judgment, based on his own puny, human capacities, he would surrender all of the authority he claims as an adherent and proponent of the "one true God." Small human vanities are fairly easy to maintain, but titanic spiritual arrogance poses a problem in honesty that only the most determined and agile of psyches can ignore.

22

Lessons of Place

The tendency toward self-deception, or the deep inclination to find evidence to support what we already believe rather than remaining open to new enlightenment, is the best reason why we must enter any spiritual thought, commitment, or even inclination to believe the unbelievable with enormous skepticism. Spiritual experience should never be easy. One should be dragged kicking and screaming into belief. Otherwise, we can't be sure whether we are indeed seeing something outside of ourselves, our own hopes and dreams, our own wishes and anxieties. You'd be surprised how many people ardently want a spiritual experience, one of those Native visions they believe you get from exposing yourself naked to the elements, starving, and dehydrating on a hilltop for four days. So they invite one, work for one, look for one, and voilà! They wind up finding one in every squirrel bite or lightning flash. You can tell by talking or even just looking at someone who is trying too hard: the overly eager aspirant to the mystic experience is gleeful when his or her hope for one is fulfilled.

The true recipient of a mystic visit, on the contrary, is frightened, confused, awed, uneasy, or reticent—but never prideful, confident, or chatty about the experience. A true contact with the Great Mysterious, experiencing a genuine mystery, is not a subject of idle conversation. Indeed, a true contact, experience, or life of spiritual involvement is personal and private, for all the world what visionaries such as Jesus and Buddha have told us and not at all the public display and personal aggrandizement that falsifiers such as Jimmy Swaggart, Pat Robertson, those who push for prayer in public schools and the public display of the Ten Commandments, or even the millions of prideful religious True Believers such as my friend Todd shout at us from street corners, in radio speeches, and from television screens.

The chaos and anarchy of formal religious structures swirling around us all the time and since all time have precious little to do with personal mystic experience. Frankly, what I know or do not know has nothing to do with what anyone else believes. Whatever attention anyone else pays to my experience, or does not pay to it for that matter, has likewise no impact whatsoever on my insights and conclusions.

My discussion of the issues here is only to lament the results of that kind of thinking . . . which is to say, nothing. While I have nothing to gain from anyone else having a mystic thought and perhaps insights or visits of the Great Mysterious, nor do I have anything to gain from anyone's general ignorance of such things. In fact, I have something to fear from the paranoia that such ignorance can inspire: pogroms, prejudice, jihads, wars, purges, and pain. Let's face it, nothing is more dangerous and destructive in this world than religion, a fact all the worse because it flies in the face of what religion should be and should mean. There is no destructive force as enormous as hatred based on religious differences, no arrogance as final as warfare waged in the name of God, no leader more dangerous than one who claims God's embrace, no death more meaningless than one given in the name of God . . . not even one in the name of the hollowest of causes, patriotism, which reflects an emptiness even shallower than that of the church.

The only thing I have to gain when people around me confess their ignorance and ask questions is that they will (1) better understand me, (2) better understand each other, (3) live fuller lives, and (4) open their eyes to the possibility of insights in the form of visions and gifts from the Great Mysterious. Is it indeed possible to be a part of a formal, structured church organization and have mystic insights? Probably. But you can be sure that in most such cases, the official authorities will judge and reject such experiences or reinterpret them to adjust them to acceptable thought because anything coming from outside official channels is a clear challenge to man's authority in such matters. And don't doubt it for a moment: the purpose of organized church structures is to impose hegemony of human authority on spiritual matters for the purposes of earthly wealth and power.

It doesn't take a lot of research or serious thought to determine the validity of that conclusion! Many churches . . . the Holy Roman Catholic Church, for example . . . have strong and deep roots in romantic mysticism, a thread that has always been dangerous to the rulers of the church and therefore has been managed, discouraged, and manipulated wherever possible. In my opinion it is entirely possible for the ardent Catholic to have mystic visions à la Native tradition, but it would require the recipient to free himself or herself to some degree from the fetters of church politics and then not bring any such mystic experience to the attention of the church. Such experiences outside church authority are not looked upon kindly.

In fact, theologies where the mystic experience constitutes a strong or principle element—Wicca, Druidism, pantheism and panentheism, naturism, the Native American Church, sun worship, most native religions—are beyond the rule of church structures; therefore, organized churches universally condemn them as heresies. There is a curious contradiction here of course because religion is in its very essence mysticism, and one would think that all religions would gain force and credibility from any other mystic experiences. And actually, all *religions* do exactly that. But *church* structures, or the humanistic, political systems imposed after the fact on legitimately mystic belief systems, have a lot to lose if word gets out that one can have mystic experiences outside their stamp of approval . . . or even without it . . . or—yikes(!)—in conflict with its established, official dogma!

This adamant rejection of divergent thought or experience may be new in the Christian theology that dominates America today. Heaven knows(!), it hasn't always been that way. To be sure, it didn't take human beings long to seize control of Jesus's offerings, to codify them, and to incorporate them into a strictly human political system. While there has always been outright hostility and physical force involved in the imposition of Christianity (or any other system) on others, there used to be . . . more . . . subtlety in doing it. Not a lot of subtlety, to be sure . . . Religion doesn't like to have such issues as murder and mayhem get in the way of imposing its gentle spiritual truth on others.

For example, if you have ever toured a European cathedral, you were probably led at some point into the deep recesses under the Christian edifice and shown the foundations of another worship center . . . maybe a Roman temple or the ruins of a pagan worship site. Maybe you were even struck by the irony that a Christian building was imposed on top of another belief system's construction. Well, once again that is not a simple matter of coincidence. Think about it: what are the chances of a Christian community unintentionally putting its altar right on top of a temple to Aphrodite or Tyr? Uh-huh . . . yeah . . . sure . . . coincidence. No, early Christians knew exactly what they were doing, and they did it universally and systematically. Step 1: you tear down the other guy's tribute to his god(s), scatter the stones as best you can, destroy statues and altars, and push over vertical stonework.

But that's not enough . . . these believers in the false god(s) are not going to forget all that easily or that soon what was located on that spot for generations, centuries, or millennia. No, that place is where people have worshiped and may continue to worship if proper steps are not taken to stop it, even without a clearly defined physical structure there. So, step 2: erect *your* building right on top of where those heathen scum had theirs. If they are going to worship and retain in their hearts allegiance to the false gods, they are going to have to do it in *your* building and in the presence of *your* god. Sooner or later, even if they don't forget, their children will. Or their children's children will.

And that desired outcome has proved to be true.

Actually, there is more to it than the simple formula of destroying one god and replacing it with another god or, for that matter, something else. Places can be sacred and not simply because some person or people decided they are or because of any particular geographic or historic feature but because of an inherent power in the geographic, topographic place or various features connected with it: a natural spring, a perspective toward another site, or memories of a nonphysical event that once happened in this hallowed place. Peoples around the world and through all time have known and felt this power . . . with the possible exception of mainstream Americans. If we feel a geographic location is somehow sanctified, we are most likely not going to attribute the power to something supernatural but to a historic event. And then curiously to an event that seems to anyone with a sense of spirituality as the least likely place on earth to be eligible for sanctification, or for the grace and blessing of the Great Mysterious. Our sanctified ground is all too often baptized in the blood of war, precisely the kind of human activity allegedly most despised by the Christ of Christianity. And how utterly beyond irony to the outer reaches of bizarre is it that we reserve special reverence for those places where brothers killed brothers, fathers killed sons . . . that is, Civil War battle sites? I admire Abraham Lincoln as a particularly wise man, one of the few such men to occupy the position of president of the United States, but when he said that both sides in a conflict cannot logically claim God's blessing because God can't possibly bless both sides at once, he was wrong. God *can* bless both sides in a conflict at the same time. Or, striking me as being far more likely, curse them both.

In fairness, I suppose I should cite Lincoln's precise statement from his second inaugural address. In speaking of warmakers' claiming the endorsement of God, specifically in the struggle at hand, he said, "Both read the same Bible, and pray to the same God; and each invokes his aid against the other. . . . The prayers of both could not be answered— that of neither has been answered fully." Without sanctimoniously arrogating to himself any special knowledge of God's intent, as has so often been the habit, even within politics and warfare today when we should know better, Lincoln further explained, "The Almighty has his own purposes." That statement suggests that we may not know what those purposes are, but it does miss the more obvious likelihood, in my opinion, that "his purposes" may not include mutual murder at all. That particular activity may be strictly the choice of the people involved, perhaps in direct contravention to God's will.

Is Lincoln's mention of the Bible even relevant? Does it matter that man kills under the aegis of the very same god or of different ones if they are all essentially elements, symbols, paradigms, or metaphors for precisely the same concept or perhaps different parts of the same concept? Surely such an argument would be a sophistry. Forgetting for the moment that the Great Mysterious does many things that defy our puny logic, Lincoln neglected in this case what strikes me as the most logical alternative to his premise: it is most likely that in war God doesn't bless either side but sees the whole enterprise as a massive failure of humanity. Far from being celebrated as sanctified, it is far more likely in my opinion that battle sites in particular are cursed by all but gods of war and evil as the least sanctified of all human efforts.

Some sacred places are seen as such because of a perceived inherent quality of divine force. Early Christians almost certainly recognized such qualities since they were much more attuned to mystic contacts than we are. Moreover, they placed their temples on top of or in place of other religions' altars not simply to transplant them but also to take advantage of the sites' inherent power, which was the original rationale for placing the previous tenancy there too.

That tactic is even more obvious in the case of similar superimpositions in calendar observances. It is not exactly news any more that Jesus was not born anywhere near December 25. Or January 6, if you prefer Old Christmas. That shepherds were "watching their flocks by night" implies better weather than December offers, even in the Middle East. Nor is there much argument that Christians . . . and, around the world, those adherents of many other religions . . . identify an important religious celebration somewhere around the third week in December by virtue(!) of that being the winter solstice, or the longest night and shortest day of the year; a time to celebrate the turn around, the arrival, or return of the sun/Son; a festival of light; a time of rejoicing. In fact, all of the trappings of those earlier pagan celebrations are still with us: a Yule log, a tree, lights, a fire, candles. Many of us relish the wonderful irony of the annual cry of the zealots, whose sense of history is ridiculously short and remarkably shallow, to restore "the original meaning of Christmas."

The situation is, to my mind, even more dramatic with the

holiday of Easter. The word "Easter" does not appear in the Bible. Small wonder . . . the origin of the word is in "Ishtar," a fertility goddess much older than Christianity. Thus the prominence of eggs, rabbits, and spring flowers in the celebration. What better way to preempt a fleshy pagan festival of fertility and lust than to put a Christian observance right smack on top of it? Even with the ancient name still staring us in the face (Easter < Ishtar), some conveniently forget the zestier origins of the day and now insist it is their own—and even more idiotically, that it always has been theirs! Perhaps just as geographic locations have a power of their own no matter who has built an altar over or within them, times of the year have the same kind of power. So far from distracting from the value of days like Christmas and Easter, the much larger importance and significance of the history and theology of these things transcend any one sect . . . even Christianity, the "one true religion" (just as all other religions are the one true religion) . . . and draw all faiths to them and in turn lend their power to whomever worships there or then.

23

Lessons from Lines

Many, perhaps most, of our problems in understanding and discussing ideas often come directly from our difficulties not with logic or understanding, not with philosophy or theology, but with language, especially definitions. President Bill Clinton was ridiculed when he said, "It depends on what your definition of 'is' is," because we Americans, in particular, have problems when it comes to dealing with definition. We tend to think there is an answer to every problem or question and, even less logically, that there is only one answer to every problem or one definition. If we took the time and used common sense to listen to people from other times and other parts of the world, we might learn that there are sometimes no answers, and other times there are many. As it turns out, it *does* depend on what our definition of "is" is! (More about this problem for the seeker later.)

I am amused when I see a map showing the distribution of Indian tribes across the central Great Plains in about 1750. There are the outlines of the current political boundaries such as state lines . . . which are pure fantasy, of course, except where they coincide with the geographic reality of rivers and shores. But even more fanciful are the dark, sharp lines showing territories of specific tribes because they are even more a fantasy concept than the line dividing one clump of grass in Kansas from another clump three feet away in Nebraska. I always wonder how non-Indians imagine the authority of those lines dividing, for example, the Pawnee Indians from the Omahas. Did an Omaha man, eager to prove his manhood, sidle up to the dividing line in some remote place or perhaps more daringly right in sight of a Pawnee war camp, dangle his foot over the boundary line, and then in an offensive demonstration of contempt actually plant his moccasin on Pawnee ground?

Of course not. That's not the way things worked then . . . and often not the way they work now.

I remember seeing a movie (in high school biology?) that showed a large aquarium divided in two by a sheet of glass. On either side was a male stickleback fish, quite content in his own little world, the proverbial large fish in a small pond. But then the experimenter complicated the lives of the sticklebacks by removing the sheet of glass between them. Slowly, unsurely, they each discovered that the restriction between them was gone, and they began to venture tentatively into the strange territory beyond the old, solid glass limitations. One fish ventured deeper and deeper into the hegemony of the other while the one whose territory was being invaded grew increasingly agitated by the insufferable incursion until . . . in a burst of fury the victim of the trespass lashed out and drove the other fish back to his own end of the tank. And now the former invadee became the aggressor and began to venture into the territory of the other, the one who previously was the boundary violator. Eventually the new defender was forced far enough back to his side of the tank that *he* lashed out and drove the offender back. And so the struggle seesawed . . . rather quickly, actually, considering that there were now no actual physical barriers deciding boundaries . . . until a de facto boundary was established by mutual probings and consent. Then both sticklebacks settled into their lives in roughly more or less the territory they had occupied previously and, instead of a physical barrier between them, observed a mutually, tacitly agreed-upon understanding of who belonged where and exactly how far each could go into the other side of the aquarium. That's the way it was with tribal territories too. Over centuries, through developing strengths and probing weaknesses, tribes established the varying degrees of jeopardy as they moved ever farther from their centers of strength. In their home villages and camps, the Omahas were almost completely safe and could relax without fear. A day's journey out of their home villages along the Missouri River, perhaps on a hunt, an Omaha band could still build a good fire, cook, and sleep without sentinels. Two days out, they might be a bit more cautious, but fear would not come to their mind. Three or four days out, as they approached what might be Pawnee country, maybe concern would be a good word for describing their condition, and maybe someone would decide to spend the night sitting up a ways from camp and keep an eye on things. Six or seven days out, they would camp in a safer, secured place, and night guards would watch for possible attackers. Eight days out, perhaps now in traditional Pawnee hunting grounds, they would not have any fires or sing any songs and sleep uneasily at night. Beyond that point, the Omahas knew their travels would be taken as a provocation, and what had been a hunting excursion became a war party. Deeper into Pawnee country they crept and stalked. The farther the Omaha raiding party went toward the Pawnees' centers of strength in their villages along the Loup River system, the more exposed the Omahas were, the more danger loomed, and the riskier their situation became. If they struck at a Pawnee settlement, at women working in a field, or perhaps at a group of hunters, they did so with speed and stealth. Then they beat a rapid retreat from the dangerous ground and headed back to the safety that grew as they returned, stickleback-like, to their own villages to the east.

Rarely were there formal, visible, acknowledged physical boundaries delineating tribal territories. There were centers of tribal strength and then gradual transitions from comfort to fear and back as the tribesmen moved between those centers. Moreover, the centers changed as tribes migrated, sometimes many hundreds of miles over generations. Drought, warfare, disease, and changing technologies all impacted the relative strengths and weaknesses of all tribes and affected the size and boundaries of tribal hegemonies from century to century and even from year to year.

It doesn't take danger and fear to establish such territories. They are in fact much more natural than the sharp, clearly delineated lines of which we Americans are so fond and to which we have become accustomed. I have been involved with similar struggles of definition where human beings demand clear and visible lines . . . but there are none. For example, defining a word like "folklore" . . . or answering such questions as what are the Great Plains? And where do the Great Plains begin and the prairies begin? Where are the lines between folklore, popular culture, individual creativity, formal custom, blah blah blah? Easy enough questions if you don't try to draw a line, because there are, in reality, no lines. These cultural concepts blend inexorably one into the other without edges. They are all part of human cultural expression. That is not to say, at all, that they are the same. They are quite different forms, in fact, and not to be confused. But to define each, you must discard the notion of drawing lines between them and think instead of what each of them are *where they are most clearly expressed*, at their center of strength, or in the "home territory," and then understand that they blend in all directions into each other.

Where are the Great Plains? If you try to draw a line around the region that goes by that name, you are playing a silly game that never ends because . . . let's say it all together . . .

"There *are* no lines." But if you draw a long line from central Canada down through the center of the Dakotas, bisecting Nebraska and Kansas, then Oklahoma and Texas, down even into northern Mexico, and say, "This spine is the center axis of the region known as the Great Plains, which spread a couple hundred miles or so to either side, gradually fading into the prairie-woodlands to the east and the mountains of the Front Range to the west . . . ," well, . . . now you are talking sense and developing a concept—that is, a definition—that is useful because it is accurate.

The same is true of every aspect of the precepts discussed in these pages, from the muddle of God-Wakonda-Coyote-Great Mysterious to the question of what exactly are the phenomena I am struggling to identify as vision, visit, epiphany, miracle, mystery, awakening. I would be willing to bet that all of these experiences and perceptions are parts of a single larger whole, that there are no lines between them, and that they fade inexorably one into the other as did the realms of two sticklebacks, the hunting grounds of two Plains Native tribes, or the grasses of the Dakotas into the grasses of Nebraska. The differences may be ones of degree, with one being simply more dramatic than another. The points fall within a range of experiences from small and simple (for example, on a whim, writing an email to an old friend only to have a message from her appear in your in-box before you have chance to send yours) to a joke from Coyote (for example, the deluge of round rocks and buffalo skulls that descended on me even after I was pretty sure I had understood the message) and to soul-shaking epiphanies bordering on trauma (my experience with the gift and the voice of the Welsh dolmen). They flow and blend inexorably one into the other, all into each.

What's more, the wide range of intensity on the spectrum of spiritual experiences isn't discrete and self-contained but, like the Great Plains or Native hunting territories, mixes inevitably into the surrounding matrix, often in many or even all directions. And as we found in our discussion of definitions, while we can clearly recognize, realize, and identify our most dramatic experience—one that falls close to the center of the scope of our understanding of what a mystic experience is—the task of defining, understanding, or perhaps most difficult of all, describing it to others becomes a lot tougher as one approaches the edges. I have used some of the clearest and most dramatic of my own experiences as examples for this book because my first task was to convince you that these events are clearly beyond coincidence. Now that I hopefully *have* convinced you of that, I have to confess too that somewhere along the edges of what are clearly supernatural (I hate that word because nothing is in fact more *natural* than these occurrences!) and externally initiated contacts there is . . . coincidence.

As much as we may yearn for definitions of god (a generic label, after all), mystic experience, or visit, those terms are clearly inadequate for the phenomenon they are intended to describe. Language is a set of symbols we use to image reality; so what do we do when we have had no previous experience with a particular reality, or when it seems even contrary to what we understand to be reality? By definition we can have no explanation for such things. We cannot describe what we cannot know, so we do what we can with approximations and metaphors to describe the phenomena: "It was like . . ." "The closest I can come to describing the experience is . . ." "Imagine a . . ." While similes and metaphors can be very useful, they can also get in the way, because whoever hears such reports can only think of the images evoked by the approximations and allusions and cannot even come close to imagining what the hell it is we are trying to say. The result is that the words we use with the intent to clarify what we want to share with others may result only in further confusion.

Naming a god or describing its character diminishes that god because our definition establishes lines around what we think that god is—listing characteristics, intentions, and taboos—and limits within human boundaries the nature of something that is far beyond humans and nature. For example, in the second book of Genesis, the Hebrew phrase *ruach elohim* is customarily translated as "spirit of God." Not much is made at that point or in any later interpretation or translation, however, that ruach is a *feminine* word, a grammatical way of completing the universality—including gender!—of the Great Mysterious. Only in translation and grammatical transduction do we get the idea that our God is exclusively male. I have discussed previously the curious custom Christians have of using a generic term, "god," while other cultures and religions see the divine spirit(s) as not a noun but adjectives and use indeterminants such as the Old Pawnee Tawadahat (This Immensity).

How many other theological errors have sprung up over the centuries from this insistence for precision where in fact there can be none? The very act of describing, defining, or even naming something limits our ability to expand our understanding of it. Once we begin to superimpose a system on an idea or set of ideas, it tends to become set in stone, and its growth slows or stops. Name something "God," applying a noun's format to it, and you have automatically removed the concept from the category of adjectives or verbs . . . a dreadful mistake, since it seems far more likely that any divine force is a quality, process, or action rather than a thing or being.

Every definition establishes boundaries and thus restrictions, often thereby excluding far more information than it is including. Note how laughable, for example, the arguments of Creationists are that the story of divine creation, or intelligent design as it is now fashionably called, should be included in school curricula. The underlying presumption—nay, *requirement!*—of their polemics is that they mean only *their* version of the creation. One cannot adopt just any biblical variant of the mythology but only the one specific model authorized by the political structure of their particular church. Or their own particular sect of their church. Or their own specific congregation of their particular sect of their church. Can Creationists really be ignorant of the fact that the concept of creation includes literally thousands of ideas of how everything came to be? Do they not realize that all of the rationale they apply to validate their own versions of our origins—faith—can also serve to support Navajo, Hindu, Maori, Bantu, or Incan stories of creation? The Creationists' definition of creation is so narrow, it excludes far, far more than it includes and with no apparent logic to the exclusions. The simple act of defining in this case has destroyed all meaning of the word "creation" and imposes a dark, heavy curtain of ignorance on any other meaningful consideration.

One of the few formal religions that recognizes this problem is the Native American Church, common to southwestern and Plains Indian tribes of North America. The Native American Church is at least nominally Christian but with a heavy layer of traditionalism enhancing that Middle Eastern religion and with a Plains chthonic spiritualism that strengthens both. While a division of the Native American Church holds ceremonies called Cross Fire, which incorporates the Bible as part of its instruments of worship, another substantial division doesn't so much as refer to the Bible or show a copy at the services. The idea is that the written word has caused only confusion, trouble, exclusion, anger, hatred, and even violence. It is of course absolutely true. Removing the physical restraints of the book and separating its written words from the belief, experience, and worship do not distract from the power of the ceremonies and its practitioners . . . Moreover, the absence of the book *enables* worshipers by removing the chains of definition from the direct, inspired information that is available to everyone, lettered or not. That is, the absence of a limiting definition with its clear lines—dictionary dogma—*frees* the seeker and opens doors for exploration, information, and inspiration.

The only way I can tell you what I want to convey about the mystic experience is with words. But in doing that I limit my description and your perceptions to the restraints set within and by the definitions of those words. It's a problem because I want to tell you something that is beyond my ability to perceive or describe and is perhaps beyond the capacity of any human understanding or communications. Most of the time the phenomena of the mystic experience are far more vast than I can grasp, but sometimes they are so close to the normal experience, the usual perception, that I struggle to differentiate the mystic from the profane.

There is, for example, sheer old luck—chance, plain and simple, or the gift of unexpected or even unmerited good fortune (or curse of ill fortune, of course). My own life is full of good luck. In fact, my life seems to me to be one remarkable stroke of good luck after another. When I was young, all eligible American males had to fulfill a seven-year military obligation. I joined the Nebraska Air National Guard the moment I was eligible, just before I turned seventeen. At my first weekend drill, I learned the unit had recently returned from active service in Korea. Seven years later at my last National Guard meeting, military units were being called into active service to respond to the Berlin Wall crisis. I somehow had the incredible good fortune to have my seven-year obligation fall precisely into the seven-year period between international crises; so while I was always ready to do my duty and never had an unexcused absence during my enlistment, I was never subjected to the disruption of active service. Pretty lucky, I'd say ... but I don't really think it can be seen as some kind of divine expression or intervention.

I entered the academic world at a time when my minimal qualifications were enough to gain a teaching appointment in higher education. Moreover, I obtained the entry-level teaching job at a small Nebraska college only, in large part, because of the school's desperation to find a one-year replacement for a teacher on leave. I was a make-do, which even at that position was probably more than my scholarship record qualified me for. If I were now entering the academic job market with the qualifications I had then, I would be laughed out of any dean's office. At that time, getting a job teaching at a college was for me, a mediocre student at best, little more than the next step. As it turned out, though anyone looking at my record and me at that point wouldn't have guessed as much, I became an excellent teacher and scholar with high honors and recommendations. I have enjoyed a life with good parents, solid children, good friends, and good decisions made not with any particular wisdom but reaping incredibly good fortune. Even what seemed at the time to be incredibly bad fortune ... a wife discarded me, we went through an ugly divorce, and I was financially gutted ... turned out in the end to be the best thing that could have happened to me, leading to incredibly good fortune in love and life. Now I look back on what seemed at the time to be crushing defeats and see that they were instead remarkable strokes of good luck.

On the one hand, surely you can see how pedestrian such events are. As important as they were to me at the time and as consequential as they have proven to be since, they are the usual stuff of life ... luck ... chance ... Almost everyone could point to exactly the same circumstances in their own lives. But I have also said that the mystic event is not unusual and that good things too happen to all of us with astonishing frequency. I think you'll agree with me, however, that while all such strokes of luck may indeed be a part of a grand pattern we mortals simply cannot see or understand, they scarcely constitute visions, visits, enlightenment, epiphanies, or transcendent moments.

On the other hand, there is something uncanny about good fortune, and it becomes all the more unsettling when it becomes common or repetitive. As we edge up the scale of such events toward even more dramatic coincidences, our goose bumps become ever more obvious. When I was in high school, some sixty years ago, I met a young fellow from Norway and became acquainted with him and his family. We struck up a pen pal arrangement, I guess you'd say. He joined the United States Air Force and was stationed at Thule, Greenland. For some reason, that place fascinated me. I increased the rate of our correspondence because I wanted to know more about Greenland. Had he seen the island's massive ice cap? Had he met any Inuits? Could he leave the base and explore the natural setting and see the wildlife of the Arctic? I devoured his letters because he answered yes to all those questions.

I was green with envy. Something drew me to Greenland and the Arctic. I have always liked winter, cold, and ice . . . My favorite movie is the virtually unknown Paul Newman–John Altman film, *Quintet*, a story of a new ice age; and my favorite poem is Loren Eiseley's "Watch the Uneasy Landlords," a prayer for the return of the Arctic ice over the North American continent. For decades I carried in my heart a lust to see arctic Greenland, the farther north, the better. Since it seemed an utterly impossible dream, however, the vigorous passion of my teenage dream faded to a dull ache in my maturity and finally in my old age dimmed into an almost forgotten fantasy that I could experience only in film and poetry. My dreams of the ice of Thule and Greenland never died, but they faded far from my conscious thought.

Then one day in 1998 I received an email message from a fan of my books about antique tractor restoration . . . a success story that is in and of itself something of an impossible stroke of good fortune. This fellow wanted to thank me because he was a neophyte amateur tractor mechanic, and he had had a hard time convincing his girlfriend that he was suitable marriage material with such a nutty hobby. He had bought and sent her a copy of one of my books, and it had done the job for him. She was now convinced that she could live both with him and with his tool shop and old tractors. He wrote that as soon as he finished his tour of duty and returned to the States, they would be married, a good fortune he attributed in part to my writing.

Well, that was flattering. Writing can be a lonely business, and it's always good to hear from a reader who has something nice to say about my work. Hmmm . . . those were curious terms my new friend used in his email . . . "tour of duty" . . . "return to the States." Let's see, he's obviously military. I wonder where he is stationed. Oh my god! There it was . . . the return address on his email was . . . Pituffik . . . the location of Thule Air Base . . . Once again it was word from the land of my lifelong dreams! I fired back a response to thank him for his kindness in taking the time and effort to write, to wish him good luck in his marital plans, and . . . to ask him the same questions I had written five decades before to my Norwegian friend. And again, all the answers came back in the positive . . . yes, he could see the ice cap (three miles thick at its center) from the window of his room; yes, he had met and knew Inuits and even had Inuit friends; and yes, he often went off the base to see archaeological ruins; to spot wildlife such as arctic hares, polar bears, "Archies" (arctic foxes), and whales; and to explore the majesty of the Arctic.

My lust for arctic Greenland was rekindled. I told my new friend about my lifelong wish to visit Thule and wondered if any outsiders ever got there. I had reason to hope. It has always been my inclination to fulfill fantasies when and where I can, and my family has always been indulgent. I once was watching a Formula One car race and sputtered that I would pay thousands of dollars to drive one of those cars just once around a track . . . It was my wife, Linda, who found a Grand Prix driving school at the Sears Point (Sonoma, California) Race Track, where fantasy drivers such as myself could learn the ropes with stock cars and then formula cars . . . and she said—and I quote—"Go!" And I did. (When a local news-paper reporter asked her what she thought about an older English professor with a wife and child going off to racing school in California, she said famously, "Well, he has always wanted to be a race car driver . . . and I've always wanted to be a rich widow.") But this dream of going to Thule, Green-land, and to the Arctic seemed completely out of reach. Not only is it an extremely expensive and difficult process get-ting to Thule, but also it is still after all a military facility with high security. You don't just walk onto a strategic mil-itary base. You need permission, clearances . . . And there is the transportation problem . . . one airplane a week, a mil-itary flight, goes to Thule. And that's it.

My new pen pal regaled me with more stories and photos and asked if I had ever thought of entertaining the troops at a place like Thule. Well, no, I never had, but at that point in my life I had left the academic world and was making my living as a writer, television essayist, and public speaker, giv-ing as many as fifty banquet speeches a year about American folk humor. My friend said the people running the recre-ational programs at the Thule Air Base were friends of his, and he'd ask them about the possibility of my visiting as a performer, teacher, and/or lecturer to the 150 Americans stationed on the ice. It seemed too much for me to hope. I tried to moderate the blazing hopes that burned in my heart. But my friend wrote, yes, the people who made such decisions were interested in having me come to Thule. "How much would you charge them for a couple performances at the base club and maybe a small class for hopeful writers among the base personnel?" he asked.

"My friend," I replied, "I am willing to pay *you* if you can get me to Thule. In fact, you don't even have to do that. Get me within ten miles of the base, and I'll swim the rest of the way."

"You won't have to do that," he wrote back. "The sea here is frozen solid all but one month of the year, so you could walk in if you had to. But the way it looks, we can fly you in and set you up to see and do whatever you want in exchange for a couple performances and a class."

I could not bring myself to believe my good fortune until the moment I set my foot on the icy surface of Pituffik's runway. A shaky flight from near my home on the first leg to Denver was almost canceled by severe crosswinds. Unless we decreased the weight on the plane . . . that is, until one passenger volunteered to remain behind . . . the flight could not continue. I saw my arctic dreams going up in smoke. To the amazement of the rest of the discouraged passengers, one passenger stood up, said he was employed by the airline, was just on the flight for fun, and would willingly stay behind so the rest of us could go on.

At Baltimore I still couldn't grasp the reality as I wandered around a near-empty airport late at night, looking for the military jump-off place for the weekly flight to Thule. At no point in the long day it took to reach Thule—actually, more than twenty-four hours when counting all the flights and layovers—could I bring myself to accept that I was actually fulfilling a dream of fifty years' duration. Besides, we all know how these things work; the realities of travel never turn out to be as good as our fantasies. It's similar to looking at seed catalogs. First there is the hope, then the disappointment. Not this time. I won't go into many details here, but every day, every moment, every experience of my time in Thule and Greenland were exciting beyond my wildest dreams. There was not a single disappointment during my stay in the Arctic. Every surprise was a good one. At every turn, things were better than I had ever conjured up in my fantasies. One of the officers at the Thule Air Base arranged for us both to go even farther north to the Inuit village of Qaanaaq, one of the northernmost human habitations on earth; to stay there; and to explore the village and surrounding country-side of ice and rock. I was also going to take my first heli-copter ride. I have spent a life in aviation and have flown on an astonishing array of military, private, and commer-cial aircraft, but somehow I had never been on a helicopter. I saw this place of absolutely unbelievable, savage beauty on my maiden chopper ride! Another notch in the glories of a week full of glories!

We landed at Qaanaaq and unloaded our gear while the Danish helicopter pilot boarded another passenger, the regional dentist. Greenland is under the governance of Denmark and enjoys the civility and common decency of universal health care, which is seen as a basic human service almost every-where in the developed world but in the United States. Over the roar of his engines (one doesn't turn off internal combus-tion engines in the arctic cold; in fact, the helicopter when it takes off and lands at the Thule Air Base operates from a flat-bed trailer pulled in and out of a heated hangar by a tractor), the pilot casually asked if I would like to take the next hop too. He was delivering the doctor to an Inuit seal hunter's village even farther north, Sioropoluk.

Uh . . . I thought Qaanaaq was the northernmost human habitation on Greenland. "Don't believe everything you read," he laughed. And an hour later when we landed at Sioropoluk, not much more than a long walk from the North Pole, again he shouted over the aircraft's engines, "Step over there . . . to the edge of the helipad." I took the few steps to the rim of the rocky area that had been cleared of snow and ice to enable the landing of the plane. "Now," he laughed, "there are only maybe ten people on earth farther north than you are."

Every day, every hour of the trip to Thule was a fulfillment of a dream and even more so. It was a surfeit of gratification. I ate seal, walrus, and whale with an Inuit woman and her friends. I stood on the ice cap and heard the scream of the ice under my feet. (I'm not exaggerating: the Greenland ice really does *scream* when you walk on it!) I walked across the sea ice to pale blue icebergs to fetch ancient geologic ice for our whiskey in the evening. It was a weeklong dream. But was it a gift of Wakan Tonka? Or just incredibly good fortune? Now we are far enough away from pure luck and close enough to a mystic experience that I don't feel comfortable making that judgment. I simply do not know. Ultimately any labeling wouldn't change the experience, either for the better or the worse. The experience simply was what it was, an incredible complex of unbelievable good fortune. Whatever the circumstances, all I could do, and probably should continue to do, is offer up my prayers of gratitude for whatever it was that brought me to that unlikely fulfillment of fifty years of wishes. (I did leave one of my prayer packets of gratitude on the ice cap.)

When I look back on one of the most remarkable influences in my life, my association with my tribal friends and family, the entire process of living appears to be one fortuitous accident after another, one stroke of good fortune followed by another. Even before my time, how about the fact that my father was struck by lightning when he was a boy and was in a coma for a week, hanging onto life by only a thread? My own life was also hanging in the balance during those long days, after all. Time and time again during my life, I have experienced incredible good luck. Yes, I have had my setbacks too, but generally speaking, the assets side of my life's ledger far outbalances the debit side. But were they by any stretch of even my own rosy imagination miracles? Or visions? Or the workings of that great Something Going On?

Still I consider myself unlucky when it comes, for example, to gambling, especially compared to my in-laws, who rarely come out of a casino and go home with less than they took with them. Their luck is uncanny. I am absolutely sure I could drop quarters into a slot machine for hours and not once come close to breaking even, let alone come out ahead. I'm just not lucky in that way. My in-laws are wonderfully modest and honest people, so I know their reports of their casino wins are legitimate. Moreover, my wife and I have accompanied them on their very modest adventures into gaming and have seen their good luck directly. They just win, and we just lose. I have no explanation for that (although my father-in-law does: he says I go to the wrong church!), but the consistency of the results does seem beyond mere chance. But is it a matter of divine intervention? A mystic message? Well, if it is, it certainly falls within the lowest levels of drama for such occurrences.

Luck may just be a point of view, at least in part. I was recently diagnosed with cancer. Not much doubt about that . . . it's bad luck. Or is it? Shouldn't I consider myself fortunate that Linda muscled me into going to the doctor's office against my will for an exam, and that the affliction was therefore caught early and had a better prognosis for cure and recovery? Then I went through the hell of a colonoscopy, prostate biopsy, Lupron hormone injections (painful, expensive, emotionally disturbing), and eleven weeks of miserable, embarrassing, disruptive radiation treatments. That certainly wasn't any fun. Miserable luck, there, one could say. Or maybe a bit of bad luck with a lot of good luck? Shouldn't I be happy that such treatments exist and are available, when twenty years ago I probably would have simply been told to put my affairs in order?

I am reminded of a nineteenth-century jest in which one fellow encounters another on the street and takes note of his dour expression. "Why are you so obviously unhappy, my friend? Is something wrong?" the first asks.

"Is something wrong?" blurts the second. "Can't you see it's raining? Why does it always rain on *me*?"

In America we too often repeat the canard, "Here you can be anything you want to be." That's not true. We are bound by many tethers, some obvious, some subtle. With my physique—short legs, long torso—I was never meant to be athletic. Okay, maybe a sumo. Now I'm seventy-eight years old, so I might aspire to things that my age and physical condition will again not allow. As much as we want to think that it is determination and hard work that get us where we want to go, sometimes it is just this thing we call coincidence or good luck. One lesson my long life and rich exposure to Native American culture has taught me is that our successes, small and large, may not be within our control at all, or may be mere strokes of serendipity, but part of the design of that master joker, Coyote the Trickster. There's no way to prepare for them but to be ever ready to recognize and accept the gifts.

We can't complain about growing old when none of us by choice would elect to take the alternative. Yet, for all we know, on the other side of death may be all the answers. A religion's or an individual's attitude toward death can tell us a lot. Absolutists are the most likely to fear meeting their God because they recognize the frailty and inadequacy of their claim to total knowledge. Those who see death as an adventure into the unknown are most likely to accept it, because their admission of ignorance leaves open all sorts of potentials while the zealot's absolutism almost ensures disappointment. The zealot knows it, tries to avoid it, and lives in fear. By the way, the treatments for my cancer worked, and I am now told I am cancer free. Is that a miracle? Does this mean Tawadahat has a mission for my coming years? Am I somehow blessed? Or that my friends who have not survived this very same form of cancer are less blessed? Or even cursed? Of course not. I am grateful, but that the treatment worked is just the luck of the draw. Nothing to see here, folks. We are all mortal. So move along . . . Move along . . .

24

Lessons from the Fourth Hill

D
eath is considered a stroke of misfortune only because of our ignorance of what lies on the other side of the curtain. (A *misfortune* is an unusually unlikely stroke of bad luck; death, so far anyway, appears from all available evidence to be common to us all.) We try to understand. We work up metaphors and paradigms to help us understand what inevitably happens to each of us, but deep down we all know that we don't know anything about death. And apparently what we pretend to know, in the end, we must admit doesn't amount to much.

For all the talk about redemption, salvation, heavenly rewards, and a better life in the Great Beyond, when someone we know dies, there is nothing but anguish, floods of tears, and a gnashing of teeth. Obviously, we are not happy for our dearly departed. I can understand and accept that we are sorry for ourselves . . . that we no longer have the company of someone we love(d). In all honesty, though, can we really be unhappy for the person who shrugs off the mortal coil (and don't we have to admire all the wonderful euphemisms we have for death and dying?) since we have absolutely no idea what has just happened to the deceased? No idea at all! And can we bemoan "God's cruelty" or even His shortsightedness in taking this person from us when we also have no idea at all of what any greater scheme might be . . . except that pretty much all of us *will* die?

Besides, perhaps our visions and mystical insights are an

effort by the Great Powers to teach us about what lies beyond or about the Something That Is Going On? Is that what ghosts are? And while we're at it, what the heck *are* ghosts, anyway? I once had an interesting conversation with a particularly bright student about ghosts. I was teaching folklore and had reached that part of my introduction to the field dealing with folk beliefs. And I had mentioned ghosts. My student's question was an excellent one: are ghosts really a matter of traditional belief or an actual observed phenomenon? Empirical data can be a part of folklore; in fact, it is the very basis of folklore.

One of the features of folklore that I felt obligated to cover at the beginning of each semester was that while the word "folklore" is sometimes used as an antonym for "fact," that is not at all the case, as those of us who have spent lifetimes studying traditional materials well know. The word "superstition" is strictly forbidden in my classrooms because it carries such a heavy load of contempt and insult. One person's superstition is another's faith, fact, truth, or life's experience. As is the case with visions and visits, this kind of labeling is a formidable detriment to learning. Once we label something as a superstition, it is automatically rejected as nonsense when the truth might be that we are throwing away very useful information by mislabeling it. And we do still have much to learn from traditional lore, if as is the case with religion and our relationships with greater forces, we are willing to confess some ignorance.

I'll admit that I have sometimes found myself slipping down that very same steep and treacherous slope I warned my students about. Once while we were discussing folk medicine, a student asked if her grandmother's treatment for warts—taping an aspirin on them with the intention of removing them—might be a form of traditional medicine. I thought about it a moment . . . and said that the determinant for what is folklore is not whether it works but if it is understood and believed to work and if the idea is passed on informally from one person to another. It seemed to be the case here: even though aspirin is intended for internal medicine, it has probably been interpreted by some people simply as *medicine* and thus has come to be held as useful even for things like wart removal. And who knows? It might even work through the placebo effect, it being generally accepted that a good deal of all medical treatment is psychosomatic in its efficacy. That is, aspirin isn't meant or useful for wart removal, but it has probably worked often enough by coincidence or psychological pressure on physiological mechanisms that some people believe it to be truly effective in a medicinal sense. Folklore is generally a system of empiricism—that is, observation—so when people see something work, or think they see it work, that information is disseminated through time and over distance and becomes what we call tradition . . . or folklore.

I imagine my students were satisfied with that suitably professorial and professional conclusion, and so was I . . . until many, many years later when I was troubled by plantar warts on my feet, and Linda picked up some over-the-counter medication to treat them. I applied the liquid to the warts and then almost by accident read the label to see what the active ingredients were. There was only one active ingredient in the medication, salicylic acid. Uuuh . . . hmmmm . . . salicylic acid . . . That would be . . . aspirin. It was my student's granny who was the scientist in the previous scenario and her professor who was the one embracing false belief based on cultural ignorance and arrogance. Coincidence, indeed! Granny knew what she was talking about. She taped aspirins on warts to remove them . . . because it worked. I rejected that truth because my mind had been closed by my ignorance. That is, my superstition.

Conversely, going back to the student's question about

ghosts, a disbelief in ghosts may be based on an individual's conclusion that since he or she has never seen a ghost personally that there are no such things. Thus, some people's belief in ghosts might only be a matter of trusting a direct observation, or a belief based on fact, right? Well, yeah, I guess so. In our penal system we can send a human being to death on the eyewitness testimony of two or three other human beings, so why do we reject out of hand the personal witness of tens of thousands, maybe hundreds of thousands of perfectly sane, bright people who insist they have seen ghosts? What kind of sense does that make? Wouldn't that, continued my student who was curious about ghosts, put the onus of superstition on people who out of hand reject the existence of ghosts in defiance of empirical evidence?

He then said that he wanted to test his thesis, as a casual experiment . . . nothing to do with any real study or research . . . He proposed making a quick survey of the professors in his department and in the building where he was pursuing his major study . . . the science building. If anyone should have an open mind and be ready to accept solid evidence, it should be a scientist, right? We agreed he would ask the question, Are there such things as ghosts? And we agreed that there could only be two meaningful responses: "In the absence of solid information, we don't know," or "There appears to be some sort of phenomena the nature of which we don't fully understand but are nominally referred to as 'ghosts.'" A hundred percent of the responses from the professional scientists responding to my student's casual question were flat-out, even adamant noes. On the basis of no evidence—or perhaps more accurately in the face of abundant supporting, albeit anecdotal, evidence—people who prided themselves on their pursuit of open inquiry quite facilely stated absolute answers in denial of even empirical evidence.

Are there ghosts? I don't know. I've had some experiences

that I can't really be sure of but that are eerily similar to what other people have reported. For example, aside from poltergeists, or particularly violent and angry spirits, people report no fear when meeting with ghosts. The real question is, what *are* ghosts? Enough people have reported experiences that they must be something. But so far we haven't established what exactly that something might be . . . emotional aberrations? Cerebral electrical shorts? Spirits of dead humans? Misinterpreted physical phenomena like methane clouds or aurorae borealis? Don't ask me. I have no idea. All I can say in honesty and logic is that we don't know what ghosts might be, but there is *Something* Going On.

Why is that such a hard admission to make? Sometimes out of belief, sometimes out of curiosity, sometimes out of desperation, people or mechanisms notoriously inhospitable to nonsense—I am thinking of police and other law enforcement agencies—have turned to so-called psychics to investigate crimes or locate evidence or victims. Perhaps we don't hear about cases where the psychics fail. I imagine there may very well be times when the alleged psychics are charlatans, and they never had a sliver of a chance for success. But how do we account for whatever proportion of situations where the "information" (I can't bring myself to say it without the disclaiming quotation marks even as receptive as I am to unconventional investigation!) turns out to be valid or even crucial? What do we say when all logic is defied by helpful guidance from a totally unlikely, illogical source? Just coincidence, I guess.

I have a good friend who insists that she communicates with her dead grandmother in an almost chatty way. This woman is a very smart person . . . highly educated (PhD), "normal," cheerful, cogent, reasonable . . . She holds down a responsible position at a major institution of higher education. What is it then that she is doing? With whom is she talking? Herself, perhaps? Some sort of radio short circuit in her dental fillings? It would be unscientific and would cut off any further information I might welcome from her or other people who do the same to say she is a nut and the voices she hears are only a pathology. They might be a pathology; they might not. The only conclusion that makes any sense for reasonable, logical persons looking at her contentions has to be that we don't know, but since we have many other such examples of this same sort of communication, there is a good chance that Something Is Going On.

I once again go back to the same conclusion I have reached throughout this book: all we can know is what we can know, and that's not much. Since so few have figured out the most basic truth—that is, Something Is Going On—it's hardly prudent to wade even deeper into the mysteries of death. In the Plains tribe where I am at home and that I know best, the metaphor of life is a passage over four hills: infancy, childhood, maturity, and old age. And beyond that is . . . well, we don't really know, do we? At no point along the previous trip have we understood what life would be like over that next horizon, so why should this last hill be any different? We don't even have the counsel of advance scouts to tell us in terms we could understand what lies over that last hill.

Richard Fool Bull did tell me once that we *do* send scouts in that direction. He said that when our elders who are approaching death behave in ways we don't understand—that is, when they lose their faculties, seem to be different people than we have known all their lives, and appear to go crazy—what is actually happening is that their souls have gone over the brow of that fourth hill to take a look at what lies beyond and to prepare their paths for the future. They leave their bodies behind without their usual guidance systems. We are left then to deal with derelict vessels without their souls, which have always been the reality of the persons to us. Is that the truth of senility? A physical mechanism running amok without its guidance system? Once again we are given a metaphor that enables us to understand the ununderstandable, true or not.

John Neihardt, the great historian and poet, once told me when he was well into his nineties that he was rather excited about dying. He knew that as he eventually—probably sooner than later—approached the unknown passage of death, he would be afraid, but at that point, still with some perspective and time, he was thinking about it precisely as a rite of passage. He said we should think about birth when considering death. He said we should try to imagine what it must be like to be a fetus in the womb. It is warm, comfortable, dark, and moist there. There are no worries. We are nourished and protected. Could anything be closer to heaven than that? Imagine the utter comfort of the womb.

Then . . . suddenly, there is pain. Lots of pain. And light and cold and deafening noise, none of which has been experienced before. All the comfort, every bit of it, is gone. There is nothing but vulnerability and the misery of life outside the womb. Now, out here in the real world, there is nothing but worry and anxiety, pain and discomfort. What a horrible, traumatic transition birth must be.

But now consider where that passage from the paradise of the womb into the fury and turmoil of the outside leads . . . to this life! To the very life that we now cling to so tenaciously and fight so hard not to lose. It seems that along the way we have decided that this new, painful existence outside the womb isn't that bad after all. In fact, anything else is terrifying. Neihardt said perhaps the next transition, the one from life through death, is the same kind of thing and terrifying in that it is unknown. No one knows what lies beyond death anymore than a fetus can know what glories and joy can come from the misery of birth and the loss of the comfort of the womb. We simply cannot know. Only our ignorance leads us to fear and fight the change.

So many religions speak of the glories beyond . . . and yet as individual human beings we lament those who make the journey and fear it ourselves more than anything else. Are ghosts only those same spirits that go ahead as scouts? For what reasons do they return? Are they trying to tell us anything? How would we possibly know? How could we possibly understand what is beyond understanding? All we can know is what we can know: Something Is Going On.

The transition between life and death is, if you think about it, a pretty small step and not at all as complicated as birth. One moment you are here . . . and the next moment some indefinable but essential part of you is gone. Only modern mechanisms and folly have made it hard to recognize when that moment of death comes and the new journey is begun. When my father died, a hospice worker said something to me so wise that it shook me almost as much as my father's actual passing. She said, "Each and every one of us is terminal from the moment we are born." We may or may not be born. We may or may not be male or female. We may or may not be a lot of things. But there's no question about whether we are going to die. To go kicking and scratching, fighting for survival seems a pretty natural position to take, but it hasn't always been looked at that way, nor is that feeling universal. There are hints in Christianity that a better life may lie beyond (or not!), but let's face it, few actually believe that so firmly that they rejoice when a tortured soul moves on. We insist we believe in a better life after death, but our behavior suggests that we may not be all that sure.

Among Plains Indians, as death threatened an elder, as often as not that person's options enabled the transition. The dying person for direct personal reasons would avoid not only enduring a long illness and lingering death but also putting the huge burden of caring for a sick elder on a family and community. The dying tribesman, for example, realizing what was happening and that as a burden he might cause considerable jeopardy for everyone he loved, would simply tell someone he needed to be moved to a nearby hillside to take the air for the day, or as a village moved to the hunt he would tell his family with a wave of his hand to move along down the trail and that he would follow shortly . . . although it was clear to everyone including himself that he would never again move from his spot. He would be left with some water and food, with love and best wishes . . . and with gratitude . . . so he could die with dignity and peace and confidence that even in this last gesture of his life, he had done what he could to make his people stronger. Then he would die. Everyone does it.

In birth there is tremendous drama . . . with the appearance of a new human being never before seen. And the drama clearly has as much impact on the newly born soul as it does on the rest of us standing around and watching this eternal drama. Wow! Talk about a transformation! Think about a step from one mode of existence to another!

But what is death? Suddenly everything simply goes silent. A few physiological mechanisms that have never been all that noticeable or understood shut down . . . a heartbeat no one paid much attention to before just as inconspicuously ceases. The soft breath goes from nearly inaudible to totally silent. Unheard and unknown processes of the brain and soul are, in death, only somewhat more of the same. Everything is there, but something we never saw anyway is gone. We see neither death coming nor the soul going. How different death is from birth in its sense of drama!

Author's note: I am gently instructed here by Linda that I myself may speak with too much confidence of my understanding. She asks me not to ask her to elaborate but reminds me that there are premonitions of death, witnesses to the departure of souls, and evidence of delays and returns of . . . of . . . of whatever it is that is our essence. And upon reflection I know she is right, not simply because she usually is, but because I had forgotten for the moment some of my own experience along these lines. And the reports I have heard from others. My apologies to Linda, and my assurances that I will not indeed ask further.

25

Lessons from Lessons

At the other end of the scale of mystic experiences we find the miracle. I imagine a miracle to be something fairly titanic, totally reversing the natural course of things, defying what seems to be the normal forces of nature . . . you know, the kinds of events that happened with surprising frequency in biblical times but seem rare today. There may be some explanations for the sudden demise of the biblical miracle . . . however, if they do happen, people don't talk about them because the world's mood doesn't seem very hospitable to miracles. Or maybe there truly are fewer. I guess that's possible. Perhaps the kind of personal experiences I and so many Native friends and others who welcome the mystic experience have had were simply embroidered through time and retellings into dramatic narratives about burning bushes that talk, rods that turned into snakes, and stone tablets that were handed down directly from the hand of God.

Despite the general reluctance to acknowledge modern miracles, however, I am uneasy about thinking that explanation alone accounts for their rarity in the modern world. People who don't know any better tend to think of the oral transmission of history or folklore as impossibly flawed. They imagine that traditional narratives (of miracles, for example) are similar to the old party game of Gossip, where one person whispers a short piece of information or a story into the ear of another, then that person tells a third person, and that person tells a fourth, and so on. The message is passed along until the transmission reaches the end of the line, and that person relates the hilariously distorted version of the item as it came to him or her at the twentieth or thirtieth telling. But that's not at all the way oral transmission, folklore, or folk history work. Oral transmissions of culturally important materials, especially religious or historical narratives, are almost never passed on in a one-to-one secret telling. Even secret materials—for example, religious instruction available only to tribal males or perhaps a select priesthood or clan elite—are never one-on-one but are recited in a company precisely to ensure their accuracy.

In some societies, with some practices, an error in recitation is held to pollute the entire process, which then must be abandoned or started over. Variation in important narratives, stories, or rituals, whether accidental or intentional, is simply not tolerated. Even personal histories must be told the same way again and again. Imagine what would happen if you were pressed for time and decided to tell a child a bedtime story about Goldilocks and the *two* bears. Or the One Little Pig. That simply would not do. The story *must* be told correctly, and that means without significant variation. Indeed, a scholarly historian and descendant of one of the combatants writing a report on the historical truth of, say, the Battle at the Little Bighorn will not only introduce his own prejudices into the battle's retelling . . . (after all, he *is* the great-great-grand-nephew of the great and legendary Lt. Col. George Armstrong Custer!) . . . but also draw his information from others who will have had their own reasons to manipulate (although perhaps unconsciously but as often as not deliberately) the data . . . military accounts, prejudicial journalists' reports, the memoirs of survivors who struggled to justify why the colonel died but they didn't. At each and every point, the individuals in telling their own versions have no trouble at all giving their own slanted impressions.

Tribal narrators who were perhaps firsthand witnesses and participants at that epic clash, however, did not have such freedom. Not only is self-aggrandizement in sacred or even historic cultural narratives discouraged in the culture itself but also any efforts to distort the account as witnessed by hundreds of kinsmen are thwarted, corrected, and even ridiculed at the time and through time by hundreds of kinsmen who may not have been there but have themselves heard the accounts from other warriors on the scene. There is a strict fabric of enforcement in oral tradition that strongly encourages . . . I would say "ensures" . . . accuracy in a way that written accounts do not.

I once heard a pompous ass read a scientific paper that discounted sightings of unidentified flying objects as so much claptrap. As with my friend Todd's theological tap dancing, this man had a wide inventory of mechanisms to explain away experiences people have insisted they have had. In no case was he willing to accept the eyewitness accounts of anyone who had experienced such phenomena, even when there were multiple observers, a situation that generally discourages dishonesty or misperception. The detractor insisted the people had probably seen the planet Venus or maybe ball lightning or hallucinations from ergot-infested rye . . . In the case of Ezekiel's ancient and detailed account in the Bible, he opined, the object that the prophet had seen and described as that fiery wheel "way up in the middle of the sky" had been only a sun dog. That casual dismissal did it for me. I rose from the audience and asked, "Excuse me, but what Ezekiel described is in no way at all like a sun dog. Have *you* ever seen a sun dog?"

"Well, no, I haven't," the speaker-detractor said. "But I have read about them."

I suggested that he really needed to step out his backdoor some crisp winter day then and take a look into the sky. Sun dogs are not rarities, after all. They are reflections off of high-altitude levels of ice crystals to either side and sometimes above a bright sun, most often seen in the winter. In fact, at night there are even *moon* dogs, or wide halos or arc segments of light around the moon. From the podium, he said he had never seen a halo around the moon either.

Doing what I could while standing in the audience to control my indignation at this idiot's presumption, I said I thought it pretty arrogant to accuse Ezekiel of not knowing what he was seeing when this guy, who thought of himself as a scientist, had not so much as stepped out into the open country air to witness the phenomenon himself. Moreover, since Ezekiel lived at a time without light pollution from streetlights, advertising signs, farmyard lights, or highway traffic, his sky was crystal clear. We can pretty much presume that Ezekiel knew the sky . . . that he could probably name a hundred stars. People in his day watched the sky. They spotted and reported on comets, meteors, and all manner of other celestial occurrences while we hardly notice when the annual Perseid meteor shower or an eclipse takes place if someone doesn't mention it as a part of the evening news. I know for a fact that we have had partial and even near-total eclipses of the sun where I happened to be, and some people didn't notice anything unusual going on . . . for example, that the sun was disappearing! The notion that Ezekiel would confuse a sun dog—he probably had ten different terms in his vocabulary for various forms of the phenomenon!—with what he describes in the biblical text is an absurdity beyond grasp.

Which is to say . . .

And I looked, and behold, a whirlwind came out of the north, a great white cloud, and a fire infolding itself, and a brightness was about it, and out of the midst thereof as the colour of amber, out of the midst of the fire.

Also out of the midst thereof came the likeness of four living creatures. And this was their appearance; they had the likeness of a man.

And every one had four faces, and every one had four wings.

And their feet were straight feet; and the sole of their feet was like the sole of a calf's foot; and they sparkled like the colour of burnished brass.

And they had the hands of a man under their wings on their four sides; and they four had their faces and their wings.

Their wings were joined one to another; they turned not when they went; they went every one straight forward.

As for the likeness of their faces, they four had the face of a man, and the face of a lion, on the right side; and they four had the face of an ox on the left side; they four also had the face of an eagle.

Thus were their faces; and their wings were stretched upwards; two wings of every one were joined one to the another and two covered their bodies.

And they went every one straight forward: whither the spirit was to go, they went; and they turned not when they went.

As for the likeness of the living creatures, their appearance was like burning coals of fire, and like the appearance of lamps: it went up and down among the living creatures and the fire was bright, and out of the fire went forth lightning.

And the living creatures ran and returned as the appearance of a flash of lightning.

Now as I beheld the living creatures, behold one wheel upon the earth by the living creatures, with his four faces.

The appearance of the wheels and their work was like

unto the colour of a beryl: and they four had one likeness: and their appearance and their work was as it were a wheel in the middle of a wheel. (Ezekiel 1:4–16)

Even presuming exaggeration on the part of Ezekiel, a misunderstanding of what he was seeing, and the possible elaboration of his story over the years by subsequent narrators, how could any sane person conceivably imagine that what he is describing is a sun dog? Never mind that Ezekiel then follows this description with a long passage of what the creature in the apparition *said* to him and that no one has even suggested in the wildest of hallucinations that sun dogs speak to mankind. (And ignoring for the moment the unsettling and obvious conclusion that what Ezekiel saw was what we now call a flying saucer, even today we must draw on a metaphor because we simply do not know what to call something with which we have no previous experience or explanation.)

The preposterous presumption that the expert debunking the biblical account was making seemed to be that Ezekiel was insane or maybe an idiot . . . when precisely the opposite seemed more likely . . . Ezekiel was only an accurate if awed reporter while the cynical expert in front of me was a fool. Two of the reasons that the stories in the Bible were included is that they were important and had credence. Now I do have my very substantial doubts about biblical stories being the Word of God, sacred texts, the Gospel, or the truth. Or, for Pete's sake, accurate historical accounts. I know way too much about how men think and manipulate, how folklore works, and, . . . well, okay . . . how the mystic experience operates. We know for a fact that many important texts were excluded from what we now know as the Bible. Somewhere along the line human beings deliberately scrubbed God and Jesus and the texts, in general, clean of a sense of humor, for one. But I have no doubts at all that the stories in that book are very significant, are very resonant with the human experience, and most important to me and our current conversation in these pages, have a foundation in a mystic experience.

That is to say, these stories are validating and verifying that lots of other people have good reason to believe that Something Is Going On. Something Was Going On in Ezekiel's day, and Something Is Going On now.

26

Lessons from the Muse

One of the most convincing bits of evidence I have found that Something Is Going On is the phenomenon of being "kissed by the Muse." For one thing, the phenomenon is more common than one might think. Second, it is not considered common (but is) because in part those who experience it are reluctant to talk about it directly. They usually talk around the topic until they can determine if their conversation is with someone who is either receptive to the notion or has experienced it for himself or herself as well. Third, it is an ancient enough experience that it has after all its classical reference . . . "kissed by the Muse." I guess, for that matter, I could list as the fourth factor attesting to the reality of receiving external inspiration from a Muse the fact that it has happened to me. That is, I can confidently vouch for the personal experience of having been driven by what seems to be external inspiration. Finally, it is unsettling enough an experience that it is never tossed aside by those to whom it happens as a mere mental aberration or curious coincidence.

The kiss of the Muse is of course generally understood to be an *artistic* inspiration. I am a writer of primarily humor or nonfiction, and while I have certainly found myself caught up in the moment of writing, saturated with the task at hand to the point where I cannot sleep or eat but am driven to write, I have a hard time thinking of that fire as derived from anything other than an internal drive system . . . my own mind powering the rest of me with its momentum. I wrote *Catfish at the Pump* (still in print with the University of Nebraska Press [1986], publisher of this book as well as many others of mine)—a book of average length, perhaps 60,000 words—from loose notes, using not a word processor but an electric typewriter (for those of you who might recall that ancient technology). Then I edited it and typed a rewrite from scratch . . . all in six days. Even now I can't imagine how that is possible . . . revising and typing 120,000 words in six days? I must have been possessed! I recall there being a lot of coffee and Jimi Hendrix while in the furies and the Beach Boys and whiskey when the brakes were on. I imagine I did some damage to my body with that exercise. I didn't get much sleep or rest until the next week, when I totally collapsed. Why did I pursue my writing with such a fury? A deadline? A sense of immediacy? Nope. It was just a fit of passion, I guess.

And maybe a hint of what was to come somewhere down the line. It was not until I wrote a work of fiction that the mind-set of writing moved from a curious preoccupation to a downright frightening possession. First I wrote a couple articles couched in a fiction format, and I backed off from doing much more along that line because the experience was unsettling enough that I was reluctant to step back through the door. Then I wrote a book of fiction. And I haven't written any more fiction in the intervening twenty years. I'm too frightened by the process. Writing fiction led me to feel a lack of personal control that I am not at all comfortable with. For the same reason I have never been attracted to drugs; they induce a loss of control and, more important, of perception. And that's for all the world what the experience of writing fiction was like for me. Yes, I am saying that for me writing fiction is comparable to using drugs. Scary.

I started my book of fiction with an outline, a solid notion of where I was going with the story, what the characters were going to do and who they would be, and how the circumstances of my imagination would move them. The book was not altogether fantasy; I had a story I wanted to tell about the cruelty of history and man and the nobility and the decency of those who are so often most despised. In short, while the book was to be fiction, it was also a polemic. Even as a writer of nonfiction, I knew for decades that writers can lie all they want in nonfiction, but what's more important, they can tell the truth in fiction. And that's what I wanted to do with that book. I found a publisher for the book on the basis of the outline (the book was published by Villard [1992] as *Touching the Fire*, which is still in print with the University of Nebraska Press) and because of the modest success of another book of mine *It's Not the End of the Earth, but You Can See It from Here* (Villard [1990] and again is still in print with the University of Nebraska Press). Then I set to writing.

It didn't take long for me to detect that something was going not at all in accordance with my plans and intentions. The characters in my book were not being who I told them to be and not doing what I told them to do. Events in the book were going out of my control. The story had gotten away from me early in the writing and had acquired a momentum and direction of its own. I would go out to my office to write, knowing precisely what I had in mind for the day and for the book, but as my fingers moved on the keys of the word processor, the messages being sent from my brain to my fingers were no longer mine. My characters were saying things that surprised me and made me laugh because they were saying funny things I would never have thought of. They were doing things I couldn't have imagined. Events happened in the book that I simply could not have conjured up on my own, and that development came to me as a total surprise. Truths emerged in the manuscript beyond what I had known or intended.

The book had gone out of my control. I am not exaggerating when I say to you that as I sat here typing, I was reading the book, not writing it. At the end of the day I would come into the house after work in tears because of a tragic turn of events or giggling about an element of humor that had developed in the plot that I certainly had not intended. No reader would ever be more surprised or moved by any part of the book than I was because I was as much an outside observer as any of my future readers might be, but I watched it develop on my word processor's screen right before my eyes rather than reading it on a printed page.

My inclination is to interpret this kind of experience, of being driven to artistic expression by what seems like an external force, to be a function of the subconscious. Just as our mind continues to work even while we sleep, it works as a self-motivated, automatic engine while we are working at other . . . or in this case, related . . . tasks. I would probably be satisfied with that interpretation if I had not experienced the phenomenon myself. But having done so, I am not all that certain. I have much more trouble understanding how I can be surprised by the products of my own mind; how can I be imagining things I can't imagine?! Why is that experience so unsettling?

As was the case with the mystic experiences I have had, I was reluctant to tell anyone, even Linda, about this bizarre loss of control I was having with my own writing. But of course she eventually noticed my peculiar behavior and how I came in from work elated or destroyed by what was happening in my writing. Finally I had to tell her what was happening and that as much as I was being emotionally shaken by the events of the plot, I was also very uncomfortable about my loss of control and the apparent independent development of character and plot that was allegedly of my creation.

As so often happens when one begins to confess a mystical experience to a compatible, sensitive, sympathetic person, far from being dismissive of my experience and my concern about it or from being troubled about my sanity, Linda began to tell me of her own similar experiences. My wife is an artist . . . a painter . . . and said she had often found her hands and brushes out of her control when she was working in her studio, that she was somehow being used by another force, and that it was always the source of her best work. The force was so powerful, she had given it an identity, calling the entity the Art Spirit, and had come to respect and revere it as well as thanking it on a constant basis for the gifts it brought to her work. She said she would lose track of hours and days, of the mechanical processes of painting such as mixing her palette, and of the creative processes such as composition. Instead, she found herself surprised at the end of the day by what had appeared on her canvas, as much in spite of her as because of her. Like me, she had found herself a third party to her own creativity.

Other factors suggest to me this matter is more than simply the creative mind working away automatically, independent of conscious control and effort on the part of the person owning it. For example, note how widespread the phenomenon is, having its foundations in classical antiquity and being shared by artists and creative writers through time and across space. As with the mystic experience, while visits of the "creative spirit" are treated as a rare occurrence—in part because those who encounter them are reluctant to talk about the experience—all you have to do is start a conversation with a serious writer or artist (the Muse doesn't seem to be all that interested in the processes of hobby artists!), and you will hear the same stories. Such conversations turn into something for all the world . . . or maybe, we should say, for all the *other* world . . . like a ghost story–telling session. In hushed voices your creative friends will tell you how eerie it is, even scary, to be possessed by the Muse, the creative spirit. It is exhilarating yet at the same time unsettling. One of the principal obstacles in my path for writing more fiction is the discomfort I felt in having my creative energies hijacked by . . . whatever it is. I guess you could call it . . . Something Going On.

While our reaction to a mystic experience might be "Wow!" I have the impression from my experiences and those of others that just as often, if not *more* often, the result is, "Huh? What?" Or even "Is that all there is?" That feeling is especially true when we expect something more remarkable or when the experience comes in the form of a series of otherwise unremarkable or only slightly remarkable events—for example, finding or receiving one small, black, round rock that looked like a marble. I think when I received the first one, I thought, "Oh. Well . . . that's strange. I wonder what *that* is about. How curious. A round, black rock. Well, I've never seen one like that before."

When the second and third small, black, perfectly round rocks came to me in equally unremarkable but very different contexts, they popped the first gift into focus and made it so enormously meaningful. Sometimes it is only in contemplation and in taking another perspective that a meaning arises that meets our expectations. I quote from my Lakota brother Charles Trimble's brilliant book *Iyeska* (Half Breed) in which he describes his initial disappointment and later realization about his own vision quest:

> In 1972, not long before I went to Washington to serve as Executive Director of the National Congress of American Indians, I was taken up a high hill for hanbleceya [*sic*]—a vision quest. In the sweat lodge after I was brought down from the hill, I told the holy man that I didn't think I had achieved a vision; but I told of my growing feeling of insignif-

icance among the stars and winds at night, and the creatures—
some of them very close, among the hills in the heat of day.
I felt alone and frightened at first, but as I stood in prayer
over the hours, I became a part of nature, and I felt at home.
The holy man said that the experience I told could be my
vision and that I should think about it and try to understand what I was being told. They could not interpret it for
me, it was up to me to determine. I thought much about it
and over time decided that I had achieved a vision after all;
that it was the realization that my tearful prayers in Hanbl-
eceya were answered: "I am nothing, I am pitiful, help me
Grandfather, Tunkasila, guide me. (28–29)

27

Lessons from the Power

There are other phenomena that beg to be appreciated as mystic but remain elusive in terms of what exactly they are and how they work. Humans continue to struggle to figure them out and nail them down but mostly in vain and to the point where their efforts become futile and even irrelevant. My own experience with mystic phenomena has been totally passive. I have received the mysteries, messages, material evidence, and assignments with no actions or anticipations of my own. I'm just standing there, and all at once—WHAM!—something out of the blue, totally unexpected, hits me. There is some evidence, however, that powers are available to us . . . or at least to some of us . . . that are somehow associated with the Great Mysterious. The notion of being kissed by the Muse may fall in or close to this category of phenomena. But some people seem to have far more control of such powers than I certainly have ever sensed for myself. Yet even people who feel or demonstrate that they have some control over the processes are mystified by them, frightened (or at least respectful) of them, and inclined to exercise them only with enormous self-control and awe. We read of such powers, of course, associated with the so-called black arts and even within conventional established religious understanding. As with all the phenomena discussed in these pages, I approach such powers with enormous skepticism. However, as is also my experience, I have found my skepticism swept aside again and again by irrefutable evidence, including and especially my own eyewitness.

A woman I know well has discovered that she has an uncanny (uncanny even to her own mind) ability to blow out light-bulbs in her presence. She has no idea how she does it. She is uneasy about working at developing the "talent," but despite (again) her *own* skepticism, she has proven beyond her own doubt that she has this ability. I trust her explicitly and know that the humility, awe, and even uneasiness with which she has told me about this ability speak to its reality.

Even more directly, I have personally *witnessed* on several occasions the ability of my wife, Linda, quite literally to blow up vehicle engines. She first experienced this facility while out driving alone on a quiet country road. A reckless truck driver passed her on a curve while there was other traffic from the nearby school . . . and there would be even more traffic when it closed for the day. She regarded the danger of the truck and wished to herself that the truck would somehow be put out of commission and off the road before it could cause a serious accident. To her own amazement almost instantly a puff of oily, blue smoke arose from under the truck's hood, and the driver pulled over to the shoulder of the road, his truck disabled for the day.

She reported this curious power to me because she already had uneasy feelings about even this one single coincidence, thinking it was just too immediate and obvious to be an accident of timing and mechanics. Within a few months of that first occurrence, I was riding with her when a truck with garbage flying from its uncovered bed passed us. The driver and his passenger blithely disregarded the mess and hazard they were presenting to other drivers on the same major highway. I mentioned to her offhandedly that it might be a good time for her to apply her new talent . . . and we laughed. But as the truck careened on and even more debris

LESSONS FROM THE POWER

fell from it onto the road, she went quiet and watched the growing problem. Within moments there was the oil smoke and smell of a blown engine, and the truck pulled over to the shoulder, done for the day.

Twice more I have witnessed Linda's gift. I have suggested that she work at developing or examining what she can and has done. I have on a couple occasions suggested that she stop other drivers who constituted a danger. But she remains very uneasy about the skill, reluctant to exercise it, unsure of what it is and how it works. As she says, "Better to leave well enough alone." But by now neither she nor I have little doubt that there is indeed something to it . . . Something Is Going On. We are part of it, it uses us, and, apparently, there are some among us who can use it. Linda could write her own book about her mystic experiences.

As I gathered the courage to share such stories with others, I find that far from being dismissive or shocked, they have such stories of their own. Perhaps we should all make more of what we learn about ourselves and our unrecognized skills. I know for sure that I make a point of staying on Linda's good side!

28

A Lesson from Prayer

Similar to my skepticism about anyone's capacity to
exercise control over unexpected forces, I have always
rejected the notion of prayer. I come to my feelings
from several points of view. Initially, as a deist, I rejected the
notion of something as immense as a god taking the time or
trouble to fuss with something as utterly insignificant as a
single human being. I still *prefer* to believe that despite growing and troubling (for me!) evidence to the contrary. When
I am moved to a specific moment of prayer, I approach it as
a moment of gratitude, figuring that the Great Mysterious
has been more than generous with me and my life as it is and
that it would be downright selfish to ask for anything more.
Moreover, as I have noted before, since my Native brother
Buddy Gilpin told me that every moment of life should be a
prayer of gratitude, wouldn't a specific, limited set of words
within a delimited moment of time—that is, what we usually
think of as a prayer—betray that ideal? With my understanding of Coyote, as the best and most complete metaphor I can
come up with to represent the Great Mysterious, then clearly
the most prudent thing I can do is not to catch his attention and not be so pretentious as to suggest I have anything
whatsoever to say in His doings.

I have spent many years working on the problem of a
prayer of gratitude I could be comfortable with. I adopted
the common device in religion and especially mysticism
of requesting the help of an intermediary in delivering my

prayers, figuring that either the prayer gets to the Great Powers, and that would be great, or it doesn't, in which case it doesn't matter. It wouldn't hurt me to be grateful in either case. In part my effort to develop a prayer suitable to my needs and feelings was self-defense. As a public speaker I found myself regularly having to participate in that most irreligious of exercises, the public prayer, usually said as a grace before a banquet meal. Living as I do in Middle America, I have found myself wincing sometimes with apparently visible embarrassment (I occasionally got a comment from someone who had watched to make sure I was appropriately respectful, head bowed, hands folded, no smirks, grins, or mutterings . . .) as whoever it was who presumed to pray for all the rest of us would say something hopelessly insensitive and stupid such as "in Jesus's name we pray." Afterward I would mutter under my breath—hopefully under my breath, at any rate—"And tough shit for any of you who happen to be Jews, Muslims, Hindus, atheists, agnostics, or deists but would still like to acknowledge and express your gratitude."

I decided that what I really needed to do was establish a formula that I could recite to myself to drown out the insipid, shallow nonsense that is usually foisted off as a prayer of thanksgiving on such occasions. I needed a way to express my own gratitude and respect for what I held to be that Something Going On.

For years I worked at this project, and I had plenty of opportunity to edit, append, emend, and delete. In an effort to express my gratitude for the food we were about to enjoy during public gatherings, I considered at some point an expression along these lines: "Thank you, my brothers and sisters, for living and dying for us." With that offering, I hoped to express my understanding that all living creatures are my kin and to acknowledge their sacrifice for my nourishment on the occasion. But then I began to feel this prayer, by speaking only to *animal* constituents, excluded so much of what was feeding us. And my good fortune was actually found not only in the food before me but also the entire beneficence I enjoyed of making my living by talking, of receiving the respect and company of large numbers of people in my audience, of having the freedom and health to speak my mind with the guarantees and wealth of living in America . . . Obviously I needed to be grateful for a lot more than was on my plate on these occasions.

I therefore tried something more abstract. In keeping with my insistence that the answers are in the questions, I decided I should instead *ask* something: "By what grace am I here?" That formula served me well for many years until I began to feel uneasy about trying to put what were for me profound feelings, actually beyond expression, into words. So I moved instead into an effort to *feel* the widest sense of my gratitude as intently as I was able to in the situation and at the time without resorting to words. And that has served me well since, even though it still falls short of what I feel the need to do. Ultimately, the ideal is to honor my Omaha brother Buddy's recommendation to me of more than forty years ago: make each moment of life a prayer of gratitude.

But the event that really jarred me, and hard, when it comes to considering the efficacy of prayer was not so much my own as those of people I love and respect. Having been adopted into the Omaha Nation Tribe in 1967, I became a part of the tribe's four separate but superimposed kinship systems. The people use the mainstream American kinship system of father, mother, grandparents, children, siblings, nephews, nieces, and so on. They also have a system of honorifics, so that a particularly influential elder might be addressed as Uncle or Aunt by anyone at all within the tribe even though there is no other relationship involved. Next there is an adoptive mechanism so a person can "adopt" a brother, sister, daughter, father, and so on. Finally there is the old, traditional tribal style in which the brothers of one's father are addressed as Father and the sisters of one's mother as Mother. Along with what else might be expected, their children are not addressed as cousins but as brothers and sisters and *considered to be precisely that*. Thus, all of my brother Buddy's children became literally my children. And still remain my family.

Bearing in mind the jeopardy of tribal life with its constant warfare and hunting, along with natural limitations on longevity, these tribal relationships reflected the necessity of caring for widowed women and men who required a support system for housing, food, clothing, and even companionship. In another related system, when a father or mother is lost, people can request becoming a relative of another tribal member. Colleen, a woman not much younger than I am, requested after her father died whether she could bestow the remarkable honor of addressing me as Dad, so she became my daughter, in every sense of that word. Jeff, one of Buddy's sons and now my son, is a traditional Omaha who is a roadman, or an ordained leader, of the Native American Church and follows its rites and rituals (and he functions seamlessly in the modern mainstream world as a respected electrical technician in nuclear power plants). Jeff's brother Pete has a daughter, Marissa, who is thus my granddaughter.

If you were to ask most Americans what is a family, they would probably respond, "A man, his wife, and their children." There is a lot of social turmoil now in the struggle to redefine the family, but for sixty years I have been trying to explain to my non-Native friends that ours is a rather restricted idea of family. Even in parts of Western culture, a family would include extended family, meaning the surviving grandparents, the husband and wife, and the children. But within Native cultures, family is much broader a concept. It in fact consists of layer upon layer of genetic

lines, adoptive connections, honorifics, and honorary relationships, all of which are taken very seriously and considered to be a part of the supportive unit. It is an important
consideration to Linda, our children, and me during important moments in our lives, especially during times of crises,
when we need all the support we can find.

A few years ago I wound up in a hospital in serious medical
trouble. I had cardiac atrial flutter, which did not respond to
any of the usual protocols and procedures. For days my doctors worked at trying to get my blood pressure under control,
and my heartbeat steadied. The worst complication, however, was that a clot had begun to form in the heart cham-
ber that was not functioning correctly, and that clot was a
major and potentially fatal problem. Finally the doctors said
that with all else failing, the next day they would have to ini-
tiate defibrillation procedures . . . you know, the dramatic
intervention on television emergency medical shows where
they put big paddles on a patient's chest, yell "Clear!" and
try to jolt the heart back into beating regularly with electric shocks. No one . . . least of all me . . . was looking forward to using this drastic procedure, but my situation was
becoming serious, maybe even grim.

It was at that point that I took the dramatic step . . . for
me, a committed skeptic, that is . . . and asked my wife to
call our son Jeff and ask him to do whatever he could do
within the procedures and powers of our Native American
Church. I don't ask for much in my prayers, and when I do,
as I have said, I try to ask only for things for others since I
have enjoyed way too much generosity already. But in this
case I was thinking I could ask Jeff and my tribal family
to think of me. Perhaps . . . in their prayers? Linda did call
and later told me that in talking with Jeff, he had said that
coincidentally(!) he had just that day received some blessed
tobacco, the smoke of which is understood to carry prayers.

He said he would burn some tobacco for me immediately upon hanging up and that he would then call the rest of my tribal family and ask them to pray for me through the night. (I might note that I have also been driven by irrefutable experience and evidence that prayer from a focused group . . . from a simple gathering of a few believers to a congregation . . . has particular potency from what seems to be a pooling of power.)

There is a lot to be said about traditional medicine. As I noted earlier, folk medicine is often as not based on empirical knowledge and, for one reason or another, works. But there is more to it. I know how it feels to be in a modern hospital . . . uncomfortable, unfamiliar, disturbing. You can't sleep in a hospital . . . that almost goes without saying . . . You are constantly bothered, there is no rest, there is no comfort, there is no dignity. Eventually you begin to wonder if anything is being done for your problem, yet everything that could be done.

But on a reservation the sick are often treated at home. They are in their own beds, comfortable and familiar. They are surrounded by their loved ones, who do all they can. During the night the patients may awaken to hear medicine songs and prayers being sung outside their home or even in the next room. There is no question about it . . . everything is being done that can be done. Even though I was in the cardiac ward of a regular in-patient hospital and my Native family was more than three hours away, it did give me comfort to know that these good, blessed, and righteous people had me on their minds . . . and in their prayers that night. It was, after all, a desperate situation for me.

Within an hour of my wife's call to Jeff and bringing me his assurances that he would immediately begin his long-distance spiritual ministrations, nurses came rushing into my room to check if the sensors attaching various monitoring devices to me had perhaps come loose or malfunctioned. Something was wrong, they said . . . suddenly my blood pressure was normal. Just like that. In fact, it occurred at the precise moment Jeff was burning his tobacco. Well . . . uh . . . I guess it could be attributed to . . . well, you know . . . coincidence. But what could I say the next morning when the doctors came in somewhat concerned because all of a sudden my heart had also resumed its normal, strong, and regular beat? My doctor said, "We can't figure out what happened that caused your heart to be suddenly put back into regularity, but there it is. We can see it on the monitor, and I can hear it right now." I explained what it might have been . . . ancient traditions and family prayer, all started with a telephone call to my Omaha son Jeff. Quite wisely and understandably the doctor said, "I want the name of that guy. We could use that kind of thing around here more often."

You can perhaps therefore understand why I am no longer quite as sure as I used to be that prayer is an idle gesture with no effect. I have seen the same kind of apparent cause and effect of prayer and apparent response since then too, primarily within Native religions but probably because that is where the foundations of my own belief lie. Maybe prayer works this way in other belief systems too. It's too early to tell as far as I am concerned. It seems such a crazy notion that this enormous power of Something Going On has any interest at all in me and my pitiful appeals. I am still sufficiently skeptical that I resist giving in easily to that idea. But at this point I at least have to concede that persuasive and growing evidence shows that prayer may indeed work.

What's more, there seems to be something to the idea of congregation . . . multiple people offering up prayers simultaneously or in tandem. We know that "schooling" (as in the biological organization of fish in schools) works astonishing efficiently. You've seen the images on television of groups of fish (or flocks of birds) suddenly shifting direction, apparently all veering at once. If there is any delay within the group to the new direction, it is so fast the eye cannot detect it. Nor is it easy for a camera to capture. The coordinated move occurs so quickly, it can scarcely be measured, in fact. The conclusion has to be that the individuals in the group have surrendered their individuality to the group and have thereby become part of a larger organism, one comprising what are still individual components that operate with astonishing, unexplained, otherwise impossible coordination.

Is this the secret of the congregation? Of group prayer? Is this again the result of empirical experience? Have human beings figured out over millions of years that coordinated group behavior, not simply in hunting in packs as wolves or lions do but also in prayer and worship, is somehow more efficacious than the power generated by the single supplicant? I realize that this question may seem to contradict my contention that organized church structures detract from mystic involvement, but it does not. What it does do, conversely, is reinforce my argument that the very foundation of religion is the mystic experience . . . including, I guess, strengthening of prayer and petition through congregation . . . but its process and advantage are hindered when it is polluted by its imposition on a humanistic, political system . . . that is, the official, structured church.

Ask Martin Luther, the Puritan Roger Williams, Buddha, Moses, Muhammad, or Jesus if you don't believe me. Each of them had personal, private, direct visions and messages from the Great Mysterious and quite understandably stressed the importance of the rest of us opening ourselves to do the same. What could be more dramatic a reaffirmation, confirmation, and validation of Something Going On than a personal experience to that effect? But people who hear about such things are perhaps impressed by them, ally with the person who had the experience, and become followers or disciples. Then, almost inevitably it seems, those who consider themselves most faithful to the idea become slaves to the dogma and foul it all up by forgetting about opening their minds and souls to their own mystic experiences and by doing what they can to make any additional individual, personal mystic experiences, of all things, *heresy*!

Talk about nutty. It's understandable, I suppose, that once men (those in charge of these structures are mostly men) set up a political authority and figure out how to use that political mechanism to gain power and wealth, they are not eager to have it challenged by the notion that spiritual inspiration and information are available to any yahoo in the street. How much better it is—for them, at any rate—to insist that the only access to that kind of spiritual event is through them or that it is simply not available to anyone at all anymore, having become only an ancient memory. The most logical and kind thing to do when confronted with this type of obstructionism is to laugh at it as gently as possible and move forward with one's own personal religious enlightenment. No one is better equipped to tell you about a true religious experience than (1) you are and (2) the experience itself.

Nothing could possibly strengthen already held religious beliefs more than a mystical experience. While I personally prefer the way I came to such experiences . . . reluctant to believe anything that was not logical, scientific, reproducible, demonstrable, and clearly within human experience . . . I also understand that most people will not take that approach. Most people already have religious beliefs, sometimes strongly held, sometimes ferociously strongly held. In a way, those beliefs can simply serve as another kind of resistance against the mystic experience. In fact, if one argues as I do that the principal avenue to such experiences is a receptive mind, then someone already equipped to believe in the mystic idea of a divine supernatural spirit, of miracles, of transcendental experiences should be all the more open to further enlightenment. The idea that Something Is Going On should be all the more acceptable to someone who already professes a belief, even if it is conventional and confined within the humanly constructed political framework of an organized church. While a popular notion, especially among church people, is that a lack of a structured spiritual life means there is no depth to that life, precisely the opposite is true. Who, after all, has the deeper spiritual commitment—someone who embraces a church for fear of otherwise suffering a horrendous fate if he doesn't (for example, in the torments of hell)? Someone who seeks rich rewards after death (heaven, perhaps, or harems of beautiful and compliant virgins)? Or the person who leads a life of decency and civility only for its own sake and follows his or her own internal ethical compulsion?

A strict dogma removes from the worshiper any need to think, wrestle, justify, doubt, wonder, ask, seek, or for that matter, accept any new experiences. All the answers are there at the end of the honeyed spoon or the bloodied whip, so why go any further? Those who discard, elude, or are lucky enough never to encounter church structure are understandably those who have the most respect for the mystic experience, for the presence of a Wakan Tonka, for the reality of the mantra Something Is Going On. If you want to find a truly religious person open to genuine revelation, look for someone who understands and acknowledges how destructive a formal church structure is to religion.

Thus, while the congregation remains a potent force for prayer and spiritual inspiration, it has been generally betrayed and weakened . . . actually, probably disabled . . . by the imposition of formal church structure on that potential. What should feed on the mystic experience and in turn nurture it has sadly become the most formidable obstacle to the mutual flow of energy. It doesn't have to be that way, but sadly it is that way in most church structures. How were the Norman invaders described when they conquered England? "They are good churchmen . . . but not very good Christians." The same could be said of most churchmen today, certainly in America.

The heart of prayer was something even Jesus, the nominal child of God, expressed clearly—a quiet, personal, private conversation between oneself and whatever it is that is beyond us . . . the Great Mysterious, Tawadahat. Actually, we may not even need to know to whom or what we express our thoughts and words. The efficacy of prayer may be in and of the expression itself. An old friend of mine, Bob Kerrey, who has surely known his own moments of prayer, in triumph and terror, delivered an address before a National Humanities Conference. I quote his words here with his permission: "I believe in praying to God. I don't expect my prayers to be answered. The act of praying is an end in itself. In prayer I acquire—at least temporarily—the humility needed to see that I know and am worth less than I think. In prayer I become thankful, grateful, and capable of loving others more than myself."

We could do worse than adopting this philosophy of prayer for everyone.

29

Still More Lessons from Lessons

Nothing is sadder and more unsatisfying than an answer. You have a question that excites your intellect and soul; it causes your mind to churn and your wonder to grow. Then you are given an answer, and all the fun of the quest is gone. When the *quest* is gone, nothing is left but a cold, dead answer. Isn't it interesting, in fact, that the root of the word "question" *is* "quest"? And the word "answer" comes to us from ancient roots meaning to speak back against—that is, to contest. An answer then was not seen as a solution to a quandary but a rejection of a concept without necessarily eliminating the original problem. Remember that to my thinking, a question is not so much a problem but an invitation or opportunity.

The excitement of life and the truth of what is beyond lie in questions, not answers. Anyone who considers a knowledge of the Great Mysterious, or gifts, visions, and visits, to be an answer is sadly wrong, and I especially emphasize "sadly," because there is no satisfaction in the answers. The only locution I can imagine better than the Lakotas' two adjectives "Great Mysterious" would be a question mark following the phrase. Wakan Tonka? Now *that* makes sense! God is a question, not an answer, and that after all is the inherent question embedded within the word "mystery."

Genuine, deep-seated ignorance wants answers because then the wonderer can relax. But once we find an answer, no further effort is needed. In a world filled with mysteries, unknowns, questions, and confusion, the medieval thinker wanted answers, and so we devised so-called answers. The traditional legends and the church (and eventually science) have provided some answers:

Jews are despised because the ritual of Passover requires the blood of innocent Christian children.

Plagues are punishments for our iniquities . . . but the officials of the church can give . . . or sell . . . you the means to escape the tortures of hell.

We human beings are not the center of the universe . . . indeed, we are just another globe circling the sun.

God has given us this land . . . and its peoples . . . to tame and subjugate to our use.

God loves us, and it is therefore your duty to fight and die for Him . . . and oh yes, by the way, to bring home the booty to your royal (and sanctified) leader and your blessed church, which have after all been given to you by God.

We now have the means to prolong life much, much longer and provide sustenance for the swelling populations of the earth, so therefore we should . . . because God and science want us to.

Religion . . . science . . . philosophy . . . today all are formulated, embraced, and expected to provide answers when the true miracles, religion, science, and philosophy are in the questions.

Let's face it, we haven't done all that well with a couple thousand years of a growing supply of answers and relying on them. There is little doubt in our new world, as evidenced in our modern folklore—for example, the so-called urban legend—that we have a growing thirst for surprise, mystery, the unknown. Medieval legends provided answers where there seemed to be nothing but questions, but the modern legend does exactly the opposite by generously supplying mysteries in a world where all amazement and awe seem to have been explained away by science.

We don't tell such stories and embrace rumors of conspiracy because we fear or hate mystery; to the contrary, we human beings *want* and *need* mystery, or perhaps more precisely, we feel deprived. And indeed, we *are* deprived where there is no mystery. Just as my Native friends have told me for decades, the white man is sadly educated out of seeing and appreciating the mysteries of life flowing constantly around him. All he needs is to reopen his eyes, to listen again, to forget false and disruptive notions such as coincidence and the official church, and accept the voices, visits, visions, messages, and gifts that are available for the taking. Will the white man's questions then be answered? No. There will only be more questions. But that is the best part of open perceptions: the answers are not simply *in* the questions, the questions *are* the answers.

And so what are we to make of all this? How are we to understand or deal with learning how to accept that we need to revel in the questions and keep learning? What do we learn from the mystic experience? What do its lessons tell us? What remains for us to learn? How can we make ourselves more receptive to it? How does it affect us? How do we respond? What with us not knowing where the experiences come from, or what they mean, or from where or whom they come, coming up with answers to any of the other myriad questions we have about them is not easy. I would however suggest the following:

1. Although it may seem contradictory advice, keep your

mind open to mysteries that are happening around you and to you while remaining nonetheless deeply skeptical about them. That is, don't be too quick to presume that you have been given a gift when it may indeed be nothing but coincidence. Still, be sensitive to those occurrences that simply defy the notion of coincidence. Remain open to such gifts while not being too quick to presume that they are indeed gifts. Watch for coincidences that only the wildest faith in circumstance could accept as such. Remain skeptical but not adamant. Do not dismiss lightly what seems to be a pattern in coincidence.

2. Your own senses are the main and best detector you have for the mysteries. Listen to them. When something uncanny happens, consider it for a moment. Rather than dismissing it out of hand as coincidence, think about what the chances are of it happening by coincidence. Is it unlikely enough that you are more than surprised but even a bit uneasy? Was your experience slightly scary? Does the hair stand up on the back of your neck when you think about it?

3. And yet almost contrary to that uneasiness, can you think of the experience as a cosmic trick or joke, the kind of thing a trickster god or trickster element of a larger cosmic entity might do by way of reminding you of your mortality, knocking you down a peg, or more important, reminding you that Something Is Going On? *Listen for the cosmic laugh.* As surely as the truly mystic experience can leave you shaking with awe, it can cause you to shake your head and mutter, "Well, I'll be damned! If that doesn't beat all!"

4. Keep in mind that a frequent element of the mystic experience is a material object, something you can hold in your hand. You may be frustrated that this gift isn't something spectacular and obviously miraculous, but there won't be any doubt in your mind that what you have is something beyond the ordinary. It will be ambiguous . . . It could be noth-

ing more significant than a rock, maybe rounder than usual, maybe interesting in one aspect or another . . . but it is not likely to be stunning to others who see it or hold it. To them it could be nothing more than a round rock; to you it will be quite clearly something more than just another round rock.

5. Don't worry about the meaning of a vision, a visit, or a gift should you be lucky enough to receive one. On the one hand, the meaning of the gift may be not only beyond you but also beyond *any* human being's understanding. It may be larger than our individual minds will ever be able to grasp, larger than our historic and collective minds can handle. On the other hand, the message may be nothing more than Vonnegut's Tralfamadorian message to the other side of the galaxy . . . a dot meaning only greetings. That, in fact, is by far and away the most likely import of the mystic experience . . . GREETINGS! Or in other words, "Something Is Going On. I am here. This is not all there is. You know nothing." That message should be enough for anyone since it is a larger concept than most people will ever receive, or accept, or understand in their lives.

6. Be especially cautious about assigning negative or positive interpretations to a visit, gift, or vision. Not only is it a mistake to consider a mystic experience to be an endorsement of you or your life or your decisions but also it is an expression of arrogance . . . and hubris, which is dangerous. Similarly, one must use caution in interpreting the mystic event as a negative statement. Even when Linda and I sensed (accurately, I would now insist) that we had made a mistake in moving the rocks from their matrix in the tipi rings to our own urban home, the bad consequences could not be read as if we were being punished or cursed or as a statement about other parts of ourselves or our lives. The rocks simply weren't supposed to be moved. The consequences had nothing to do with anything but the rocks. The same

must be said of all mystic events. As much as we might want them to say more or fear that they say more, the fact is they are in and of themselves the message. "Greetings!" It would be vain to second-guess or outguess the Great Mysterious, after all. Don't try to understand. Just accept.

When you have an uncanny sense that an outer, greater force is telling you what to do or where to go, it is important not to reject that direction. You don't need to know its meaning . . . in fact, it is inevitable and implicit that it won't make any sense to you because you may be only a minor element in a larger process that even then is not a significant part of the grander scheme. Or perhaps, for all I know, the *grandest* scheme! My friend John, who gave me the round grindstone his aunt had given him and that he had been using to hold open his garage door, knew only that he was to bring the stone to me. To his enormous credit, he did not dismiss what he was being told simply because it made no sense to him; indeed, somehow he realized that the instruction made no sense *only to him*. To me it was a clear and profound message: Something Is Going On . . . He was simply a messenger. In turn, that is what I was when a silent voice instructed me to send the pipestone pipe to my son Jeff. The only reward in fulfilling such assignments is, once again, nothing more than another validation of the ultimate message, "Something Is Going On." Believe me, if you wind up being nothing more than the messenger for someone else's mystic experience, it will not only be in and of itself sufficient reward for your trouble but also one of the most important events in your life.

7. Remember, these events are not of your world, your experience, or your expectations. They are beyond your realm of experience or understanding. The point is not that they should be understood but that they be accepted. A real problem of anticipating the mystic experience by trying to imag-

ine what it must be like, reading about it, or talking with others who have had them so you know what to expect is that you can't know what to expect. It is one of the reasons they are genuinely *mystic* experiences and not coincidences or simply another part of the human experience. They are by their most basic nature beyond the human experience and therefore beyond human imagination. Don't waste your time trying to prepare for what is going to be given to you. Just accept it when it arrives. There it is—"Well, I'll be darned. All I can figure is . . . Something Is Going On."

8. The only appropriate response upon receiving a vision, gift, or visit is gratitude and respect. You won't need words or actions, just an attitude of gratitude. As my brother Buddy so eloquently put it, "Every moment of life should be a prayer of gratitude." Let the gift that Wakan Tonka gives you be an incentive and reminder to do precisely that in your life. If you fulfill that part of the bargain, you will have done all you can . . . or more, since again few other human beings have managed to bring themselves even that far in their spiritual thought.

9. When material gifts are a part of the mystic experience, they should be considered with respect but not reverence. They are not holy relics or sacred talismans. They are not magical. They do not have powers that you are likely to understand or be able to control. As far as I have been able to determine, they are simply to be respected, and the principal way to pay that respect is to maintain a posture of gratitude for them and to whatever brought them to you. Any feelings or demonstrations of pride in regard to visions, visits, or gifts strike me as being very dangerous and flirting with hubris. The word "hubris" is modified as often as not by the adjective "fatal" for a reason. Fatal hubris. It's not something to be invited or encouraged.

10. When one is tempted to broadcast news of having been

given a mystic experience, not only is this kind of pride a risky exercise in hubris but also it is likely to carry with it its own repercussions. People who hear voices (especially talking rocks!), see things, interpret items like bones as a gift from the gods, and find mystic messages in events that are nothing more than mere coincidence are liable to find themselves not being taken very seriously in other matters. The experience is between you and . . . whatever . . . Wakonda, Wakan Tonka, Ateus Tawada, Tawadahat, the Great Mysterious, Coyote . . . Jesus knew this, as did Moses, Roger Williams, and Martin Luther. As tempted as you might be to call up the local newspaper to report your magical experience or your incredible awe in having been given a vision by mystic forces swirling around you, resist the temptation unless you are ready to be ridiculed and ostracized for a long time to come. The Great Powers around us do not need or expect PR!

11. Whatever other reaction you might have in the event of an experience with the Great Mysterious, you definitely do not want to carry an account of your adventure to so-called church authorities. In all but a few cases, the power, wealth, and authority of churchmen lie in the basic rule that *they* control, approve, and even experience all such divine events. Anyone else who comes waltzing along and claims to have what appear to be divine revelations is a clear threat to the authorities' status as exclusive recipients, possessors, guardians, and interpreters of the truth and will therefore not be welcomed. Throughout history where there has been a formal church establishment and individuals have come forward who have had their own sacred experiences, the words that quickly—too quickly—arose from the church were "heresy," "witchcraft," "demons," "blasphemy," and "apostasy." Not long thereafter, especially if the recipients of those gifts persisted in making their reports and accepting the gifts, the heretics

and infidels faced having their bones broken on the wheel and their flesh burned on pyres in the village square.

What I am saying is that if you must share reports of what you have found or felt after a mystic visit, be cautious about who is in your audience. Perhaps my best advice would be that you keep the information to yourself as a private treasure. I know what you're thinking: if I am counseling that *you* might best keep *your* mystic experiences private, why am *I* making my own experiences so public in these pages? Believe me, I have asked myself the same question. It's probably because I now have a circle of friends so compatible and accepting of what I know and feel about such things that I do not fear social expulsion, and now I am old enough that whatever negative consequences I might have for making these experiences public will not be with me long.

12. Perhaps most important, and yet another lesson I have learned from my apprenticeship in tribal circles, is that in writing out my experiences, feelings, and conclusions about mysticism and religion, I can impose in some small degree the Indian mode of discourse on the mainstream American model. Watch a television panel show, a political debate in your local tavern, or a discussion about anything at your next family reunion. Our usual style of debate, or even casual conversation, is instant rebuttal and response. We don't even let someone finish a sentence before jumping in with our own opinion. There is only expression, no listening . . . therefore, no real exchange. All discussion is one way but in both directions at once and usually winds up with people yelling at each other with not even an illusion of being heard, much less understood.

One of the first things that impressed me in tribal debates was how wonderfully and truly intellectual they are. I was once at a very important meeting where a vital cultural issue was going to be discussed. I was already impressed because my Omaha Indian friends were talking about an issue the seriousness of which I had never heard approached even within academic circles. The Kiowas had offered to give the Omaha Tribe a major dance "society"—the Tiapiah Society, or Gourd Dance Society. I could imagine a typical group of white folks being offered membership in the next town's Rotary Club and saying, "Okay, sure . . ." This proposal was a much more serious issue and assuredly of enormous import to the Omahas. For example, the society had hereditary posts, so if we accepted the gift, we would be obligating our descendants to the requirements of those posts. To what degree would the rituals and intellectual properties of this new cultural society affect traditional Omaha groups? For example, are the blue-and-red shoulder blankets of the Tiapiah Society dancers somehow an offense to the same style of blankets used in Native American Church rites?

Clyde Sheridan, my friend to whom the Kiowas had offered the society, presented the issue. And then there was a long silence from the group that had gathered to consider it. A good quarter hour of silence passed as serious people weighed serious questions. Eventually someone raised one of the potential problems I mentioned in the previous paragraph, and again a long silence followed as we considered the new matter. Long into the night the debate continued, with each important point followed by a length of time commensurate with the point's seriousness. Now and then someone would rise with a trivial factor—for example, the bother of investing in another blanket, rattle, and the other paraphernalia for this new society—and we would not pause. In short, the importance of the various subjects raised was acknowledged by the amount of time devoted to thinking about that point before rising to speak next. As I watched this process, I was drenched in awe, thinking yet once again how my own middle-class, white, mainstream culture could learn from these people who had come to be my friends and family!

This book lets me follow the same system in presenting my ideas to you and to introduce the idea of this debate system to the white culture. Instead of our talking at and over each other, these words on the page give you time to think about what I am saying and then a chance to respond without my speaking before you have finished saying your piece. Feel free to shout, even dismiss these ideas . . . but give them at least a moment's consideration first.

13. Be slow to broadcast your mystic discoveries, but be as open as you can be to any and all incoming information. Reject anything within you that rejects anything during the process, and for an absolute certainty do not let anyone else keep you from opening your mind. Only someone or something with a pernicious agenda is going to tell you to exclude or ignore what is clearly new information. An insistence on maintaining the status quo means that whoever is doing the insisting has something to gain from keeping things as they are and something to lose with any change. That stance precludes a search for the truth. Any organization . . . church or political . . . that works to restrict information and discourage incorporating new discoveries into traditional understandings is working only to protect itself, not to discover and celebrate truth.

14. Do as you are told—not by any human authority but by the voice of the Great Mysterious. I do not know how to explain this concept. If you haven't "been told," you're not going to understand what that means; if you have heard the voice, then it is obvious to you. The point is, listen to what your senses tell you and follow the path that seems to be pointed out to you. I am not suggesting that one simply follow one's own whims and inclinations, however; that's not what I mean by "being told."

And I most assuredly would not suggest that anyone throw oneself into the discipline of official church dogma! A few years ago a dear Catholic friend of mine lectured me sternly and at length about the importance and liberation of blind obedience to the authority of the Catholic Church. That surprised me, coming as it did from such a bright, modern, open, intellectually liberal person, but what other people believe is their own business in my opinion. Moreover, as is the case with my friend Todd, I am interested in the processes, logic, and history of other peoples' spiritual lives. I listened to my friend's enthusiasm for orthodoxy, dogma, discipline, and church authority even though it was certainly not compatible with my own attitudes or approach. Within a year she was in a sexual relationship with her priest. Later she left her husband and married the reverend father, who apparently joined her in a changing attitude toward the importance and comfort of papal authority! He left his position in the church but to my knowledge did not apologize to all those he had previously chastised and condemned through the years from the lofty perch of his churchly authority.

I could draw other conclusions from the thoughts that I have shared with you in these pages . . . but as with so much of what seems to be the processes of the Great Mysterious, I don't know exactly what they are. All I know is that there are more. *That* is the exciting part and is another reason why the answers are questions: Now that I know these little bits, what else is there? If there is indeed Something Going On, what is it, and what does it mean? For example, if one detects that he or she has a special skill like blowing out lightbulbs, sensing animal thought, detecting spirits, killing truck engines, what is one to do with that ability? I don't know. I don't have a comparable skill, for one thing, but even most of the people I know who do have such powers are mystified and a bit uneasy about them. Should one work to enhance or focus the skill? How dangerous is it? Should such abilities be used only for good ends, and how exactly does one determine what ends are good? All I know is that such skills exist and that they are powerful and disturbing to those who have them. I wish I could offer more, but I can't. Further, I don't believe there is more to be offered. I started my journey into mysticism as a skeptic, and I remain one because I believe that is the best place to begin with inherently unlikely and unfamiliar experiences and coincidences. But my mind is also open, and I will listen. Indeed, I am excited and hope I will be around and perhaps graced to be included in even more of the wonder before I leave this life.

Some suggest that animals are better at such experiences than we humans are. We know scientifically that animals have physiological capabilities well beyond our own: the sense of smell in dogs and deer is much more highly developed than a human being's, and an eagle or falcon's vision makes ours seem puny in comparison. But is there more, perhaps skills that are beyond the senses science understands? People who work with animals intimately and directly almost always come away with precisely that impression. A Native friend, a dedicated and worshipful manager of a tribal bison herd, said it well, as he so often does, in a personal communication to me: "The creator speaks to us through animals, so we must listen and observe their behavior. Indians are always touching each other when they meet and are together, [an activity I have also seen in] my experiences watching buffalo. I've been in a large crowd in the big city surrounded by total strangers and know there is another Indian around by the way they reach out and touch me. It's hard to describe to those who don't understand." The "touch" my friend refers to is not a physical tap on the shoulder but a cultural and psychic nudge of his soul. They are impossible to describe to those who refuse to understand, I might add. How often that very phrase "it's hard to describe to those who don't understand" winds up being the ultimate expression of these great mysteries!

The electromagnetic spectrum, which includes light we humans see, radio and television transmissions that we know of and use, and segments that other creatures that share this earth with us know and use, is immense. But our perceptions within that range are minuscule. If that range were arrayed in a display stretching from New York City to San Diego, what we detect of it would be measured in fractions of an inch. It is yet another example of how limited our perceptions are (although we may subconsciously detect more of that spectrum than we are consciously aware of).

It is one thing to know. For some that may be the most comforting condition. There is a sense of stability and superiority in *knowing*. The knower can relax, stop wondering, let the mind rest, laze confidently in the sun . . . But there is far more excitement (and legitimacy) in wondering. The bottom line in science is the curiosity of the human mind. And it is the most important and valuable asset in the best purposes of religion . . . seeking, wondering, respecting, and being in awe of, amazed by, and surprised by the wonderfully funny punch line of the truth. The unifying element for belief, religion, philosophy, art, skepticism, literature, agnosticism, deism, science, and virtually *all* of the meaningful conclusions of man is, plain and simple, the one homely, inevitable, wonderful truth: Something Is Going On.

You might ask . . . and rightly so . . . isn't all this just a rehash of Buddhism? A mainstay of Buddhism is that the answer is the question. There is substantial overlap, agreement, even exchange between religions, and there are many reasons for that. For instance, two of the Ten Commandments are codified in our law, prohibiting theft and murder, and they can be found in the tenets of most religions, including many preceding Mosaic or Christian ethical formulations or the Code of Hammurabi . . . Indeed, they even exist in some that plainly contributed to Mosaic or Christian formulations. In December Jews celebrate their festival of light right on top of the Christians' observance of Jesus's birthday. Now the Wiccans mark solstice during the Christmas season too. About this time of year the Zunis and Hopis open pueblo kivas to start the kachina seasons, with the lighting of fires. At this same time of year, Zoroastrians celebrate Yalda, their festival of light. (My favorite, for no other reason than its wonderful name, is the ancient Roman winter festival of Natalis Solis Invicti, or "the Birth of the Unconquerable Sun.")

We all celebrate a season of light at that time of year. It does not belong to any one faith. It is indeed a matter of "happy holidays" and not simply all about a "Merry Christmas." Offering kind wishes to others who may celebrate the event under a different name is not acting out of "political correctness" but according to that old idea of the Golden Rule.

Do we all see the same god? I don't know. It may be similar to that story of the blind men describing an elephant, with all of us simply exploring different parts of the same thing. Whatever this great power is after all, it is the most enormous thing we have to deal with. Even if we see something of it, we most assuredly (despite the zealots' insistence to the contrary) cannot guess from our small samples, even if they are somehow connected, the nature of the whole. Moreover, we are all seeing this "elephant" through different eyes. Some of us are monocular, some color blind; some have only the sense of smell, some only hearing. No one perceiver is right or wrong, and none has the complete answer. Also no one impression is more important than another. The real key to whatever understanding we can have is the realization, and admission, that there are other perceptions, and they may be as valid as our own.

Imagine it all as an enormous jigsaw puzzle to be assembled without the advantage of the entire picture available to go by. We have one piece but have no idea what the larger image might be. We do know that any one piece is no more important than any other. The puzzle will never be completed without all the other pieces. If we somehow have the enormous good fortune or skillful eye to find a piece that interlocks with the one we are holding, the most important thing once they are joined is to preserve their unity. It is helpful when more eyes and hands contribute to the solution; it is not at all helpful when one person pockets a piece, insisting that it is the only piece that counts, that it somehow trumps all others, and that it is the exclusive property of the current holder. Even more foolish would be for that person to claim knowledge of the entire image from the exclusive possession of its one small piece. It will be immediately obvious to everyone else that in fact the exact opposite is true: once the puzzle hog has decided not to pursue any further solving activities, any real solution becomes impossible for everyone.

Of course, one can never discount the very real possibility . . . perhaps probability . . . that we are actually working on several jigsaw puzzles at once. With all the pieces jumbled together. Or for that matter, that every piece before us is from a different puzzle, with none fitting together in any meaningful way. A lot of the pieces look alike . . . but that doesn't mean they are identical or even associated in any meaningful way other than they lie before us on our table.

30

Lessons in Brief

am a storyteller, so I tell stories. I like to think my audiences draw the same conclusions from the tales that I do, but just in case they don't, sometimes it's a good idea to strip away the ornamentation and state more simply what I believe the conclusions of the longer discussions might be. Believe me, I do not offer them as fact or even the most logical conclusions. They are my guesses. We are dealing with curious experiences seen only through my eyes. What would you have seen if you were given one of these experiences? I don't know. What would you have taken as the message(s)? I don't know. But I will tell you what I think.

As wisely suggested by my old friend Richard Fool Bull, the white man's religion seems to put so much faith in coincidence. Conversely, Mr. Fool Bull felt (and I feel) that it ignores patterns that offer deeper insights than mere accidental occurrences might give us.

1. For example, more than enough evidence indicates that there *is* a power moving around and beyond human beings. The Western world timidly refers to this immense power with the generic term "God," in part because there is danger in words and in making casual reference to such powers. One does not use the name of God to avoid trivial blasphemy but to avert possible danger to oneself. "Speak of the Devil [and he may appear]," some say. In ancient times one might speak of Old Nick instead of Satan lest

he should be summoned. Native terminology captures our ignorance of such greater powers better—the Lakotas' Wakan Tonka, or Great Mysterious; the Pawnees' Tawadahat, or This Immensity.

2. This power (or perhaps these powers) is sentient—that is, self-aware—as is evident from what appears to be its clear interaction with external things. Such as us. This power is not an ordinary physical force like wind, cold, good, and so on.

3. The power interacts with human beings as a whole and as individuals and uses us as agents in its intentions and designs, which are rarely if ever apparent to us.

4. It also interacts with animals and uses them as agents.

5. It provides ample physical evidence of its presence and nature.

6. For reasons I cannot guess, rocks seem especially useful to it.

7. It has a clear sense of irony and humor.

8. It does not reveal its greater intent easily. On those occasions when some intent is suggested, it may still be obscure, or it may be clear and surprisingly specific. Neither can be expected.

9. It hears our entreaties and prayers and may or may not respond, or it may answer us in ways not at all expected or understood.

10. It responds to group prayer proportionally or perhaps more directly and strongly. I am not at all clear about this matter and still want to doubt the very idea.

11. Quite aside from its own nature, we can trust least of all those who most loudly claim their own knowledge of the presence's intent and meaning and their own exclu-

sive, infallible, or total access to it. I believe we can judge the grasp of any religion's, or person's, understanding of these powers by the inverse degree to which it claims to have that knowledge or understanding.

12. The political structure of a church is a good place to look for the nature of man but not a useful source of information about the nature or presence of these Great Powers.

A concept that baffles me is boredom. I haven't been bored for at least forty years and only rarely beforehand. When someone remarks that he or she is bored, if I say anything at all, I suggest that perhaps one escape from boredom is to venture out and find something interesting. And plenty around us is interesting. In fact, I would say much around us is downright amazing. Boredom results from a closing down of receptors, a self-imposed sensory numbing, a reliance on stimulation initiated by something or someone else. I can imagine, but only with real effort on my part, someone never noticing that Something Is Going On. Richard Fool Bull said that some of us are "educated out" of realizing the wonders that swirl around us. But that observation too implies that the insensitivity comes from somewhere, something, or someone else. While I have suggested throughout this book that I don't think we can seek out the mystic experience or appeal to a formula to invoke communication with the Great Powers, I have the impression we can work on our own minds and senses to keep the doors open and our eyes bright to recognize and appreciate, perhaps with laughter, when those coveted experiences come our way.

Can there be any doubt that there is more that we don't know than there is that we do? There's a good chance there is not only a lot we don't know but a lot we will never know. All we have to do to grasp some of that idea is to look into a clear night sky. While even the brightest and most focused of us can't understand that we see in that sky, we certainly can understand that it is there. So it is with that Something That Is Going On. I am a latecomer to this new age of computers, social communication, cyber technology, "smart phones," and all that goes with it. But I do know how my life and work changed when I bought that first desktop computer in the mid-1980s, began to store my writing on floppy disks (does anyone even remember floppy disks that were actually floppy?), and printing material on the slogging, pounding typewriter printer. To this day I don't understand how it all works, but I know it's there. And I know how wonderful and interesting it is.

So it is with that Something Going On. My Omaha brother Buddy Gilpin told me in 1967 that we are too small, even collectively, to understand the wonders of the Great Mysterious, and now, nearly fifty years later, I have affirmation through my own experiences that it most certainly is the case. But as with staring into the clear Nebraska night sky and wondering at what a ride it is to be on this speck of blue dust we call Earth, and home, I have no doubt that what the Old Pawnees called Tawadahat, or This Immensity, *is* there. Further, even in our innocence, the most profound prayer we can give is open-eyed wonder.

The Lessons of Others

A Selected and Annotated Bibliography

You are not going to encourage or understand a mystic experience by reading about it. You can't get there by asking for it, looking for it, or somehow manipulating your mind to be more receptive. (Others, however, including friends and kin within my Native circles for whom I have great respect, would disagree with me on this point.) Nothing in the books I am suggesting here will do any of those things for you. What they will do is give you some idea of what the mystic experience is and has been for others, but they will in no way prepare you for your own. Nothing will. When it happens, you will say, "Of course! That's it! Now I understand!" But nothing can prepare you in advance or explain in retrospect. There are no models, ideals, formats, or accepted qualifications for either having experiences or interpreting them. While mystic experiences do seem to share some characteristics, they defy prediction or description in terms of anything typical. In reading the following suggested texts, however, you may gain some perspective on the incredible scope of such experiences and thereby perhaps . . . if you walk the careful balance between being skeptical and being intellectually receptive . . . be better prepared for whatever happens whenever and if it happens.

The Teachings of Don Juan: A Yaqui Way of Knowledge by Carlos Castaneda (New York: Ballantine, 1968) has been widely condemned as inaccurate, a baseless bit of fiction, or pure charlatanism. Frankly, I don't care whether the book is true. It is inspired. It may not be good science—I neither know nor care—but it is superb theology. As I have said earlier, in fiction you can tell the truth. Did Castaneda actually study under a Yaqui shaman? Are these indeed his experiences? Are they only drug-induced hallucinations? It doesn't matter. As I read his work for the first time during my earliest years in the company of Native peoples, I thought over and over again, "That's it! He got it!"

Castaneda's experiences were not precisely the same as mine—not even close—but the *nature* of them was the same. I never met Castaneda, but I wish I had. I would have liked to ask him if he wasn't perhaps protecting people and practices by wrapping them in a literary metaphor. I've done that—telling the truth through fiction. No doubt about it, Castaneda had a much greater impact with his work published indeed as fiction than he would have had with yet another crushingly boring doctoral dissertation monograph (which is what *The Teachings of Don Juan* was originally meant to be). Read his words and works not with an idea of imitating his fieldwork but with the intent of preparing yourself for experiences just as jarring to your own psyche and sense of logic as Castaneda's should you ever be fortunate enough to find yourself in a Native context.

I have insisted that all my children (and many of my friends) read *Siddhartha* by Hermann Hesse (the editions I prefer and use are the translation by Hilda Rosner [New York: Bantam Books, 1951; Bantam reprint edition, 1991]). It is a superb and poetic story of the Buddha and one among a long cycle of literary and folk narratives about the search for self and the mystic experience. The moral in each and every one of these narratives is the same: there is no place like home. And, of course, they all tell us Something Is Going On. For some, I suppose such morality tales never have much of an impact and never will. They are too obvious and ordinary.

We will continue to make the same mistakes over and over and learn the same lessons again and again. But I still consider this book important enough to recommend nonetheless. This book has helped to explain a lot about life to me and to millions of others.

All I can figure is that Kurt Vonnegut had some sort of mystic experience of his own before he wrote *The Sirens of Titan* (New York: Delta, Dell, 1959). I cannot imagine coming up with the genius of this book's plot and its incredible, mystic, cosmic implications with nothing in the mix but a normal (and yet incredible!) human mentality. It is too precise, too incisive to be the product of mere literary creativity. I never read this book without laughing all over again at what must surely be as close an explanation of the meaning of life as has ever been put in words. And Vonnegut's explanation contains an important secret that almost no other thinkers or writers have remembered when discussing the nature of God and the meaning of life: they are *funny*. And if you have even a vestigial sense of humor, you'll have to admit that life is funny. Vonnegut nails down that reality as no one else ever has. You don't have any sort of grasp of life or the role of mysticism or the nature of God if you haven't read this book. It is that important.

You cannot imagine the number of people I have said this same thing to who then read *The Sirens of Titan* and consequently questioned my sanity. And Vonnegut's. They wonder, how can his ideas possibly make sense? How can this book possibly be funny? Isn't it the most depressing set of ideas— even though couched in fiction or, for that matter, in science fiction!—ever inflicted on readers? Vonnegut believes we are nothing but mechanisms? Tools? *Delivery boys?!* Our most profound thoughts are empty? Our every truth is false? We don't in fact even know how insignificant we are?!

Well, those ideas are neither surprising nor depressing

for me. I don't find the thesis of Vonnegut's book the least bit depressing. I think it is perfectly delightful, probably because it is so thoroughly within the nature and tradition of the Cosmic Trickster, Coyote. There isn't the slightest doubt in my mind that Vonnegut tells us the real meaning of life in these pages. And if you have any questions at all about the role of the messenger or facilitator in the process of the mystic experience, Vonnegut answers your questions. Among the epigraphs I include in the opening pages of this book is the key to Vonnegut's tale, a quote from the rock group Steppenwolf's lead singer John Kay: "If all of this should have a reason / we would be the last to know." We humans are not up to that kind of knowledge, and maybe we should be grateful we don't have to deal with what is clearly and impossibly beyond us.

Lame Deer, Seeker of Visions: The Life of a Sioux Medicine Man by John (Fire) Lame Deer and Richard Erdoes (New York: Simon & Schuster, Touchstone Books, 1972) is a useful introduction to Native mysticism in large part because it conveys so well the ease with which Native peoples experience and accept the mystic event. In a very conversational way, the Lakota holy man Lame Deer tells the reader the life of a contemporary and yet traditional Native spiritual leader and his understandings and experiences with the Great Mysterious.

I once asked John Neihardt if *Black Elk Speaks: Being the Life Story of a Holy Man of the Oglala Sioux, as told to John Neihardt* (Lincoln: University of Nebraska Press, 1961) should be considered his work or Black Elk's. Black Elk told Neihardt about his life and his own mystic visions, but the text clearly resonated with Neihardt's sense of poetry while still reflecting Lakota eloquence. Neihardt was evasive when answering my question, but he insisted that the truth of the narrative and the essence of the mysticism in the book were Black Elk's . . . but that perhaps the *poetry* of the transliteration was his own. It's not easy to tell, probably not even for Nei-hardt, where the truth of any particular part of this work lies.

One of the deepest and most bitter ironies of our long and sad relationship with Native peoples is our perception and depiction of them as inarticulate and reticent ("Ugh . . . me Tonto . . . heap big red man . . .") when in fact eloquence is a prized talent in tribal life, and its practice within Native contexts far exceeds that of mainstream Americans. It would therefore be very hard to determine where Black Elk's elo-quence ends and Neihardt's poetry begins. Whatever the case, *Black Elk Speaks* is an excellent introduction to one Lakota elder's understanding of the intersection between the Great Mysterious and mortal man.

The Adventures of a Simpleton: Simplicius Simplicissimus (That Is an Account of the Life of a Strange Vagabond Called Melchior Sternfels von Fuchsheim) by Hans Jakob Christof-fel von Grimmelshausen (as translated by Walter Wallich [New York: Frederick Ungar, Continuum Publishing, 2002]) is more than three centuries old but is as relevant now as it was so long ago. Like *Siddhartha* and *The Sirens of Titan* and the films *Joe Dirt* or *The Jerk*, it is the story of a simple pilgrim who wanders the world seeking the answer to the meaning of life only to find that it doesn't lie in the directions we humans tend to think and hope it does—wealth, plea-sures of the flesh, aestheticism, commerce, religion, learn-ing, power, the discipline of military life—but rather in the simple life where we are most at home, within our origins, and where we can easily slip into a state of surrender to what-ever mystic gifts that come our way.

Grimmelshausen so wonderfully describes it when intro-ducing us to the mind of his protagonist: "So perfect was my ignorance that I was not even in the least aware of it." Of course with this statement, he betrays that the worst of vices—being unaware of one's ignorance, which then all too often translates into arrogance—was not at all his hero's failing because he obviously *was* aware of it, and that is the greatest virtue a human can have: recognizing and admitting his *ignorance*, which then becomes *innocence*. This long, complicated, repetitive, foreign, medieval text isn't the easiest reading and, like so many picaresque narratives of the period, is repetitive to the point of becoming tiresome, but there are some wonderful surprises. It is refreshing and reassuring, for example, to find that the same failures of faith and misunderstanding of those who insist on remaining blind to the mystic three hundred years ago are precisely the same as those of us who are befuddled skeptics now. The book opens with a line that brings a chuckle of recognition even to the modern reader: "In recent years (when many people think we shall soon see the end of the world!) . . ."

Virginia Irving Armstrong's *I Have Spoken: American History through the Voices of the Indians* (published originally by the Swallow Press [New York, 1971] in a larger format and in a smaller edition by Pocket Books [New York, 1972]) is an excellent and inexpensive anthology of Indian speeches throughout American history and an excellent path into a deductive understanding of Native thought and the mainstream misunderstanding of it. A more elegant volume (largely because of its excellent photos, quality binding, and rich paper) with much the same idea—focusing on Native eloquence as a way to understand Native values and dispel mainstream ignorance of them—is the book I mention so often in these pages, T. C. McLuhan's *Touch the Earth: A Self-Portrait of Indian Existence* (New York: Promontory Press, 1971). It has been particularly important in my own journey, and it might be helpful for you too. I recommend both books cited in this paragraph very highly, whatever your interest, or even disinterest, in Native thought and spiritualism.

The Lakota Way: Stories and Lessons for Living by Joseph

Marshall (New York: Viking Compass, 2001), himself a Lakota traditionalist, is an insider's look at the intellectual and spiritual life of one major Native tribe as expressed by an articulate insider. Marshall's more recent book, *Returning to the Lakota Way: Old Values to Save a Modern World* (Carlsbad CA: Hay House, 2013), is an even deeper exploration of Native spirituality.

I strongly recommend Vine Deloria's series of books that look at life and spiritualism from a Native point of view, most specifically: *God Is Red* (Golden CO: Fulcrum, 1973); *Red Earth, White Lies: Native Americans and the Myth of Scientific Fact* (Fulcrum, 1997); *Spirit and Reason: The Vine Deloria, Jr., Reader* (Fulcrum, 1999); and *The World We Used to Live In: Remembering the Powers of the Medicine Men* (Fulcrum, 2006).

My Lakota brother Charles Trimble's wonderful book *Iyeska* (Half Breed) (Indianapolis: Dog Ear Publishing, 2012) provides the non-Indian with a superb view of life while growing up on a reservation (Pine Ridge) and a context for understanding the role of a very modern Native intellectual who remains true to tribal traditions. One has to read between the lines in most places (except the one excerpt cited in my own text while dealing with the nature of visions), but it is precisely this subtlety that gives us a basis for understanding the ancient spiritual experience in a modern context.

The following titles are not so much lessons from other writers as they come from the same old guy—me. My work *Touching the Fire: Buffalo Dancers, the Sky Bundle, and Other Tales* (New York: Villard, 1992) is labeled fiction, but it is clearly based on solid historical and anthropological fact. I assert in this book that one can tell the truth in fiction, and that is clearly what I try to do, revealing a good deal about Native culture, religion, and life without exposing my resources to the destructive elements of mainstream analysis.

Some of the ideas in this book you are holding have been

introduced in my book *Embracing Fry Bread: Confessions of a Wannabe* (Lincoln: University of Nebraska Press, 2012). Think of it as a companion piece for this volume or perhaps a more cautious, earlier effort in much the same direction.

The most obvious and yet probably the most unlikely resource for the reluctant pilgrim is . . . the holy Bible, read not as a text for orthodoxy, not seen through the corrupting lens of official interpretation, not used in fragments and pieces to support already established conclusions, but insofar as possible with a fresh eye and open mind. The Bible is clearly a metaphor, especially in its original languages. It is brilliant, subtle, and almost subversive in its revolutionary nature . . . which is to say, in the ways in which it is almost never read or interpreted by sanctioning authority. People such as Job and Ezekiel did their best to interpret what they saw, experienced, knew, thought, and heard, using language that, like our own today, is utterly inadequate for the task. Read in this way, not only is the book full of evidence supporting Native mysticism, but also it can help us all deal with whatever mystic wonders and revelations we may have the good fortune to be granted in our own pilgrimages. Read the books of the Bible in their entirety. Read them as if you were seeing them for the first time. Read them slowly. Think about what they say and what they might be struggling to explain or describe. I think you will find anew that the Bible is worth reading and is indeed a spiritual guide corrupted by two thousand years of distortion and misinterpretation but in which the core of the mystic experience can still be discovered. ·

Other works by Roger Welsch